STUDIES
IN ANCIENT TECHNOLOGY

BY

R. J. FORBES

VOLUME VII

WITH 36 FIGURES AND 14 TABLES

SECOND EDITION

LEIDEN
E. J. BRILL
1966

CONTENTS

STUDIES IN ANCIENT TECHNOLOGY

VOLUME VII

PREFACE

Like the other volumes of this series this survey of ancient geology and mining does not pretend to be more than a summary of our present state of knowledge of this subject together with a selected bibliography for the historians, archaeologists and scientists interested in these matters. No attempt has been made to present a complete bibliography, for, after all, what bibliography is complete? This depends entirely on the approach to these problems which will differ from case to case and from period to period as the gaps in our knowledge are slowly filled. The books and articles mentioned will serve to guide the reader towards the particular data he is looking for.

Throughout the text the transliteration of Egyptian words is completed by figures between brackets referring to volume, page and line of A. Erman and H. Grapow's Wörterbuch der Aegyptischen Sprache (6 vols. Leipzig, 1926—1950), where the reader will find the correct hieroglyphic version of these words.

Unfortunately many mines have been studied in the past by archaeologists or travellers, who were no mining experts or geologists and subsequent diggings or reopening of the mines have often destroyed valuable evidence for ever. On the other hand there is still ample material to make more detailed and comparative studies in regional developments possible and thus many problems indicated in these pages will probably be solved in the near future. Should this be the case the labour spent in collecting and publishing the data presented in the following chapters will be amply rewarded.

Amsterdam, January 1963   R. J. FORBES

PREFACE TO THE SECOND EDITION

Apart from the consistent valuable help from Mr. F. W. Leemans we have received many details on local problems and data from such experts like Mr. John C. Allan (Lisbon), Mr. L. U. Salkield (Rio Tinto Mines), Mr. Michael G. Diallinas (Heraklion) and Dr. Beno Rothenberg (Tel Aviv) who have contributed materially to the revision of the text now presented to the reader who is invited to follow the example of the above-mentioned experts and to suggest corrections and additions to the contents of this book.

Amsterdam, September 1966   R. J. FORBES

CHAPTER I

ANCIENT GEOLOGY

1. *Introduction*

Modern geology, the science of the earth, its composition, structure and history, has become a very broad field of knowledge with many subdivisions, usually grouped under two headings, physical and historical geology. *Physical geology* embraces the following main subjects:

a. *mineralogy*, the systematic study of minerals;

b. *petrology*, the study of the physical and chemical properties of rocks and their origin (igneous, sedimentary and metamorphic rocks);

c. *geomorphology*, the study of land forms and the process of development of such forms (weathering, erosion, sedimentation, etc.);

d. *geotectonics* (structural geology), the study of the form and arrangement of strata and their changing shape as a result of deformations and dislocations (mountain structure, etc.), and

e. *economic geology*, the study of mineral deposits of practical value and their industrial uses.

The main subjects of *historical geology* are:

f. *stratigraphy*, the study of the succession and chronology of stratified rocks, with the help of fossils, and the successive changes in the distribution of land and sea in the past;

g. *palaeontology*, the study of fossil animals and plants and their location in the historical sequence of the earth in order to arrive at a time chart of the earth and absolute dating; and

h. *geological mapping*, the mapping of bedrock units defined by their physical characteristics and geological age.

There are of course many more branches of geology, which has now become a closely integrated body of knowledge with a language of its own. Fortunately, a recent dictionary in four languages will help the archaeologist to understand such geological terms as he might find on his way (1).

2. *The scope of ancient geology*

Ancient geology was not such an integrated body of knowledge.

We must remember that, like other fields of science, geology never was anything but an auxiliary subject to the ancient philosophers. More than often they discussed geological phenomena as part of their cosmology or philosophy rather than as natural phenomena as such. The perusal of any general history of geology (2) or such books and essays devoted to the discussion of geology in Antiquity (3) will instantly reveal the lack of integration of the various geological phenomena known to the ancients. From our point of view their observations seem haphazard and most of their hypotheses baseless. Strangely enough, no ancient author follows up the evidence to be derived from ancient mines and quarries with their distinctive succession of strata and discusses the structure of the rocky crust of the earth. Neither do they study the fossils, on which they report, as evidence from which the story of the earth might be written. Their discussion of gems and minerals, their origin and properties, of earthquakes and volcanoes, of the formation of alluvial deposits by rivers, of the origin of rivers, the saltness of the sea and like subjects is always disconnected and anecdotical.

We shall see, that only few authors have devoted basic studies to any of these subjects, nor should we expect any such treaties in greater quantity before the sixteenth century. In his Dedicatory Letter to his De Natura Fossilium (1547) Georgius Agricola cites no less than twenty-seven earlier authors on geology (4), still Nicolaus Steno (Niels Stensen, 1638—1686) was the first author to outline the history of the earth by inductive reasoning based on exact studies in the field (5). This essay on the "Dissection of a Shark's Head" (1667) was followed by a more detailed geology in his "De solido" of 1669.

Therefore our data are to be culled from a long list of authors on widely different subjects (Appendix I) and we will be discussing geological topics rather than an integrated doctrine of geology. First, however, a few general points should be made clear.

Nearly all ancient philosophers, geographers or historians have something to say on the shape of the earth, its structure and the atmosphere surrounding it, however vague such statements may sometimes be. In the ancient mind, cosmology, geology and meteorology are often thrown together in a way which astonishes us, but we here should remember how Galileo still takes meteors to be meteorological phenomena. Like every ancient philosopher he is still tempted to regard our "sublunary world", our planet and its atmosphere, as the only scene of sudden erratic changes. When the ancients discussed phenomena of change, which we now call geological, they were always tempted to derive arguments from cosmological theories and thence we must needs mention some of their opinions on these matters (6) before we can deal with specifically geological subjects.

In the ancient Mediterranean world the contrasts of the seasons made the cycle of growth and decay more spectacular than in Northwestern Europe. The cold and the wet seem to encroach on the hot and the dry, who in their turn drive away the other pair of opposites. In the preclassical world such common observations had no effect beyond the world of philosophy and religion. To the Egyptians and Sumerians Heaven and Earth had been created by the gods "in the beginning"; broadly speaking no changes, such as they observed on earth, had any lasting effect on the divine creation and they did not speculate on the mechanism of such geological phenomena as they knew. The Greek philosophers of the sixth century B. C., however, sought to explain these phenomena, searching for their "archè", the primary substance or rather substrate (Freeman), their material cause (Burnet). Early Greek science is the "istoria" of the "stuff things are made of" and later "its general character or constitution"; their "theoria" still being closely linked up with "seeing" rather than with the "observation" of modern science.

The thesis "water is the archè of all things" enounced by Thales of Miletus (c. 585 B.C.) would come natural to an inhabitant of the coastal area of Asia Minor, observing the evaporation of water from the sea by the heat of the heavenly bodies, coming down again in rain and, as early cosmologists believed, turned into earth, which then later changed into water again, as dew, night mists and subterranean springs suggested. The waters under the earth were an independent source of moisture. According to Seneca, Thales thought that the earth floated about like a ship on the great ocean, which also surrounded it, and the tossing about on this water was what we felt when there was an earthquake. Seneca himself disbelieves this explanation of earthquakes. However it seems certain, that Thales believed that water was the indispensible element in the material world. Possibly he thought of the earth growing in the water, growth being dependent on moisture, and all things being nourished by that of which they were composed.

His contemporary, Anaximander (c. 560 B.C.) derives the cosmos from the "apeiron" (the spatially infinite (Burnet), the non-limited (Freeman)) from which arise the four elements forming the world and returning to it again and again. The "archè" of Anaximenes (c. 546

B.C.) is "pneuma", air or rather vapour, from which the other elements
differ in degree of density. When pneuma is condensed it first forms
wind, then cloud, then water, earth and lastly stones. Heracleitus
(c. 500 B.C.) makes "fire" play the part of Anaximenes' "pneuma".
Fire condenses and becomes water, water condenses and becomes
earth; this is the downward path. Earth rarifies to water, water rarifies
into exhalations, some bright and akin to fire, some dark and akin to
moisture. Anaxagoras (c. 460 B.C.), possibly Anaximenes' pupil, said:
"The dense and moist and cold and dark (elements) collected here,
where is now Earth, and the rare and hot and dry went outwards to
the furthest part of the Aether. From these, while they are separating
off, Earth solidifies; from the clouds, water is separated off, and from
the water earth, and from the earth stones are solidified by the cold, and
these rush outward rather than water". His contemporaries, Archelaus
of Athens and Diogenes of Apollonia (in his On Natural Science)
propound much the same ideas. In his "On Being" Melissus of Samos
(c. 440 B.C.) defends Parmenides and states: "It seems to us that the
hot becomes cold and the cold hot, and the hard soft and the soft hard,
and the living thing dies and comes into being from what is not living,
and that all things change, and what was and what now is are not all
the same, but iron which is hard is worn away by contact with the
finger, and gold and stone and whatever seems to be entirely strong is
worn away; and from water, earth and stone come into being".

All these philosophers recognize the four elements, fire, air, water
and earth, choosing one as the primary substance from which the
others are believed to arise, but in this material world these four are
seen to play their part and material changes are related to them. The
various early theories about the size of the earth and its form have been
ably summarized by Taylor (7). The pre-classical world, generally
speaking, believed the earth to be a disk with certain elevations (mountains) floating on the Waters of the Deep, from which it arose. In the
classical world the sphericity of the earth was taught by certain philosophers, but this was doubted by many. Plutarch in his dialogue "The
Face appearing in the Moon" ridicules it, but Ovid (8) believes it.
Saint Augustine, who is more of a scientist than many of his contemporaries and who will only relate "what I was told by one whom I
trust as I trust mine own eyes", believes in the spherical earth and he
regards as a matter of scientific proof, whether "antipodes" can exist
on it (9). Strabo too is convinced of it and he stresses the relative insignificance of such irregularities as mountain ranges: "And so, after he

(Eratosthenes) has stated that the earth as a whole is "sphere-shaped" — not spheroidal indeed as though turned by a sphere-lathe but it has certain irregularities of surface — he proceeds to enumerate the large number of its successive changes in shape — changes which take place as the results of the action of water, fire, earthquakes, volcanic eruptions, and other similar agencies; and here too he does not preserve the proper order. For the spheroidal shape that characterizes the earth as a whole results from the constitution of the universe, but such changes as Eratosthenes mentions do not in any particular alter the earth as a whole (changes so insignificant are lost in great bodies) though they produce conditions in the inhabited world that are different at one time from what they are at another, and the immediate causes which produce them are different at different times". (10).

Schwarcz stated that the Pythagoreans believed in a "central fire within the earth", but this is wrong. The "central fire" stood in the centre of the Universe, the Earth (as a planet) and the "Counter-earth" (Antichthon) revolving around it with the other planets. When Aristotle and his school considered this theory unsatisfactory they took his "central fire" to be at the centre of the earth, whence it gave life to all and warmed the parts which had cooled down.

Aristotle is the first author who was left us more than just fragments on geological subjects. The essay De Mineralibus, which we know only in its medieval Latin version, was definitely proved to be partly a direct translation and partly a summary of Avicenna's Kitâb al-Shifâ, written in 1022. However, in his De Respiratione we find references to fossil fishes and in his De Generatione et Corruptione some notes on subjects treated in more detail in his main work on geological subject, the Meteorologica (11).

In the introduction to the first book of the Meteorologica Aristotle gives this work a place between the Physics, De Caelo and De Generatione et Corruptione and his works on biology. From our modern point of view it is a strange mixture of subjects now considered to belong to the fields of astronomy, geography, geology, seismology and meteorology. Only a few chapters are of interest to the historians of geology. The first chapter of Book I discusses the place of meteorology in the natural sciences, the second recapitulates Aristotle's theory of the four elements as laid down in his De Caelo, the third deals with the relative dispositions of air and fire in the terrestial atmosphere. In chapter 13 he discusses winds, rivers and springs and in the next one climatic changes, coastal erosion and silting. All other chapters of

Book I (4—12) deal with such subjects as shooting stars, aurora bore-
alis, comets, the Milky Way, rain, clouds and mist, dew, hoarfrost,
snow and hail, part of which we now consider to be cosmic phenomena
rather than terrestial. In Aristotle's world, however, these were all
"sublunar" phenomena, which happened in the spheres of fire and air
which surround the surface of the earth.

The first three chapters of Book II deal with the sea, its origin, place
and saltiness. Chapters 4—6 and 9 interest us less here as they deal
with the winds, thunder and lightning, but chapters 7—8 merit our
attention as they give Aristotle's views on earthquakes and their causes.
The third book contains little of interest to our subject, it discusses
hurricanes, typhoons, firewinds, haloes, rainbows, rods and mock suns,
but the concluding chapter 6 ends with the author's views on the
generation of rocks and ores, which theory had a profound influence
on Arab and medieval mineralogy.

Book IV, which is now generally held to be authentic, gives the
application of Aristotle's doctrine of the four elements to the phenomena of chemical change. It is an important document in the
history of chemistry.

Like so many other works by Aristotle his Meteorologica seems to
be a body of lecture-notes which the author constantly revised and
brought up to date. The internal evidence for the date of composition
is inconclusive, but Lee suggests that this work was not started before
Aristotle's period of residence in the Troad and Lesbos (344—342
B.C.), but it also contains references to the archonship of Nicomachus
(340 B.C.).

In the second chapter of the first book Aristotle says: "These four
bodies are fire, air, water and earth: of them fire always rises to the
top, earth always sinks to the bottom, while the other two bear to each
other a mutual relation similar to fire and earth — for air is the nearest
of all to fire, water to earth. The whole terrestial (sub-lunar) region
then is composed of these four bodies, and it is the conditions, which
affect them ,which, we have said, are the subject of our inquiry."

In the next chapter Aristotle argues that "earth" is comparatively
small in bulk and lies, with water, at the centre of the universe. The
celestial region is composed of a divine fifth element, which we may
identify with the traditional "aether". Then he goes on to explain his
theory of the two exhalations and the part they play in the genesis of
ores and minerals, to which theory we will revert in the chapter dedicated to this subject. This theory is given at the end of the third book,

but there is no attempt at any detailed description of the mineral kingdom of Nature such as Aristotle gave of plants and animals in other works. The origin of certain groups of ores and minerals is discussed in general without any reference to their specific character or properties.

Aristotle's Meteorologica stands in plain contrast with Theophrastus' excellent little essay "On Stones" (12) which we will discuss together with other data on ancient mineralogy. With Adams one can say "Theophrastus On the Stones remained for 1800 years a most valuable and authoritative book on minerals, referred to and quoted by all. It shows that even at this early date there existed, probably among miners, quarrymen and other men engaged in the technical trades and industries a body of knowledge of mineralogy, especially on its practical side, which had been drawn upon by Theophrastus in the compilation of this work".

Theophrastus also seems to have written a work on mining, which Diogenes Laertius (V. 44) mentions, but it must have gone the way of many of Theophrastus' manuscripts, the story of which is given by Strabo (13) in the following passage:

"Neleus the son of Coriscus was a pupil of Aristotle and Theophrastus, and also inherited the library of Theophrastus, which included that of Aristotle... Neleus took it to Scepsis and bequeathed it to his heirs, ordinary people, who kept the books locked up and not even carefully stored. But when they heard how zealously the Attalic Kings (notably Eumenes II of Pergamum, 197—159 B.C.) to whom the city was subject were searching for books, they hid their books underground in a kind of trench. But much later, when the books had been damaged by moisture and moths, their descendants sold them to Apellicon of Teos for a large sum of money (before 84 B.C.), both the books of Aristotle and those of Theophrastus. But Apellicon was a bibliophile rather than a philosopher; and therefore, seeking a restoration of the parts that had been eaten through, he made new copies of the text, filling up the gaps incorrectly, and published the books full of errors... Rome also contributed much to this for, immediately after the death of Apellicon, Sulla, who had captured Athens, carried of Apellicon's library to Rome, where Tyrannion the grammarian, who was fond of Aristotle, got it in his hands by paying court to the librarian, as did also certain booksellers who used bad copyists and would not collate the texts — a thing that also takes place in the case of books that are copied for selling, both here and at Alexandria".

In the second book of his Natural History Pliny treats of the universe, heavenly bodies, meteorology and the chief agents, such as earthquakes and tides, at work in changing the relation of land and sea on the earth's surface. However, he does so in a much less critical and systematic fashion than other authors. The thirty-seventh book deals with "stones" far more extensively but much less systematically than Theophrastus, whose work is also free from fable and magic, which Pliny's essay is certainly not. Pliny takes much for granted, for instance he mentions that we know by experience that the land is entirely surrounded by water (II. 66) and this "does not require investigation by arguments"! Hence we can cull interesting data from Pliny, but we must always be aware of the fact that he is primarily an encyclopedist and not a scientist!

Seneca's Naturales Quaestiones (14) is a much more systematic book dealing mainly with meteorological manifestations, such as winds, rain, hail, snow, comets, rainbows and what he regards as allied subjects, such as earthquakes, springs and rivers. This essay seems to be one of Seneca's last works dedicated to his friend Lucilius Junior, procurator of Sicily, the probable author of the didactic poem "Aetna". Seneca wrote this work between the end of AD 63 and the beginning of 65, as he mentions the earthquake of 62 which damaged Pompeii! This work is more or less a parallel to Aristotle s Meteorologica; Seneca describes the "decreta", the scientific truths observable in the natural phenomena, from which he draws, from time to time, the "praecepta", the lessons which one can derive from them.

Though he deals with many subjects also discussed by Aristotle in his Meteorologica, he does not seem to have first-hand knowledge of this essay. The quotations from this work seem to show that Seneca drew them from Poseidonius or Asclepiodotus rather than from the original. Still the work has much in common with the Meteorologica. Like Aristotle Seneca quotes his most important predecessors in the field before he gives his own views. The great difference consists in the moral precepts and conclusions with which Seneca has chosen to elaborate the purely scientific discussion of natural phenomena.

In Seneca's work too the larger part deals with subjects which have little bearing on geology. Book I discusses the luminous aerial phenomena (haloes, rainbow, meteors, mirrors), Book II thunder and lightning, Book V the winds and Book VII the comets. The third book is entirely devoted to the "terrestial waters", here Seneca discusses the flow of waters on our globe and concludes that it is impossible that the rivers derive their waters from rain alone. There must be immense reservoirs of water in large subterranean caverns where conditions apply under which large amounts of air present can be changed into water too. Like the human body the earth is full of channels and conduits, which bring the water to the surface to feed the rivers. The book ends in describing the Last Flood and World Conflagration which will destroy the world, which is to be reborn again to start a new cosmic cycle.

Apart from these few essays no other book on geological subjects was published in classical Antiquity, our further information comes from historians, geographers, philosophers and poets, who often have not personally observed the phenomena they describe. Still the variety of terms used by the ancients for the phenomena we are discussing shows that they must have observed many details, which did, however, not form subjects of scientific study.

The Egyptians, for instance, were familiar with different forms of mountains. Where the Assyrians use the word šadû (Sum. KUR,ḪUR -SAG) they speak of h3ś. t (III. 234. 7), when they want to contrast the mountains with their flat country (Coptic ⲁ̄ⲧⲱⲟⲩ, Greek ὀρεινός). The oldest word for mountain was ḏw (V. 541. 7, or sometimes ḏw. t (V. 545. 2), Coptic ⲧⲟⲟⲩ) mostly used in the sense of the mountains where there were quarries or mines. A much later term śt3 (IV. 554.12) was used for such mountains whence precious stones came. Another late term was mn (.t) (II. 69.11), usually written mn. tj, to indicate the two mountain ranges enclosing the Nile valley. An older word ṭs.t (V. 401.6) indicates mountains in general. The word for mountain-top, dhn. t (V. 478.11, Coptic ⲕⲟⲟϩ) designates "precipice" too, for which later texts use the term nw. w (II. 214.18, Copt. ⲛⲟⲩⲛ), which usually designates the ocean, the netherworld (abyssos), just as the Sumerians denote a precipice by ABZU (Akkad. apsû), later also using KI-IN-DAR (Akkad. nigiṣṣu), which really means "crevice". The valley in the desert is called in.t (I. 93.2), but the chasm between mountains is termed šrh (IV. 528.13, Copt. ⲱⲗϩ), whereas the mountainpass was called g3w. t (V. 152.18). The distinction between the different Coptic terms for precipice ⲩⲱⲙⲉ and ⲝⲁⲝⲣⲓⲁ, ⲝⲟⲓⲩⲝⲉⲓⲩ escape us, though the latter seems to mean "foot of a mountain" too. The word "shivering of the earth", nwr-t3 (II. 223.1, Coptic ⲕⲙⲧⲟ, ⲕⲉⲙⲟⲟ) designates an earthquake, which the Sumerians called ᵈNUN-GAL (Akkad. rêbu, râbu). The Copts also use "tottering" (ⲥⲟ̄ⲙ) to render our "earthquake". The Egyptians being well-acquainted with the annual floods used a special term to designate underground water "breaking through" (śd, IV. 375.6), just as the Sumerians distinguished URÚ (Akkad. abûbû), deluge from NAG-KUD-MAḤ (devastating flood, Akkad. butiqtu). More such examples would be easy to find, but these few terms may be sufficiently convincing to demonstrate to the readers, that such phenomena were properly observed in detail.

3. *The changing face of the earth*

The preclassical and classical civilisations rose and flourished in an area of seismic disturbances. The ancients were well aware of such natural convulsions, which they often report though they never draw any general conclusion from them but treat them as separate cataclysms. They observed changing shorelines and beaches, tidal waves and volcanic islands rising and disappearing again. As Ovid has it (15):

> "Even places alter — with uncertain gales
> Where once was land the bounding vessel sails
> And where the sea once spread, on steady land
> Now houses, trees and men securely stand.
> Shells far from sea removed are often found
> And anchors buried in the mountain ground.
> Torrents a valley of the plain have made
> And mountains headlong to the sea conveyed."

The stories about the Pillars of Hercules (16) are well-known, but tradition has it also that Euboea was rent from Boeotia (17) and Ceos from Euboea (18), etc. (19). Miss Semple pointed out that in some cases such data may be of importance to the modern seismologist. Thus the rupture of the Strait of Rhium admitting the Ionian Sea into the deep-running Gulf of Corinth is described carefully by Pliny (20), but ancient authors of various periods mention different widths for these straits. Thus Thucydides (21) says that it measured seven stadia, Strabo (22) five, Pliny (23) a mile, and Scylax ten stadia (24) and she concludes that "these variations in a busy ferrypoint in an active earthquake-zône should not be overlooked."

The Vale of Tempe was formed by an earthquake according to Herodotus (25), another made a channel for the river Ladon from a mountain-basin in Arcadia to the Alpheus (26). In this light Plato's story of the destruction of Atlantis must have come quite natural to people accustomed to see volcanic islands rise from the sea or disappear in it (27). Pindar (28) claims that when all the rest of the land was already in existence "from the waters of the sea arose an island (Rhodes), which is held by the father of the piercing beams of light".

Both Eratosthenes and Poseidonius agree that such changes are caused by the action of water, fire, earthquakes and volcanoes (29), but only Aristotle believes that "we must suppose these changes to follow some order (taxis) and cycle (periodos)" (30). However, all seemed to agree that even upheavals, like mountains, were "mere dust on a ball" (31). Such theories of elevation and subsidence were often based on observations of sea-shells and salt-deposits far inland in the mountains. Strabo (32) is convinced that "formerly at various periods a large portion of the mainland has been covered and again uncovered by the sea", thus confirming an earlier statement by Aristotle (33), that "inroads and withdrawals of the sea have often converted dry land into sea and sea into dry land".

Tertullian mentions the washing-down of soil from the mountains, the alluvial deposits laid down by rivers and sea-shells on mountain-tops as a proof that Noah's Flood once covered the whole earth. Still the flood was not the only main catastrophe (34), lands like Sicily have been torn off or engulfed like Atlantis and he seems to have had in mind some kind of geological evolution. On the other hand Isidore of Seville (35) uses the fossil shells embedded in remote mountains as witnesses to the truth of the Noachian tradition without mentioning other changes of the face of the Earth.

It is interesting to compare this classical hint at a constantly changing face of the earth with Chinese tradition, recently published by Needham (36). Chu Hsi in his Chu Chhüan Shu (c. 1170) recognizes the fact, that the mountains had been elevated since the days when the shells of living animals had been buried in the soft mud of the sea bottom. Somewhere between AD 200 and 600 something like our modern concept of "geological time" came to be denoted by "sang thien" (the long period of centuries during which the sea turned into dry land). In the History of the Chin Dynasty (AD 222—284), which was written down before 635 we find the following interesting passage expressing the Chinese idea of the changing face of the earth: "Ty Yü often used to say that the high hills will become valleys and the deep valleys will become hills. So when he made monumental stelae recording his successes he made them in duplicate, burying one at the bottom of a mountain and placing the other on top. He considered that in subsequent centuries they would be likely to exchange their position."

4. *Sea, water and rivers as geological agents*

In older classical tradition the "Waters of the Deep", the Tihom of Genesis and the Tiamat of the Sumerians constantly reoccur, they are mentioned by Hesiod's Theogony and play their part in Plato and many other authors, who assume that all water comes from the Ocean and ends there again. Anaximenes calls the "sea the source of the water and the source of the wind. For neither could the force of the wind blowing outwards from within come into being without the great main sea, nor the streams or rivers, nor the showery water of the sky, but the mighty main is the begetter of clouds and winds and rivers". Also "we all have our origin from earth and water". Somehow water percolates the earth for "in certain caves water drips down". In a fragment of the writtings of Hippon of Samos (c. 450 B.C.), quoted by a scholiast on Homer, we read: "Homer says that all rivers, seas, springs and wells have their source in the Ocean, and Hippon among others supports this view, because the sea is deeper than our wells; the assumption being that water rises from a lower to a higer level".

St. Basil (AD 329—379) held (37) that the sea formed one body of water, but that it was separated from certain pools and lakes, for it was evident from Genesis I that "all the waters did not flow together in one place. Although some authorities think that the Hyrcanian and Caspian Sea are enclosed in their own boundaries, if we believe the geographers, they communicate with each other and discharge themselves into the Great Sea, the vast ocean so dreaded by navigators, which surrounds the isle of Britain and Western Spain". Still "sea-water is the source of all moisture on earth".

The philosophers generally agreed that the mass of water is greater than that of the land. Apollonius gets this answer from his Brahmin informant (38): "... Apollonius resumed by asking Iarchus, which they considered the bigger, the sea or the land and Iarchus replied: "If the land be compared with the sea, it will be found to be bigger, for it includes the sea in itself; but if it be considered in relation to the entire mass of water, we can show that the earth is the lesser of the two, for it is upheld by the water".

Many asked themselves why the sea was salt, some holding that it was the relic of a vast water-mass reduced and made salt by the sun. Sea shells and salt deposits found far inland were rightly understood to indicate old sea-bottoms, e.g. in the Egyptian oases and the Lybian depression or in the heart of Asia Minor. Democritus held that the saltness of the sea was due to the same cause as the accumulation of salt on the land. Like atoms have sought like and coagulated, the process being assisted by evaporation, for the sea was becoming smaller and smaller and would finally dry up. Anaxagoras gave a more plausible explanation, holding that it was due to the percolation of water through the earth, which contains salt (salt and soda for instance being mined!), and as the water flows into the sea evaporation would help to accumulate the salt there. Metrodorus of Chios (fourth century B.C.) who wrote an "On Nature" held that the sea is salt because its water trickles through the earth (itself the sediment or "dregs" of the original watery mixture) and takes part of the solid substance through which it passes like a fluid percolating through ashes.

A theory of an immense underground reservoir of water, supplied and reinforced by seepage from the sea, the earth absorbing salt as the water percolated, was held by several ancient authors such as Seneca (39). Geikie rightly points out that Seneca evidently had no idea of the structure of the earth's crust and was misled by a few spectacular caves and underground structures known to the ancients. Aristotle had already given a far better picture of the hydrological cycle of water evaporating from the seas and lakes to return as rain and snow by the way of brooks and rivers (40).

In the first three chapters of Book II of this Meteorologica Aristotle discusses the sea and its nature. He quotes the ancient theologians who believed that the sea, like rivers, had sources, whereas the secular philosophers believed that it had a beginning in time and gave various accounts of its saltness (Anaximander, Diogenes of Apollonia, Anaximenes). Aristotle then argues that the sea cannot have sources, for water from sources is either running or artificial, the sea is neither. Nor have sources ever been found in the land-locked seas known to the Greeks. If the sea does flow on places this is either due to confinement in narrow straits or to difference in depths. The place occupied by the sea is the natural place for water. The sun evaporates the fresh water, which subsequently falls as rain, the salt water is left. Aristotle compares this proces with the digestion of food and criticizes the account of rivers and the sea given by Plato in the Phaedo (111 c ff.):

"Plato's description of rivers and the sea in the Phaedo is impossible. He says that they all flow into each other beneath the earth through channels pierced through it, and that their original source is a body of water in the centre of the earth called Tartarus, from which all waters running of standing are drawn. This primary and original mass causes the flow of various rivers by surging perpetually to and fro; for it has no fixed position but is always oscillating about the centre, and its motion up and down fills the rivers. Many of them form lakes, one example of which is the sea by which we live, but all of them pass round again in a circle to the original source from which they flowed; many return to it again at the same place, others at a point opposite to that of their outflow, for instance if they flowed out from below, they return from above. They fall only as far as the centre, when once that is passed all motion is uphill. And water gets its tastes and colour from the different kinds of earth through which it happens to flow."

Evaporation and rainfall balance each other. The sea is therefore constant in volume but the water composing it changes. Its saltness is due to the dry exhalation, says Aristotle, which exhalation is analogous to the residue left in digestion and combustion, and like them salty. This dry exhalation is mixed with the moist exhalation and is carried down with it in rain, thus causing the saltness of the sea. Examples quoted by Aristotle show that the saltness is due to an admixture of an appropriate substance. These then are his actual words:

"Some (Empedocles, Democritus and Antiphon) believe that the sea is, as it were, the sweat of the earth which it sweats out when the sun heats it which is the reason why it is salt because sweat is salt. Others (Xenophanes, Anaxagoras) suppose that the earth is the cause of its saltness just as water strained through ashes becomes salt, so the sea is salt because earth with this property surrounds it.

Water surrounds the earth just as air surrounds water: and the sun evaporates fresh water, which subsequently falls as rain. The fresh water, then, is evaporated, the salt water left. The process is analogous to the digestion of liquid food. The place occupied by the sea is the natural place of water: and fresh water evaporates more easily and quickly when it reaches and is dispersed in the sea. The sea is not salt either because it is a residue left by evaporation or because of an admixture of earth; nor is it any explanation to call it the sweat of the earth. The sea is constant in volume though the water composing it constantly changes. Its saltness is due to the dry exhalation, which is analogous to the residues left in combustion and digestion, and like them salty. This dry exhalation is mixed with the moist exhalation, is carried down by the rain, and so makes the sea salt. Hence south winds and autumn winds are brackish. So the sea increases in saltness, for little or no salt is lost in the process of evaporation. Examples show that saltness is due to an admixture of an appropriate substance."

Though some believed that rivers flow from subterranean reservoirs fed by rainfall, Aristotle criticized this view as such reservoirs would have to be impossibly large. Condensation produces water below the earth as well as above it. "The process is rather like that in which small drops form in the region above the earth, and these join again others, until rain water falls in some quantity; similarly inside the earth, as it were, at a single point, quantities of water collect together and gush out of the earth and form the sources of rivers. A practical proof of this is that where men make irrigation works they collect the water in pipes and channels, as though the higher parts of the earth were sweating it out. So we find the sources of rivers flow from mountains, and that the largest and most numerous rivers flow from the highest mountains. Similarly the majority of springs are in the neighbourhood of mountains and high places, and there are few sources of water in the plains except rivers. For mountains and high places act like a thick sponge overhanging the earth and make the water drip through and run together in small quantities in many places. For they receive the great volume of rain water that falls (it makes no difference whether a receptacle of this sort is concave and turned up or convex and turned down): and they cool the vapour as it rises and condense it again to water."

Aristotle then discusses the geographical evidence for his thesis that the largest rivers flow from the highest mountains and finally summarizes his theory in the following words:

"We can now see that the supposition that rivers spring from definite hollows in the earth is false. For, firstly, the whole earth, we might say would hardly be room enough, nor the region of the clouds, if the flow were fed only by water already existing, and if some waters were not in fact vanishing in evaporation, some re-forming all the time, but all were produced from a ready-made supply. Secondly, the fact that rivers have their sources at the foot of the mountains proves that the place accumulates water little by little by a gradual collection of drops, and that the sources of rivers are formed this way. It is of course not at all impossible that there do exist such places containing large amounts of water, like lakes; but they cannot be so large as to act in the way this theory maintains, any more than one could reasonably suppose that their visible sources supply all the water for the rivers, most of which flow from springs. It is thus equally unreasonable to believe either that lakes or that the visible sources are the sole water supply. But the rivers that are swallowed up by the earth prove that there are chasms and cavities in the earth...".

Most ancient authors are perfectly aware of the hydrological cycle of evaporation, condensation and rainfall, followed by the flow of water back to the sea (41), "the sun drawing water to feed its flames", but they do not always state it clearly. Thus Lucretius (42) tells us:

"For the rest, that sea, streams and springs are ever filling with new moisture, and that waters are ceaselessly oozing forth, there is no need of words to prove: the great downrush of waters on every side makes this clear. But the water which is foremost is ever taken away, and so it comes to pass that there is never overmuch moisture in the sum, partly because the strong winds diminish it as they sweep the seas, and so does the sun in heaven, as he unravels their fabric with his rays, partly because it is sent hither and thither in every land. For the brine is strained through and the substance of moisture oozes back, and all streams together at the fountainhead of rivers, and thence comes back over the lands with freshened current, where the channel once cleft has brought down the water in their liquid march" and omits the parallel process of the return of water from the clouds in the form of rain!

Like the modern Greeks the ancient inhabitants of that country were very "water-conscious" and the quality of the water of various springs must have been as lively a topic then as it is in modern Greece (43). Some waters were said to be fatal, like the water of the river Styx, which was supposed to kill instantly and to corrode all vessels except those made of horn (44). In observing these springs and rivers they came across the often recorded phenomenon of "*lost rivers*". The widespread limestone formations of the Eastern Mediterranean and especially the karst regions of Arcadia, Epirus and Liguria would give rise to stories about lost rivers so frequent in classical mythology and other literature (45). Rivers suddenly disappear in swallow-holes and are supposed to flow underground for many miles or to feed an underground lake or reservoir. On the other hand the abundance and volume of many limestone springs could be explained only by supposing that they were the issue of subterraneous streams or drainage channels of katavothra lakes. The earth must be riddled with caverns and channels, so the ancients thought. It was quite natural to regard the subterraneous outlets of the Pheneus Lake in Arcadia as the work of the engineering hero Heracles (46), when one was confronted with such a wonder. In the same passage Pausanias tells us that the Stymphalus Lake of highland Arcadia had its outlet in an underground rift but reappeared twenty-two miles away in Argolis as the Erasinus river which washed the town of Argos. Strabo mentions the "Erasinus which now flows

underground from the Stymphalian Lake and issues forth into the
Argive country, although in earlier times it had no outlet, since the
"berethra" (lit. pits), which the Arcadians call "zerethra" were stopped
up and did not admit of the waters being carried off". Similar stories
are told about the Ladon and the Anias, both in Arcadia.

This type of speculation is very frequent in ancient literature. Thus
the river Styx, rising on Mount Aroania of northern Arcadia, flows
over a cliff and looses itself in a mass of broken rock, but is said to
emerge at some distance as a tributary of the "ever-flowing" Cartis,
the hidden part being in Tartarus (47). Similar stories are told about
the Acheron and Cocytus rivers of Thesprotia and others of the old
katavothra district of Epirus (48). The Eridanus (Po) was said to spring
from the lower world, where Aeneas saw it flowing through the Ely-
sian fields (49). The Fons Timavus at the head of the Adriatic was
claimed to be a subterranean offshoot of the Danube (50) and a similar
story is attached to the Rheti near Eleusis (51). "Lost rivers" are also
mentioned in descriptions of Syria and Cilicia (52) and in Western
Spain (53). Sometimes a mythological reason is given. Thus the river
Helicon ran three miles underground in its course from Mount Olym-
pos to the sea, because the river dipped underground on its own account to avoid pollution when Orpheus was murdered (54).

Again, fresh-water springs are common of the Mediterranean coasts,
and the ancients knew many of them such as the spring between the
island of Aradus and the Phoenician mainland (55), one off the coast
of Lycia (56), the submarine spring of Deine in the Argolic Gulf (57),
"Dulcis Portus" on the west coast of Epirus (58), one between Baia
and Ischia (59), near Puteoli (60), near Gades in the Atlantic Ocean
(61) and also ten miles south-east of the port of Massilia. Coupling
these fresh-water springs with the "lost rivers" the ancient authors
made up some very famous and tenacious tall stories such as that of
the river Alpheus going underground near Olympia (Greece) to reappear in the fresh-water spring Arethusa near Syracuse (Sicily) (62)
"which casts up filth every fourth year on the very days when the
victims are slaughtered at the Olympic Games". This story is rejected
by Strabo and Polybios. Strabo (63) mentions that "the mouth of the
river empties into the sea in full view and there is no mouth (whirl-
pool) on the transit, which swallows it up. "He cites further fables of
this type, such as the Asopus in Sicyon rising in Phrygia, the Alpheus
rising in Tenedos and the Inopus crossing over from the Nile to Delos. There was also a story of the river Nile feeding a fresh-water spring

off the coast of Delos (64): "the Maeander descending from Ce-
laenae through Phrygia to Miletus goes through to the Peloponessus
and forms the Asopus. The Delians state that the stream which they
call Inopus comes to them from the Nile. There is even a story that
the Nile itself is the Euphrates, which disappears into a marsh, rises
again beyond Aethiopia and becomes the Nile" and Pliny in the second
Book of his Natural History argues:

"But some rivers so hate the sea, that they actually flow underneath
the bottom of it, for instance the spring Arethusa at Syracuse, in which
things emerge that have been thrown into the Alpheus which flows
through Olympia and reaches the coast in the Peleponnese. Instances
of rivers that flow underground and come to the surface again are the
Lycus in Asia, the Erasinus in the Argolid and the Tigris in Mesopotamia; and objects thrown into the spring of Aesculapius at Athens
are given back again in Phaleron Harbour. Also a river that goes
underground in the Plain of Atinas comes out 20 miles further on, as
also does the Timavus in the district of Aquilea."

Hence also, rivers with the same name flowing in different countries
are supposed to have underground connection, thus the various rivers
with the name Lethe (65) and the Inachus river of southern Epirus,
which is thought to be the same as the Inachus of Argolis (66).

The interest awakened by these "lost rivers" led to the exploration
of some underground caves and the discovery of *stalagmites and stalactites*, about which we have several reports. Thus in a work ascribed to
Aristotle (67) we are told: "In the island of Menonesus, Chalcedon,
there a cave which is called the Pretty Cave. In this pillars have been
formed by the congelation of the water and this becomes evident from
their being contracted towards the ground, for the narrowest part is
there." Pausanias describes the Corycian cave on the way between
Delphi and Parnassus (68): "It is larger and you can go a great way
through it even without lights... water is dripping from the roof, so
that everywhere the marks of the droppings are visible on the floor
of the cave" and in a cave at Pylus "in which it is said the cows of
Nestor and of Neleus before him were stalled" the same phenomena
were observed. Pomponius Mela says that they were also found in
the Rock of Gibraltar cave.

In China the study of caves and the formations found in them have
been pursued for many centuries, they were of particular interest to
the early Taoist hermits. Stalactites (and staglamites) are included in
lists of inorganic and chemical substances from the fourth century

B.C. onwards. Ko Hung describes them plainly in connection with one of the varieties of his "magical mushrooms" (AD 300).

5. *Sedimentation, erosion and denudation*

Aristotle is convinced of the part which water plays in shaping the surface of the earth and he expresses it in this way (69):

"The same parts of the earth are not always moist or dry, but change their character according to the appearance or failure of rivers. So also the mainland and sea change places and one area does not remain earth, another sea, for all times, but sea replaces what was once dry land, and where there is now sea there is at another time land. This process must, however, be supposed to take place in an orderly cycle. Its originating cause is that the interior parts of the earth, like the bodies of plants and animals, have their maturity and age. Only whereas the parts of plants and animals are not affected separately but the whole creature must grow to maturity and decay at the same time, the parts of the earth are affected separately, the cause of the process being cold and heat. Cold and heat increase and decrease owing to the sun's course, and because of them acquire different potentialities: some are able to remain moist up to a certain point and then dry up and become old again, while others come to life and become moist in their turn. As places become drier the springs necessarily disappear, and when this happens the rivers first dwindle from their former size and finally dry up: and when the rivers are removed and disappear in one place, but come into existence correspondingly in another, the sea must change too. For wherever it has encroached on the land because the rivers have pushed it out, it must when it recedes leave behind it dry land: while wherever it has been filled and silted up by rivers and formed dry land, this must again be flooded.

But these natural changes escape our observation because the whole natural process of the earth's growth takes place by slow degrees and over periods of time which are vast compared to the length of life, and whole peoples are destroyed and perish before they can record the process from beginning to end."

Aristotle then discusses some examples such as the formation of Egypt by the Nile deposits and the silting up of Lake Maeotis (Sea of Azov). Finally, this is his conclusion: "It is therefore clear that as time is infinite and the universe eternal that neither Tanaïs (Don) nor Nile always flowed but the place whence they flow was once dry: for their action has an end whereas time has none. And the same may be said in truth about other rivers. But if rivers come into being and perish and if the same parts of the earth are not always moist, the sea must necessarily change correspondingly. And if in places the sea recedes while in others it encroaches, then evidently the same parts of the earth as a whole are not always sea, nor always mainland, but in process of time all change."

The ancients were of course aware of movements of the land and some speculate on the part such movements played in shaping the face of the earth, for, as Lucretius has it (70): "Plains sank down, lofty mountains grew in height; for indeed the rocks could not settle down, nor could all parts equally subside". Nowever, the changes due to the action of the sea or rivers was much more obvious to them. Pliny discussing the coastline of southern Spain says (71): "During so long a period of time the seas have been encroaching on the land or the shores have been moving forward, and rivers have formed curves, or have straightened out their windings". They were even more familiar with *sedimentation*, with the silting action of their rivers in an area where the tides are far too feeble to scour the harbours. This is what Thucydides has to say about the silting up of the mouth of the river Achelous (72): "Most of the Echinades islands lie opposite the Oeniadae at no great distance from the mouth of the Achelous, so that the river, which is large, keeps making fresh deposits of silt, and some of the islands have already become part of the mainland, and probably this will happen to all of them in no great while. For the stream is wide and deep and turbid, and the islands are close together and serve to bind to one another the bars as they are formed preventing them from being broken up, since the islands lie, not in line, but irregularly, and do not allow straight channels for the water in to the open sea", a phenomenon also commented upon by Pliny and Strabo (73). The latter also mentions the extension of the delta of the Maeander into the high seas (74): "The soil is not only friable and crumbly but it is also full of salts and easy to burn out. And perhaps the Maeander is winding for this reason, because the stream often changes its course, and carrying down much silt, adds the silt at different times to different parts of the shore; however, it forcibly thrusts a part of the silt out to the high sea. And, in fact, by its deposits of silt, exceeding forty stadia, it has made Priene, which in earlier times was on sea, an inland city", and the silting up of the Po delta (75): "Not only is it (the Padus) the largest of these rivers but it is oftentimes filled by both the rains and the snow, although, as the result of separating into many streams near the outlets, the mouth is choked with mud and hard to enter".

Strabo (76) discusses sedimentation in general in the first book of his Geography before he goes on to speak about the Nile Valley and its history, a problem which held the attention of many ancient authors: "Now the reason why the alluvium brought down by many rivers does not reach the open sea in its forward course is that the sea, which is naturally refluent, drives it back again; for the sea is like animated beings, and just like they inhale and exhale their breath unremittingly, so in like manner the sea too is subject to a certain recurrent motion that proceeds from itself and returns to itself unremittingly. This is apparent to any one who stands on the beach at the time when the waves break; for no sooner are one's feet washed than they are left bare by the waves, and then again they are washed, and this goes on unremittingly. And close upon the wash comes a wave, which, however gentle it may be, possesses an certain increase in power as it rushes in, and casts all foreign matter out upon the land—"and casteth much tangle out along the sea". Now while this takes place to a greater extent when there is wind, yet it occurs both when there is a calm and when the winds blow from the land; for the wave carries to the land none the less, even against the wind, as though it were subject along with the sea itself, to the sea's own motion. This is what Homer meant when he said: "And goes the arching crest about the promontories, and speweth the foaming brine afar", and "the shores cry aloud as the salt sea belches forth".

Accordingly, the onset of the waves has a power sufficient to expel foreign matter. They call this, in fact, a "purging" of the sea — a process by which dead bodies and bits of wreckage are cast upon the land by the waves. But the ebb has not power sufficient to draw back into the deep sea a corpse, or a stick of wood, or even the lightest of substances, a cork (when once they have been cast by the waves upon the land) from places on the shore that are near the sea, where they have been stranded by the waves. And so it comes about that both the silt and the water fouled by it are cast out by the waves, the weight of the silt cooperating with the wave, so that the silt is precipitated to the bottom near the land before it can be carried forward into the deep sea; in fact, even the force of the river ceases just a short distance beyond its mouth. So then, it is possible for the sea, beginning as its beaches, to be entirely silted up, if it receives the inflow of rivers uninterruptedly. And this would be the result even if we assume that the Euxine Sea is deeper than the Sea of Sardinia, which is said to be the deepest of all the seas, that have been sounded — about one thousand fathoms, as Poseidonius states."

Strangely enough the Egyptians had little to contribute to the *problem of the Nile and its annual rise* or to the geology of the Nile valley, which was a matter of life and death to them (77). Anaxagoras had given the correct solution of the problem when he maintained that this flooding was due to the melting of the snow in the Aethiopian mountains, but this view was dismissed by Herodotus and the most popular theory in Antiquity was that of Oenopides of Chios (c. 425 B.C.), who believed that it was due to underground water being less consumed by internal heat in summer: "the waters below the earth are hot in winter, cold in summer; this can be seen from deep wells, the water of which is cool in the hot season, but remains unfrozen in winter. The Nile waters therefore diminish in winter, owing to the heat below, but in summer when this cause is not operating, they fill their channel without hindrance." Diogenes of Apollonia maintained that the summer floods were "drawn up along secret channels by the heated earth"; Ephorus that this flood of waters "sweated through the sun-cracked surface". Democritus reverted again to the theory of Anaxagoras and said that the floods were due to "the rains which fill the lakes and the Nile", in which passage we may see a hint at the source lakes in Central Africa. Seneca in his fourth book of the Naturales Quaestiones does not believe in the rain-fed floods, but here our manuscript breaks off and we do not know what solution he proposed.

However all authors agree that the land of Egypt was built up by the sediment brought down by the river Nile, or as the famous phrase of Herodotus runs, that it was "a gift of the river". This is what this oldest Greek historian has to tell us about Egypt's geological history (78):

"The greater part of the country (Egypt) seemed to me to be, as the priests declare, a tract gained by the inhabitants. For the whole region above Memphis, lying between the two ranges of hills that have been spoken of, appeared to have formed at one time a gulf of the sea. It resembles (to compare small things with great) the parts about Ilium and Teuthrania, Ephesus, and the plain of the Maeander. In all these regions the land has been formed by the rivers, whereof the greatest is not to compare for size with any of the five mouths of the Nile. I could mention other rivers also, far inferior to the Nile in magnitude, that have effected very great changes. Among these not the least is the

Achelous, which, after passing through Arcanania, empties itself into the sea opposite the islands called Echinades, and has already joined half of them to the continent.

In Arabia, not far from Egypt, there is a long and narrow gulf running inland from the sea called the Erythraean, of which I will here set down the dimensions... My opinion is that Egypt was formerly very much such a gulf as this — one gulf penetrated from the sea that washes Egypt to the north and penetrated towards Ethiopia; another entered from the southern ocean and stretched towards Syria; the two gulfs ran into the land so as to almost to meet each other, and left between them only a very narrow tract of land. Now if the Nile should choose to divert its waters from the present bed into this Arabian Gulf, what is there to hinder it from being filled up by the stream within, at the utmost, twenty thousand years? For my part, I think it would be filled in half that time. How then should not a gulf, even of much greater size, have been filled up in the ages that passed before I was born, by a river that is at once so large and so constantly at work?

This I give credit to those from whom I received this account of Egypt, and am myself, moreover, strongly of the same opinion, since I remarked that the country projects into the sea further than the neighbouring shores, and I observed that there were shells upon the hills, and that salt exuded from the soil to such an extent as even to injure the pyramids; and I noticed also that there is only a single hill in all Egypt where sand is found, namely the hill above Memphis (Giza!); and further I found the country to bear no resemblance either to its borderland Arabia, or to Libya, nay, nor even to Syria, which forms the seaboard of Arabia; but whereas the soil of Libya is sandy and of a reddish hue, and that of Arabia and Syria inclines to stone and clay, Egypt has a soil that is black and crumbly, as being alluvial and formed of the deposits brought down by the river from Ethiopia."

Aristotle has a short passage on the Nile valley filling up (79): "Egypt is a land which is obviously in a process of getting drier, and the whole country is clearly a deposit of the Nile; but because the adjacent peoples have only encroached on the marshes gradually as they dried up, the beginning of the process has been lost in the lapse of time. We can see, however, that all the mouths of the Nile, except the one at Canopus, are artificial and not formed by the action of the river itself, and the old name of Egypt was Thebes... the higher lands were inhabited before the lower-lying, because the nearer a place is to the point where silt is being deposited the longer it must remain marshy, as the land last formed is always more waterlogged. But this land changes in its turn, and in time becomes thriving. For as places dry they improve, and places that formerly enjoyed good climate deteriorate and grow too dry."

Strabo (80) reports a most interesting theory propounded by Strato, Theophrastus' successor as head of the Lyceum and a famous physicist: "The same thing, Strato says, happened in the Mediterranean basin also; for in this case the passage at the Pillars was broken through when the sea had been filled by the rivers, and at the time of the outrush of the water the places that had hitherto been covered with shoal-water were left dry. Strato proposes as a cause of this, first that the beds of the Atlantic and the Mediterranean are on different levels, and secondly, that at the Pillars even at the present day a submarine ridge stretches across from Europe to Libya, indicating that the Mediterranean and the Atlantic could not have been one and the same formerly. The seas of the Pontus region, Strato continues, are very shallow, whereas the Cretan, the Silician, and the Sardinian Seas are very deep; for since the rivers that flow from the north and east are very numerous and very large, the seas there are being filled with mud, while the others remain deep; and herein also is the reason why the Pontus is sweetest, and why the outflow takes place in the direction of the inclination of its bed. Strato further says it is his opinion that the whole Euxine Sea will be silted up at some future period, if such impourings continue; for even now the regions on the left (western) side of the Pontus are already covered with shoal waters; for instance, Salmydessus, and the land at the mouth of the Ister, which the sailors call "the Breasts" and the desert of Scythia; perhaps too the temple of Ammon was formerly on the sea, but is now situated in the interior because there has been an outpouring of the sea. Strato conjectures that the oracle of Ammon with good reason became so distinguished and well-known as it is if it was situated on the sea, and that its present position so very far from the sea gives no reasonable explanation of its present distinction and fame; and that in ancient times Egypt was covered by the sea as far as the bogs about Pelusium, Mount Casius and Lake Sirbonis; at all events, even today when the salt-lands in Egypt are dug up, the excavations are found to contain sand and fossil shells, as though the country had been submerged beneath the sea and the whole region round Mount Casius and the so-called Gerrha had once been covered with shoal-water so it connected with the Gulf of the Red Sea; and when the sea retired these regions were left bare, except that the Lake Sirbonis remained;

then the lake also broke through to the sea, and thus became a bog. In the same way, Strato adds, the beaches of the so-called Lake Moeris (Birket al-Karun) more nearly ressemble sea-beaches than river-banks."

As to the structure of the Nile valley before the river began to deposit its mud we have an interesting theory of Xanthus of Lydia (c. 500 BC), that there was an early connection between the Mediterranean and the Red Sea, a theory which is also held by Eratosthenes (81). Strabo believes it too and considers it probable that (82) "at some future time the isthmus which separates the Egyptian Sea from the Erythraean Sea should part asunder or subside, and becoming a strait, should connect the outer and the inner seas, similarly to what has taken place at the Pillars".

The river Nile carried much silt into the sea and this phenomenon attracted much attention (83): "Moreover, those pecularities of each several country which are in some way marvellous and most widely known, and manifest to everybody; such is the case with the rising of the Nile and also the silting up of the sea... To those who visit Egypt... the nature of the country becomes quite clear to one who has learnt about the river..."

Herodotus (84) gives some exact data on the situation in his day: "The Egypt to which the Greeks go in their ships is an acquired country, the gift of the river. The same is true for the land above the lake. to a distance of three days' voyage, concerning which the Egyptians say nothing, but which is exactly the same kind of country. The following is the general character of this region. In the first place, on approaching it by sea, when you are still a day's sail from the land, if you let down a sounding-line you will bring up mud, and find yourself in eleven fathoms water, which shows that the soil washed down by the stream extends to that distance."

Strabo compares this with the silting up of the Pyramus Delta (85): "In passing out through the mountains it (the Pyramus) brings down so much silt to the sea, partly from Cataonia and partly from the Cilician plains, that even an oracle is reported of having been given out in reference to it as follows: "Men that are to be shall experience this at the time when the Pyramus of the silver eddies shall silt up its sacred sea-beach and come to Cyprus". Indeed, something similar to this is taking place also in Egypt since the Nile is always turning the sea into dry land by throwing out silt. Accordingly, Herodotus (II. 5) calls Egypt "a gift of the Nile", while Homer (Od. 4.354) speaks of Pharos as "being out in the open sea", since in earlier times it was not, as now, connected with the mainland of Egypt."

Plutarch, in his De Iside et Osiride, points out that mollusca (kog-chylia) are found on the mountains and in the mines, which proves that all Egypt was once sea, but he also states that the flat riverland was formed by continual deposition of mud from the Nile "all of which has the testimony of sense to confirm it. For we see at this day that the river pours down fresh mud and adds new earth unto the old, the sea by degrees gives way and the salt water runs off as the parts in the bottom gain height by new accessions of mud. Moreover, we see that the island Pharos, which Homer in his time observed to be a whole day's sail from Egypt, is now a part of it; not because it changed position or came nearer to the shore than before; but because the river still adding to and increasing the main land, the intermediate sea was obliged to retire."

The *silting up of the Sea of Azov* and the formation of the Hellespont and the Straits of Gibraltar was another frequent theme of discussion, for many ancient philosophers saw these problems as a logical sequence of happenings in the past. Aristotle even believed that there was a connection between the Caspian and the Black Sea (86): "There is the lake beneath the Caucasus, which the inhabitants call a sea: for this is fed by many rivers, and having no obvious outlets runs out beneath the earth in the district of the Coraxi (east coast of the Black Sea) and comes up somewhere in the so-called deeps of Pontus. This is a part of the sea whose depth is unfathomable; at any rate no sounding has yet succeeded in finding the bottom". He also argues that the waters of Lake Maeotis (the Sea of Azov) flow into the deeper Black Sea and thence into the still deeper Aegean and thus through the Mediterra-nean into the Ocean. We noticed that Strato, head of the Athenian school from 287 B.C., amplified this theory, arguing that the Black Sea was originally a lake, which burst its bonds when its bed was gradually raised by silt, then the same happened to the Mediterranean, which fed by many rivers, finally broke through the Straits of Gibraltar. Afterwards its level fell uncovering the present coast-line and leaving shells and salt deposits far inland as well as a submarine reef in the Straits. The present opinion seems to point to an original Mediter-ranean land-area with two big lakes, which were united with the ocean when the Atlantic rose after the melting of the ice-cap and broke through the limestone dike at the Straits (87). Polybius agrees with Strato's picture of the slow secular process forming the Bosporus and the Straits of Gibraltar (88):

"The silting up of the Pontus has gone on from time immemorial and still continues. In the course of time both this sea and the Palus Maeotis will be entirely filled, if the existent local conditions remain the same and the causes of the alluvial deposits continue to act. For time being infinite, and the area of these basins being certainly limited, it is evident that even if the accretions were quite insignificant, the sea would be filled up in time; for by the law of nature if a finite quantity continuously grows or decreases in infinite time, even if the increase of decrease is infinitsemal — for this is what I now assume — it stands to reason that the process must be finally completed. But when, as in this case, the increase is no small one, but a very large quantity of soil is being deposited, it is evident that what I state will not happen at some remote date, but very shortly. And it is indeed visibly happening. As for the Palus Maeotis it is already silted up, the greater part of it varying in depth between five and seven fathoms, so that the larger ships can no longer navigate it without a pilot. And while it was once, as all ancient authorities agree, a sea continuous with the Pontus, it is now a fresh-water lake, the salt water having been forced out by the deposits and the inflow from the rivers prevailing. Some day it will be the same with the Pontus; in fact the thing is actually taking place and although it is not very generally noticed owing to the large size of the basin, it is apparent to any one who gives some slight attention to the matter."

Diodorus (89) maintains that the tradition of the Black Sea breaking through the Hellespont was still alive in his day: "And the Samothracians have a story that, before the floods which befell other peoples, a great one took place among them, in the course of which the outlet (of the Black Sea) at the Cyanean Rocks was first rent asunder and then the Hellespont. For the Pontus, which had at that time the form of a lake, was so swollen by the rivers which flow into it, that, because of the great flood which had poured into it, its waters burst forth violently into the Hellespont and flooded a large part of the coast of Asia (Minor) and made no small amount of the level part of the land of Samothrace into a sea; and this is the reason, we are told, why in later times fishermen have now and then brought up in their nets the stone capitals of columns, since even cities were covered by the inundation. The inhabitants who had been caught by the flood, the account continues, ran up to the higher regions of the island; and when the sea kept rising higher and higher, they prayed to the native gods, and since their lives were spared, to commemorate their rescue they set up boundary stones about the entire circuit of the island and dedicated altars upon which they offer sacrifices even to the present day. For these reasons it is patent that they inhabited Samothrace before the flood."

However, Pliny begs to differ (90) and puts something like the modern version in these few words: "The Euxine (Black Sea) formerly because of its inhospitable roughness called the Axine, owing to a peculiar jealousy on the part of Nature, which indulges the sea's greed without any limit, actually spreads into Europe and Asia. The Ocean was not content to have encircled the earth, and with still further cruelty to have reft away a portion of her surface, nor to have forced an entrance through a breach in the mountains and rent Gibraltar away from Africa, so devouring a larger area than it left remaining nor to have swallowed up a further space of land and flooded the Sea of Marmara through the Dardanelles; even beyond the Straits of Constantinople it widens into another desolate expanse, with an appetite unsatisfied until the Sea of Azov is linked on its own trespass to its encroachments."

Strabo contradicts Strato's theory in much more detail (91): "Eratosthenes says further that this question in particular has presented a problem: how does it come about that large quantities of mussel-shells, oyster-shells, scallop-shells, and also salt-marshes are found in many places in the interior at a distance of two thousand or three thousand stadia from the sea — for instance (to quote Eratosthenes) in the neighbourhood of the temple of Ammon and along the road three thousand stadia in length, that leads to it. At that place, he says, there is a large deposit of oyster-shells, and many beds of salt are still to be found there, and jets of salt-water rise to some height; besides that, they show pieces of wreckage from seafaring ships which the natives said had been cast up through a certain chasm, and on small columns dolphins are dedicated that bear the inscription: "Of Sacred Ambassadors of Cyrene". Then he goes on to praise the opinion of Strato, the physicist, and also that of Xanthus of Lydia. In the first place he praises the opinion of Xanthus, who says that in the reign of Artaxerxes there was so great a drought that the rivers, lakes and well dried up; that far from the sea, in Armenia, Matiene and Lower Phrygia, he himself had often seen, in many places, stones in the shape of a bivalve shell, shells of the pecten order, impressions of scallop-shells, and a large salt-marsh, and was therefore persuaded, that these plains were once sea. Then Eratosthenes praises the opinion of Strato, who goes still further into the question of causes, because Strato says he believes the Euxine formerly did not have its outlet at Byzantium, but the rivers which empty into the Euxine forced and opened a passage, and then the water discharged into the Propontis and the Hellespont.

Now one may admit that a great part of the continents was once covered by water for certain periods and was then left bare again; and in the same way one may admit also that the whole surface of the earth now submerged is uneven, at the bottom of the sea, just as we might admit, of course, that the part of the earth above water, on which we live, is subject to all changes mentioned by Eratosthenes himself; and therefore, so far as the argument of Xanthus is concerned, one cannot bring against it any charge of absurdity.

Against Strato, however, one might urge that, although there are many real causes of these changes, he overlooks them and suggests causes that do not exist, for he says their primary cause is that the beds of the Mediterranean and the Atlantic Ocean are not on the same level, and that their depth is not the same. But I reply that the cause of the rising and the falling of the sea, of its innundation of certain tracts of country, and of its subsequent retirement from them, is not to be sought for in the varying levels of the beds of the sea, in that some are lower and others higher, but in the fact that the beds of the sea sometimes rise themselves, and, on the other hand, sometimes sink, and in the fact that the sea rises or recedes along with its beds, for when the sea is lifted up, it will overflow, and when it is lowered, it will subside to its former level. Indeed, if what Strato says is true, that the overflow will necessarily follow every sudden increase in the volume of the sea: for instance, at every high tide of the sea or whenever the rivers are at their flood — in the one case the water having been brought from other parts of the sea, in other cases the volume of the water having been increased. But neither do the increases from rivers come all on the same time and suddenly and thus cause a swelling of the sea, nor do the tides persist long enough to do so (they are not irregular, either), nor do they cause innundations either on the Mediterranean Sea or anywhere else. Therefore, it remains for us to find the cause in the floor of the sea, either that which underlies the sea or that which is temporarily flooded, but preferably the submarine floor. For the floor that is saturated with water is far more easily moved and is liable to undergo more sudden changes; for the air-element, which is the ultimate cause of such occurences is greater there. But, as I have said the immediate cause of such occurences is that the beds of the sea are sometimes elevated and sometimes undergo a settling process, and not, that some beds are high, while others are less so. Strato, however, assumes this, believing that what happens in the case of rivers also occurs in the case of the sea, namely that the flow is away from the high places; otherwise, he would not have suggested that the bed is the cause of the current at Byzantium, saying that the bed of the Euxine is higher than that of the Propontis and the sea next after the Propontis, and at the same time adding the reason, namely, that the deeps of the Euxine are being filled up by the mud which is carried down by the rivers, and are becoming shallow, and that, on this account, the current is outward. He applies the same reasoning to the Mediterranean Sea as a whole as compared with the Atlantic Ocean, since, in his opinion, the Mediterranean Sea is making its bed higher than that which lies beneath the Atlantic Ocean; for the Mediterranean Sea too is being filled up with silt from many rivers, and is receiving a deposit of mud similar to that of the Euxine Sea. It should be also true, then, that the inflow at the Pillars and Calpe (Rock of Gibraltar) is similar to the inflow at Byzantium. But I pass this point by, for people will say that the same thing does occur here, but the inflow is lost in the ebb and flow of the tides and thus escapes observation."

On the other hand we must remember that Pliny (92) hesitates to ascribe the formation of the Straits of Gibraltar to natural causes and continues the passage we quoted above with these words: "These were the limits of the labours of Hercules, and consequently the inhabitants call them the Pillars of that deity, and believe that he cut the channel through them and thereby let in the sea which had hitherto been shut out, so altering the face of nature."

We have only one report of an attempt to cut such a rocky ledge separating to inland gulfs, the words which Apollonius of Tyana (93) is said to have uttered as a prophecy of Nero's attempt to cut the Isthmus of Corinth: "And he was at the Isthmus, when the sea was roaring round Lechaeum and hearing it he said: "This neck of land shall be cut through, or rather it shall not be cut". And herein he uttered a prediction of the cutting of the Isthmus which was attempted soon afterwards, when Nero in the seventh year of his reign projected it... It is said that he then (at Olympia) formed the novel project of cutting through the Isthmus, in order to make it possible for ships to sail right round and by it, and to unite the Aegean with the Adriatic Sea. So instead of every ship having to round Cape Malea, most by passing through the canal so cut could abridge an otherwise circuitous voyage. But mark the upshot of the oracle delivered by Apollonius. They began to dig the canal at Lechaeum, but they had not advanced

more than about four stadia of continuous excavation when Nero
stopped the work of cutting it, some say because Egyptian men of
science explained to him the nature of the seas, and declared that the
sea above Lechaeum would flood and obliterate the island of Aegina,
and others because he apprehended a revolution in the empire."

This passage shows that the ancients had little or no exact data on
the level of different gulfs and seas, for instance they always claimed
that one could not cut the Isthmus of Suez because the Mediterranean
and the Red Sea differed several feet in level (94). However, we know
that the Egyptian king Necho (609—549 B.C.) dug a canal connecting
the Nile and the Red Sea as a continuation of the irrigation canal leading from the Nile to Lake Timsah through the Wadi Tumilat. This
"Suez Canal" was certainly reopened by King Darius I (522—485
B.C.), three stelae along it testify of the King's efforts to make shipping
from the Nile to Persia feasible. Herodotus reports on this feat of engineering (95): "This prince (Necho) was the first to attempt the construction of a canal to the Erythraean Sea — a work completed afterwards by Darius the Persian — the length of which is four days'
journey, and the width such as to admit of two triremes being rowed
along it abreast. The water is derived from the Nile, which the canal
leaves a little above the city of Bubastis, near Patamus, the Arabian
town, being continued thence until it joins the Erythraean Sea. At
first it is carried along the Arabian side of the Egyptian plain, as far
as the chain of hills opposite Memphis, whereby the plain is bounded,
and in which lie the stone quarries; from here it skirts the base of the
hills running in a direction from west to east; after which it turns, and
enters a narrow pass, trending southwards from this point, until it
enters the Arabian Gulf. From the northern sea to that which is called
the southern or Erythraean, the shortest and quickest passage, which
is from Mount Casius, the boundary between Egypt and Syria to the
Gulf of Arabia, is a distance of exactly a thousand furlongs. But the
way of the canal is much longer, due to its crookedness. A hundred and
twenty thousand Egyptians, employed on the work in the reign of
Necho lost their lives in making the excavation. He at length desisted
from his undertaking in making the excavation in consequence of an
oracle which warned him that he was "labouring for the foreigner".
The Egyptians call by the name of foreigners all such as speak a language different from their own."

Strabo (96) wrongly states that "Darius, too, having been persuaded
by a false notion, abandoned the work when it was already near com-

pletion: he was persuaded that the Red Sea was higher than Egypt, and that if the intervening isthmus were cut all the way through, Egypt would be inundated by the sea. The Ptolemaic kings (Ptolemy II), however, cut it through and made the strait a closed passage, so that when they wished they could sail out without hindrance into the outer sea and sail in again. Pliny and Diodorus (97) too report on the canal, but we know that Darius completed the work, but that the canal was no succes due to the adverse winds and the many reefs in the Gulf of Suez and also because of political reasons.

We also have an interesting report (98) on the action of the Rhone waters on a Pliocene bed of pebbles, 17—20 M thick, in the Plain of La Drau, near the mouth of the Rhone, which attracted attention because of the large pebbles of quartzite standing out abundantly on the surface. Aristotle believed that they had been thrown up by an earthquake, Aeschylus calls them "stones sent from heaven to serve as missiles", but Strabo gives more details: "Between Massilia and the outlets of the Rhodanus there is a plain circular in shape, which is a far distant from the sea as hundred stadia, and is also as much as that in diameter. It is called the Stony Plain from the fact that it is full of stones as large as you can hold in your hand, although from beneath the stones there is a growth of wild herbage which affords abundant pasturage for cattle. In the middle of the plain stand water and salt springs, and also lumps of salt. Now although the whole of the country which lies beyond, as well as this, is exposed to the winds, the Black North, a chilly and violent wind, descends upon this plain with exceptional severity; at any rate it is said that some of the stones are swept and rolled along, and that by the blasts the people are dashed from their vehicles and stripped of both weapons and clothing. Now Aristotle says (De Mundo 4) that the stones, after being vomited to the surface by those earthquakes that are called "brastae", rolled together into the hollow places of the districts. But Poseidonius says, that, since it was a lake, it solidified while the waves were dashing, and because of this was parted into a number of stones, as are river-rocks and pebbles on the sea-shore; and by reason of the similarity of origin, the former, like the latter, are both smooth and equal in size. And an account of the cause has been given by both men. Now the argument in both treatises is plausible; for of necessity the stones that have been assembled together in this way cannot separately, one by one, either have changed from liquid to solid or have been detached from great masses of rock that received a succession of fractures."

The ancients had no clear idea of the *erosive of action rivers* and currents. The Vale of Tempe and other such formations are generally a-scribed to earthquakes. Erosion is suggested in a few passages only like that by Polybius describing a vale in Arcadia(99): "When he (Philip of Macedonia) observed the great strength of the town of Psophis (Arcadia), the king was at a loss what to do; for on its western side there descends a violent torrent, impassable for the greater part of the winter, and rendering the city very strongly protected and difficult of approach on this side, owing to the depth of the bed it has gradually formed for itself, descending as it does from a height". Much later we find Philo (100) saying, that the earth can not have existed from all eternity as the action of rain-drops, torrents and rivers through the ages would have smoothed and levelled the entire earth, or poets claiming that "cascades hollow out the scurvy tufa".

It is interesting to compare this with Chinese reports on similar phenomena (101). Shen Kua in the Mêng Chhi Pi Than (c. 1070) discussed the eroded cliffs of Yen-Tang Shen near Wenchow off the coast of southern Chekiang and says: "Considering the reasons for these shapes (peaks, cliffs and gorges) I think that for centuries the mountain torrents have rushed down, carrying away all sand and earth, thus leaving the hard rocks standing alone" and also "In the west of Shensi and Shansi the waters (of the great muddy silt-bearing rivers) run through gorges as deep as a hundred feet. Naturally mud and silt will be carried eastwards by these streams year after year and in this way the substance of the whole of the continent must have been laid down".

The mountain-forming process was believed to be of a seismic or volcanic nature, water and wind were said to play a minor part only. Here again we are struck by the lack of proper data on the height of mountains as is apparent from two quotations taken from Pliny (102) and Plutarch (103):

"Yet it is surprising that with this vast level expanse of sea and plains, the resulting formation is a globe. This view has the support of Dicaearchus, a savant of the first rank, who with the support of royal patrons took the measurement of mountains, and published that the highest of them was Pelion, with an altitude of 1250 paces (6000' instead of the true 5340') inferring that this was no portion (a negligible fraction) of the earth's general sphericity. To me this seems a questionable guess, as I know that some peaks of the Alps rise to a height, not less than 50,000 paces!" and "Olympus is ten furlongs and a hundred feet in height according to Xenagoras, but the geometricians say that no mountain has a height, and no sea a depth of more than ten furlongs (2000 M)".

The earliest more consistent discussion of the subjects we mentioned can be found in the tenth-century Rasâ'il Ikhwân al-Safâ of the Brethern of Sincerity, who debated changes in sea-level, denudation, peneplanation, river evolution and the like. More can be gleaned from the Latin treatise "De Congelatione et Conglutatione Lapidum" (104), long ascribed to Aristotle but now known to be the translation of part of Avicenna's Book of the Remedy (Kitâb al-Shifâ), written in 1022. The author describes the petrifactive process and goes on to discuss the mountain-building, which he ascribes to earthquakes and the like, which suddenly raise part of the land, or to a lengthy erosive action of winds and floods carrying away part of the formation and leaving the mountains as a core.

To the classical scholars the mountains remained a kind of framework on the surface of the earth "to restrain and keep within bounds that unruly element, water" as Pliny has it. Still the problem of *denudation* was very much with them. The Mediterranean region was formerly covered with a copious natural growth of forest. The Greeks and Romans had taken much interest on decorative and shade-giving trees. They had introduced the palm and the plane-tree with many others and the Romans even carried the latter as far north as the English Channel. But they also displayed a culpable negligence in the preservation of their forests. The large requirements of timber for house-construction, ship-building and charcoal-burning made them cut down these forests without adequate replacements by fresh plantation or care to protect the saplings from the depradations of the numerous goats. By the fourth century B.C. The Athenians had laid bare the flanks of the Attic border ranges and Plato (105) was well aware of this:

"Why are we right to call Attica as it is now a remnant of the land of those days? It is one long projection running out from the main body of the continent into the open sea, like a headland, and as we know, the marine basin that borders it is extremely deep. So, while there have been formidable deluges in the course of the nine thousand years — that is the interval between the date we are speaking of and the present — the soil washed away from the higher levels in these periodical convulsions does not deposit a noticeable sediment, as in some other regions, but is regularly carried off and lost in the depths... At the time we are speaking of the present mountains were high crests, what we now call the plains of Phelleus were covered with rich soil, and there was abundant timber on the mountains, of which traces may still be seen. For some of our mountains at present will only support bees (i.e. are heather-clad), but not so very long ago trees fit for the roofs or vast buildings were felled there and the rafters are still in existence. There were also many lofty cultivated trees which provided unlimited fodder for beasts. Besides which the soil got the benefit of the yearly water from Zeus, which was not lost as it is today, by running off a barren ground to the sea; a plentiful supply of it was received into the soil and stored up in the layers of non-porous potter's clay. Thus the moisture absorbed in the higher regions percolated to the hollows and so all quarters were provided with springs and rivers."

But, as A. C. Johnson has pointed out (106), they could still make up the loss fairly easily by imports from the northern Aegean area. This abuse of the forest by men and beasts turned many a hill-side, once richly wooded into a mantle of maquis or even a completely bare rock. The former mean annual rainfall and temperature seem to have been maintained but certainly the seasonal variations became more extreme. By the end of the Republic the Romans had stripped Italy in the same way, later generations turned to Corsica and north-west Africa with the same results. The natural re-growth of the forests was retarded, and in the denuded areas the heavy winter rains carried off the original coating of humus. Heavy water consumption has lowered the water table too and in some modern afforestations in the region it has been found necessary to blast holes in the rock so as to provide a safe bedding for the saplings. Glover (107) has given an excellent picture of this fateful denudation process.

Partsch (108) has pointed out that we have several ancient observations of wind-blown *sand-dunes*. The word "dunos" is first found in early medieval sources such as Prudentius of Troyes (839) and it seems related to the Anglo-Saxon "dun" (hill, mountain, English "down", Celtic—dunum). Its basic meaning appears to be "something collected by the wind" and it is connected with the Greek "dín" or "dís", which, however, means just "heap" and not specifically "dune". The Romans seem to have had no special words for dunes, but the Berbers used the word "gedea".

Herodotus tells us about the sand-dunes covering the Persians (109) "sent to attack the Ammonians, they started from Thebes having guides with them... It is certain that they neither reached the Ammonians, nor even came back to Egypt. Further than this, the Ammonians relate as follows: that the Persians set forth from Oasis across the

sand, and had reached about halfway between that place and themselves, when, as they were at their mid-day meal, a wind arose from
the south, strong and deadly, bringing with it vast columns of whirling
sands, and caused them wholly to disappear."

Strabo (110) describes the difficulties of Alexander's march into
Asia: "In addition to the resourcelessness of the country, the heat of
the sun was grievous, as also the depth and the heat of the sand; and
in some places there were sand-hills so high that, in addition to the
difficulties of lifting one's legs, as out of a pit, there were also ascents
and descents to be made". Then there were dunes accumulated on the
coast of Arabia (111): "Next is a gulf with scattered islands; and continuous with the gulf are three exceedingly high banks of black sand;
and after these lies Charmothas Harbour, about one hundred stadia
in circuit, with an entrance that is narrow and dangerous for all
kinds of boats."

Other authors (112) have observed them on Greek territory and
foreign countries like Syria. Herodotus, when discussing the formation of the Nile Delta mentions accumulations of sand on the mountains over Memphis. He, and other classical authors, always relate
them to coastal areas. The phenomenon of quicksands was well-known
to Diodorus (113):

"For between Coele-Syria and Egypt there lies a lake, quite narrow,
but marvellously deep and some two hundred stadia in length, which
is called Serbonis and offers unexpected perils to those who approach
it in ignorance of its nature. For since the body of water is narrow,
like a ribbon, and surrounded on all sides by great dunes, when there
are south winds great quantities of sand are strewn over it. This sand
hides the surface of the water and makes the outline of the lake continuous with the solid land and entirely indistinguishable from it. For
this reason many who are unacquainted with the peculiar nature of
the place have disappeared together with whole armies, when they
wandered from the beaten track. For as the sand is walked upon it
gives way but gradually deceiving with a kind of malvolent cunning
those who advance upon it, until, suspecting some impeding mishap
they begin to help one another only when it is no longer possible to
turn back or escape. For anyone who has been sucked in by the mire
cannot swim, since the slime prevents all movement of the body, nor
is he able to wade out, since he has no solid footing; for by reason of
the mixing of the sand with the water and the consequent change in
nature of both it comes about that the place cannot be crossed either

on foot or by boat. Consequently those who enter this region are borne towards the depth and have nothing to grasp to give them help, since the sand along the edge slips with them. These flats have received a name appropriate to their nature as we have described it, being called "barathra" (e.g. chasm. from a root meaning "to devour"). He goes on to recount the loss of part of the Persian army in these sands during the campaign against Egypt in 350-49 B.C. (114) and the part they played in the attack made by Antigonus on Demetrius in 306 B.C. But nowhere their morphology is studied in more detail than in the passage quoted above.

6. *Earthquakes and seismic phenomena*

Earthquakes were universal phenomena in the Eastern Mediterranean particularly along its coasts (115), they are discussed in details by Thucydides, Aristotle, Eratosthenes, Strabo, Pliny and Pausanias. The zone of seismic unrest proved to be running across Sicily, southern Italy, Greece, the Aegean islands, western Asia Minor and Cyprus

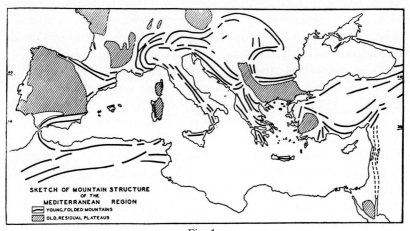

Fig. 1.
The mountain structure of the Mediterranean region.
(After Semple)

to the north-Syrian coast (Fig. 1). Along this line there are countless active faults due to the vast subsidences of the Quarternary Period.

We have several *records of earthquakes* from pre-classical times (116). James Mellaart believes that a volcanic eruption is already attested in a drawing of the seventh millennium B.C. found at Çatal Hüyük in southern Anatolia. A tablet (BM 123358) excavated at Niniveh in 1930-31 reads:

"Unto the king, my lord, thy servant Nabû-šuma-ukin, the A-BA. Greeting unto the king, my lord; may Nabû and Marduk be gracious to the king, my lord! On the 21st of Elul an earthquake took place; all the back part of the town is down; all the wall at the back of the town is preserved (except) 30½ cubits therefrom being strewn and fallen on the near-side of the town. All the temple is down, (but) I am glad (to say that) the gods of the king are all safe. The casing(?) of the window of the temple... Of the portico, of one cubit of... has fallen. One of the... therefrom of this temple has fallen. As for the namiru of the Great Gate near by, of the Great Gate... have fallen. (Of) Bît...; (Of) the keep (guard-house) of the town one or two houses therefrom have fallen. Let the Chief(-Architect) come and inspect".

From Sumerian times onwards earthquakes (rêbu, râbu) are generally attributed to the god Adad, but in a few Assyrian letters, such as this one from Balasî, Ea is blamed for them: "Let them perform whatever are the rites for an earthquake; thy gods will cause (it) to pass away; (what) Ea has given release (therefrom). Whoever causes the earthquake, the same provides an incantation for release (therefrom). Was there no earthquake during the times of the fathers or the grandfathers of the king? As for me, since I was (then) too small, I did not notice earthquakes".

We have reports of various earthquakes in the Niniveh area in the days of Shalmaneser I (c. 1280 B.C.) and then again in the time of Ashurdân (c. 1187—1150). As earthquakes were due to the gods they form a subject of omen literature (117), one could draw forecasts from these divine warnings, also they could be predicted by astrological calculations.

In Egypt, which like the Russian platform, the land of the Scythians is remarkably free of earthquakes, the inbahitants regarded earthquakes as contrary to the laws of nature (118). The Egyptian word for earthquake, nwr-t3, "shaking of the earth" (119) occurs in a few Pyramid texts and inscriptions in the Royal tombs only, but in no instance in texts referring to the land of Egypt itself.

Apollonius of Tyana regarded an earthquake at Antioch as a divine warning (120) and Pliny, though he does not definitely accept it, mentions the Babylonian tradition that they are due to influences of the planets Saturn, Jupiter and Mars (121). Generally speaking, however, the Greeks attributed earthquakes to Poseidon, but Herodotus is the first to query this belief (122).

Strabo mentions earthquakes in India (123) and Rhagae in Medi

(124), but they were fairly frequent, much closer to home, in Palestine (125) as reported in the Bible and by classical authoririries. The descriptions are sometimes very graphic (126):

"The sea saw it and fled, Jordan was driven back.
The mountains skipped like little rams and the little hills like lambs".

In the Bible an earthquake is usually an expression of God's wrath, e.g. when the Lord descended on Mount Sinai (127). Amos records an earthquake which must have taken place about 770 B.C. (128) and other earthquakes played their part in the life of Jesus (129).

In ancien Syria and throughout the Lebanon trough seismic disturbances were fairly frequent too, notably at Tyre and Antioch (130), the latter town suffering much damage in 184 B.C.

Many earthquakes were also reported from Asia Minor (131), notably at Magnesia (132), Sardis (133) and Mysia (134), that of AD 71 was particularly severe as Tacitus tells us graphically.

In their homecountry the Greeks were only too familiar with earthquakes and auxiliary phenomena. In the Aegean the island of Delos, which Pindar calls the "wide world's immovable wonder", because Zeus anchored it to the sea floor himself, was struck twice by earthquakes, once in 490 B.C. before the Persian invasion and again in 431 at the outbreak of the Peleponesian War! Both were regarded as particularly ominous as they happened on the island sacred to the prophet god Apollo (135). Nisyros was shaken (136) and so were Cos 412 B.C. (137) and Rhodes in 224 B.C. (138), the latter island profiting of the sympathy of the entire Hellenic world. In fact they were very common in the Aegean as on the mainland (139)!

A severe earthquake shook Orchemenos in 427-6 B.C. (140) and Corinth in 426 and 420 B.C. (141), Sicyon (142) and Achaia (143). At Delphi seismic disturbances were recorded in 480, 373, 353 and 279 B.C. (144). The Saronic Gulf region (145), Argos and Argolis (146), Laconia (147) and Boeotia (148) were among the regions frequently by earthquakes.

Neither were they rare in Italy (149) and Sicily, the very name "Rhegium" suggests the break of Sicily from the mainland by earthquake action which so many ancient authors uphold (150). The earthquake of Messina in 1908 has certainly shown this region to be a deep fracture of the earth's crust. But even on the mainland of Italy they were frequent, Pliny (151) mentions that no less than 57 earthquakes were reported near or at some distance from Lake Trasimenus in 217 B.C.

The ancients also knew that certain phenomena were connected
with earthquakes or heralded them. According to Strabo (152) Demetrius of Callatis noticed that hot springs at Aedepsus and Ther-
mopylae ceased to flow, though they were far from the centre of the
earthquake. Recently similar phenomena were noticed in Portugal
before the earthquake of 1755. Then there was the violent agitation
of the sea, its vast reflux from the shore and its quick return overflowing
the beaches and causing a tidal wave up the river mouths (153). Sometimes Poseidon is blamed for the earthquake, which is believed to be
due to the tidal wave (154), but by the time of Thucydides (155) it was
agreed that the tidal wave was a secondary phenomenon. Pindar in the
fragments of his Song on the Eclipse of 643 B.C. ascribes the "empty-
ing of the sea upon the land" to the wrath of Zeus. The tradition of the
"Dardanian Flood" was very much alive at Samothrace (156). Chalcidice was damaged by a tidal wave in 479 B.C. (157) and again around
AD 62 (158). Most Greek authors localised the Deucalion flood in the
northern part of the Euboean Sound and the Strait of Oreus (159).

Strabo (160) discusses the engulfing of land and the formation of
new islands due to earthquakes in these terms: "Now deluges (as we
have seen, are caused by upheavals of the bed of the sea) and earthquakes, volcanic eruptions, and upheavals of the submarine ground
raise the sea, whereas the settling of the bed of the sea lowers the sea.
For it cannot be that burning masses may be raised aloft, and small
islands, but not large islands; nor yet that islands may thus appear,
but not continents. And in a similar way settlings in the bed of the sea,
both great ones and small, also occur, if it be true, as people say, that
yawning abysses and engulfments of districts and villages have been
caused by earthquakes — as happened in the case of Bura and Bizone
and several other places; and as for Sicily, one might conjecture that
it is not so much a piece broken away from Italy as that it was cast up
from the deeps by the fire of Aetna and remained there; and the same
is true for both the Lipari Islands and of the Pithecussae."

Pausanias classifies earthquakes (161), the most serious forms of
which are those accompanied by an advance of the sea such as at Helice
in Achaia in 373 B.C. The signs of earthquakes are: "Warnings, usually
the same in all cases, are wont to be sent by the god (Poseidon) before
violent and far-reaching earthquakes. Either continuous storms of rain
or else continuous droughts occur before earthquakes for an unusual
length of time, and the weather is unreasonable. In winter it turns too
hot, and in summer, along with a tendency to haze the orb of the sun

presents an unusual colour, slightly inclining to red or else to black. Springs of water generally dry up; blasts of wind sometimes swoop upon the land, and overturn the trees; occasionally great flames dart across the sky, the shape of the stars too appear such as has never been witnessed before, producing consternation in those that witness them; furthermore there is a violent rumbling of winds beneath the earth — these and many other warnings the god is want to send before violent earthquakes occur. The shock itself is not of a fixed type, but the original inquirers into such matters, and their pupils have been able to discover the following forms of earthquakes. The mildest form — that is, if such a calamity admits of migitation —, is when there coincides with the original shock, which levels the buildings with the ground, a shock in the opposite direction, counteracting the first and raising up the buildings already knocked over. In this form of earthquake pillars may be seen righting themselves which have been almost uprooted, split walls coming together to their original position; beams, dislocated by the shock, go back to their places, and likewise channels and such like means of furthering the flow of water, have their cracks cemented better than they could be by human craftsmen. Now the second form of earthquake brings destruction to anything liable to it, and it throws over at once, as it were by a battering-ram, whatever meets the force of its impact. The most destructive kind of earthquake the experts are wont to liken to the symptoms of a man suffering from a non-intermittent fever, the breathing of such a patient being rapid and laboured. There are the symptoms of this to be found in many parts of the body, especially at each wrist. In the same way, they say, the earthquake dives directly under the buildings and shakes up their foundations, just like molehills come up from the bowels of the earth. It is this sort of shock alone that leaves no trace of the ground that men ever built and dwelt there."

The younger Pliny mentions the earthquakes preceding the great volcanic eruption of the Vesuvius in AD 79 (162), but "they were less alarming as they are frequent in Campania", and Livy tells us about two "cave-ins" during the second Punic War, though he does not classify them as seismic phenomena (163). Though the ancients never found the true cause of earthquakes, the slipping of the crust rocks along lines of previous faulting, many did discuss the *origin of earth-quakes* and Strabo tells us that Demetrius of Callatis devoted a special treatise to this subject (164). The early myths blamed Poseidon, the "Earth-Shaker", for them, who also caused the tidal waves (165) but even in the days of Aulus Gellius, when the philosophers had already rejected this myth and were discussing natural causes (166), no agreement had yet been reached: "what is regarded as the cause fo earthquakes is not only not obvious to the ordinary understanding and thought of mankind, but it is not agreed even among the natural philosophers whether they are due to the mighty wind, that gathers in the caverns and hollow places of the earth, or to the ebb and flow of the subterranean waters in its hollows, as seem to have been the view of the earliest Greeks, who called Neptune "the Earth-Shaker"; or whether they are the result of something else or due to the divine power of some god — all this, I say, is not yet a matter of certain knowledge". Cicero impresses on his readers (167) "not even Pheredydes, that famous Pythagorean master, who predicted an earthquake when he saw that the water had disappeared from a well which was usually well filled, should be regarded as a diviner rather than a physicist".

Aetius reports (168) that Anaximenes held that "the cause of earthquakes was the dryness and moisture of the earth, occasioned by droughts and heavy rains respectively" and also underground passages overfilled with water.

According to Anaxagoras the flat earth is maintained in the middle by the force of an eddy going round it, the same force that originally caused it to settle in the middle, as large bodies do in a whirling pool of liquid or an eddy of air. The earth can, however, be disturbed when the air which bouys it up on the under side rises through heat and impinges on it, causing it to toss like a ship on the sea and this results in an earthquake. To Democritus of Abdera (420 B.C.) the gathering of water in the hollows of the earth causes earthquakes. As the water accumulates, the spaces cannot hold it all and it beats against the enclosing earth, causing it to move. Metrodorus of Chios held that earthquakes were caused when the air enclosed in the caves of the earth is struck by air from above. He compares the phenomenon with the precussion set up when someone sings in a hollow jar, and says that a solid substance like earth cannot move of itself but must be moved from without.

These earlier theories, which are known to us only from the fragments reported by other authors, are discussed in detail in the chapters 7—8 of the second Book of Aristotle's Meteorologica. In the first of these he examines the theories held by Anaxagoras, Anaximander and Democrites; "Anaxagoras says that the air, whose natural motion if upwards, causes earthquakes, when it is trapped in hollows beneath the earth, which happens when the upper parts of the earth get clogged by rain, all earth being naturally porous... Democritus says the earth is full of water and that earthquakes are caused when a large amount of rain water falls besides this; for when there is too much for the existing cavities in the earth to contain, it causes an earthquake by forcing its way out. Similarly, when the earth gets dried up water is drawn to the empty places from the fuller and causes earthquakes by the impact of its passage.

Anaximenes says that when the earth is in process of becoming wet or dry it breaks, and is shaken by the high ground breaking or falling. Which is why earthquakes occur in droughts and again in heavy rains, for in droughts the earth is dried and so, as just explained, breaks and when the rains make it excessively wet it falls apart". Aristotle spends but few words to refute this opinion and proceeds to explain his own views in the next chapter. He holds that the earth of itself is dry, but, on account of the rains, becomes moist, so that being subjected to the action of the Sun's heat and its own internal heat, a large quantity of "pneuma" is generated both within and without, and this vapour flows sometimes into and sometimes out of the Earth (II. 8. 1). Hence most earthquakes will occur in calm weather, having exhausted all available wind. Should it be accompanied by wind it is likely to be much less violent, seeing that the motive cause (wind) is divided. Earthquakes are due to be the severest where the earth is hollow. They are most frequent during spring and autumn and during rains and droughts, for these are the conditions in which exhalations are produced in maximum quantities. Again Aristotle draws analogies from the human body and gives examples which confirm his theories. After a severe earthquake the shocks may last for some time. They are due to occur during an eclipse of the moon, the subterranean noises are caused by the wind. Sometimes they are accompanied by an outbreak of water, but their cause is nevertheless air. Tidal waves may accompany them, but they are far more local than winds. Horizontal and vertical shocks have been observed, also they are rare in islands at a distance from the mainland. Aristotle believed that earthquakes were more violent and also more frequent in districts where the land was cavernous or where the coast was much broken (II. 8. 8). He points to the Hellespontine region, Achaia, Sicily and Euboea, where the sea appeared to flow into narrow passages under the earth (II. 8. 9). From this part of the Meteorologica it would seem that after all Aristotle is not yet completely satisfied with the theory he built up.

Pliny in his Natural History (169) blames underground storms for earthquakes in the following words: "The theory of the Babylonians deems that even earthquakes and fissures in the ground are caused by the force of the stars which is the cause of all other phenomena, but only by that of those three stars (Saturn, Jupiter and Mars) to which they assign thunderbolts; and they occur when these are travelling with the sun or are in agreement with him, and particularly about the quadratures of the world (i.e. when they are distant from him one quarter of the heaven)". He then observes that Anaximander of Miletus warned the Spartans against an impeding earthquake and that Phere-cydes, teacher of Pythagoras expected one when a well fell dry. Pliny himself attributes their cause to the winds: "for tremors of the earth never occur except when the sea is calm and the sky so still that birds are unable to soar because all the breath that carries them has been withdrawn; and never except after wind, doubtless because then the blast has been shut up in the veins and hidden hollows of the sky. And a trembling in the earth is not different from a thunderclap in the sky, and a fissure is no different from when an imprisoned current of air by struggling and striving to go forth causes a flash of lightning to burst out. Consequently earthquakes occur in a variety of ways and cause remarkable consequences, in some places overthrowing walls, in others drawing them down into a gaping cleft, in others thrusting up masses of rock, in others sending out rivers and sometimes even fires and hot springs, in others diverting the course of rivers. They are, however, preceeded or accompanied by a terrible sound, that some-times ressembles a rumble, sometimes the lowing of cattle or the shouts of human beings or the clash of weapons struck together, according to the nature of the material that receives the shock and the shape of the caverns or burrows through which it passes, proceeding with a smaller volume in a narrow channel, but with a harsh noise in channels that bend, echoing in hard channels, bubbling in damp ones, forming waves in stagnant ones, raging against solid ones. Accordingly even without any movement occuring a sound is sometimes emitted. And sometimes the earth is not shaken in a simple manner but trembles and vibrates. Also the gap sometimes remains open, showing the objects that it sucked in, while sometimes it hides them by closing its mouth and drawing soil over it again in such a way as to leave no traces; it being usually cities that are engulfed, and a tract of farmland swallow-ed. Although seaboard districts are most subject to earthquakes, and also mountain regions are not free from disasters of kind: I have ascertained that tremors have somewhat frequently occured in the Alps and Apennines."

Pliny then observes that earthquakes are less frequent in summer and winter and hence Gaul and Egypt are free of them, as these seasons are much longer in such countries. Sailors can anticipate them by observing the birds, sudden waves and a thin streak of cloud over a wide space of the sky. In wells the water becomes muddy and dries up. The most dangerous types of earthquakes are those with "a waving bend and a sort of billowy fluctuation or when the movement drives in one direction only". The consequences are in many cases inundations of the sea, birth of new land formations (Echinades Islands near the mouth of the Achelous, Delos, Rhodes, several islands in the Cyclades and the bay of Campania), islands being torn from the mainland (Sicily from Italy, Cyprus from Syria, Euboea from Boeotia), encroachments of the sea and collapse of mountains.

Seneca (170) states that he wrote in his youth an essay on the subject. After having quoted many older authors on the causes of earthquakes Seneca avows that he cannot regard air to be the only cause, for there are three different types; shocks, oscillations of the earth's surface and vibrations. The first type is probably due to the subsidence of subterranean crevices or caverns from which the imprisoned air escapes, but this explanation is insufficient to explain earthquakes of the other two types. However, Seneca does not discuss these in detail but observes that earthquakes are restricted to certain localities and that large parts of the earth are known to be free of them. He mentions the noxious gases liberated by earthquakes and the fissures and dislocations of buildings and monuments caused by them. Though he agrees that fire sometimes accompanies earthquakes he is not willing to relate seismic to volcanic phenomena.

Lucretius devotes a long passage (171) to this subject in which he points out that the causes of earthquakes are: 1) the dislodgement of masses of rocks and earth inside subterranean caverns and chasms, 2) dislodged masses of earth falling into a subterranean lake and thus causing agitation and oscillation of its waters, 3) subterranean winds upsetting the balance of the earth, or 4) such winds themselves causing dislocations. These are his words: "Come now and hear what is the law of the earthquakes. And first of all let yourself suppose that the earth below, just as above, is full on all sides of windy caverns and that it bears in its bosom many lakes and many pools and cliffs and sheer rocks; and that many rivers hidden beneath the back of the earth roll on among their waves and submerged stones. For clear fact demands that it should be in all parts like itself. When these things, then, are placed and linked together beneath it, the earth above trembles, shaken by great falling masses, when beneath time has caused huge caverns to fall in; nay, indeed whole mountains fall, and at the great shock tremblings creep abroad thence far and wide. And with good reason, since houses by the roadside tremble when shaken, whole houses by waggons of no great weight, and the waggons leap none the less whenever a stone in the road jolts on the iron circles of the wheels on either side. It comes to pass too, when a vast mass of soil loosened by age from the earth, rolls down into huge wide pools of water, that the earth too tosses and sways beneath the wave of water; even as a vessel sometimes cannot stand still, unless the liquid within has ceased to toss with the unsteady waves.

Moreover, when the wind gathering through the cavernous places of the earth blows strong from one point, and with all its weight presses on the lofty caves with mighty strength, the earth leans over to where the swooping force of the wind presses it. Then the houses that are built upon up the earth, yea, the more they are severally raised towards the sky, bend over in suspense, tottering towards the same quarter, and the timbers driven forward hang out ready to drop. And yet men fear to believe that a time of ruin and destruction awaits the nature of the great world, even when they see so great a mass of earth bowing to its fall. Why, unless the winds breathed in again, no force could put a curb on things or avail to pull them back from destruction as they fall. As it is, because turn by turn they breathe in and then grow violent, because as it were, they rally and charge again and then are driven back and give ground, for this reason the earth more often threatens a fall than brings it to pass: for it leans over and then sways back again, and after falling forward, recovers its position to a steady poise. In this way, then, the whole building rocks, the top more than the middle, the middle more than the bottom, the bottom but very little.

There is this cause, too, of that great same shaking, when suddenly wind and some exceeding great force of air, gathering either from without or within the earth itself, have hurled themselves into the hollow places of the earth, and there first rage among the great caves in turmoil, and rise, carried on in a whirl; and when afterwards the moving forces driven forth burst out and at the same time cleave the earth and cause a huge chasm. Even as it came to pass at Sidon in Syria, and as happened at Aegium in Peleponnese, cities overthrown by this issue of air and the quaking of the earth which arose. And, besides, many walled towns have fallen through great movements on land, and many cities have sunk down deep into the sea, inhabitants and all. And even if it does not burst forth, yet the very impulse of the air and the fierce forces of the wind are spread, like a fit of shivering, throughout the riddling passages of the earth, and thereby induce a trembling: even as cold, when it comes deep, into our members, shakes them against our will and constrains them to tremble and to move... "Lucretius then goes on to describe the terror inspired by an earthquake.

It is interesting to compare these classical theories of earthquakes with those from ancient China (172), which is certainly one of the world's areas, where such seismic disturbances are very frequent. Needham reports that up to 1644 908 shocks were recorded. The earliest of these are mentioned in the Shih Chi, it interrupted the course of three rivers (780 B.C.): "In the second year of the reign of King Yo of Chou, the three rivers of the western province were all shaken and their beds raised up. Poyang Fu said: "The dynasty of Chou is going to perish, It is necessary that the chhi of heaven and earth should not lose their order; if they overstep their order it is because there is disorder among the people. When the Yang is hidden, and cannot come forth, or when the Yin bars its way and cannot rise up, then there is what we call an earthquake. Now we see that the three rivers have dried up by this shaking; it is because the Yang has lost its place and the Yin has overburdened it. When the Yang has lost its rank and finds itself subordinate to the Yin, the springs become closed, and when this has happened the kingdom must be lost. When water and earth are propitious the people make use of them, when they are not, the people are deprived of what they need. When the Ho dried up the dynasty of the Shang perished. Now the virtue of the Chou is in the same state as that of these dynasties was in their decline... The Chou will be ruined before ten years are out; so it is written in the cycle of numbers".

The "chhi" mentioned in this passage is equivalent to the "pneuma" or "subtle matter" of the classical philosophers. The Chinese believed that earthquakes could be predicted astrologically like the Babylonians did. We must mention the brilliant mathematician, astronomer and geographer Chan Hêng (AD 78—139) who constructed the first seismograph, which is recorded in the Hou Han Shu and which is discussed in full by Needham. This is a remarkable achievement, for no classical philosopher ever thought of an instrument to record earthquakes!

7. *Volcanoes*

The Ancient Chinese had no direct knowledge of volcanoes, the first report can be found in the late third-century Shih I Chi: "In Tai-Yü Shan there is an abyss a thousand miles deep, in which water is always boiling. Metals or stones thrown into it are attacked and reduced to mud. In winter the water dries up and yellow smoke billows forth from the ground many yards high. People who live amoung these mountains dig down to the depth of several tens of feet and get scorched stone like charcoal, which will burn with flames. It can be ignited by a candle, and the flames are blue. The deeper they dig, the more flames they get". Needham believes that this is a description of Mount Etna brought by Syrian traders, but it could just as well be a report from merchants to the southern seas, who saw volcanoes in Sumatra or Java.

The early classical myths call them the smithy of the Fire God (173) though there is no sign of a volcano at Lemnos the Fire-God's favourite home. Other myths describe them as prisons of vanquished giants (174) such as Enceladus under Mount Etna and Typhoeus under Aenaria (Ischia). Apollonius of Tyana holds both mythical explanations up to ridicule in the following passage (175): "What then is the explanation of such mountains. It is this: the earth by affording a mixture of asphalt and pitch, begins to smoke of its own nature, but it does not belch out fire yet; if however it be cavernous and hollow and there be a spirit or force circulating underneath it, it at once sends up into the air as it were a torch; this flame gathers force, and gets hold of all around, and then like water it streams off the mountain and flows into the plains, and the mass of fire reaches the sea, forming mouths, out of which it issues, like the mouths of rivers. And as for the place of the Pious Ones around whom the fire flowed, we will allow that such exist even here, but at the same time let us not forget that the whole earth affords secure ground for the doers of holiness, and that the sea is safely transversed not only by people in ships but even by people attempting to swim."

The earliest picture of a volcanic eruption was found at Çatal Hüyük (Level VII, c. 6200 B.C.) in a shrine. It seems to depict the then active volcanoes of Karaca Dağ and Hasan Dağ at the eastern end of the plain and may have something to do with the part which this ancient settlement played in the obsidian trade, which we will discuss later on (175a).

It was generally held that volcanoes and earthquakes were logically related phenomena, the volcanoes acting as safety valves for the forces which generated earthquakes (176), though Anaxagoras was tempted to suggest that fiery ether gets into the hollows below the earth and seeks its way out. Ovid and other poets, however, speak of "vis fera ventorum...". Strabo (177) has a good description of the volcanic phenomena below the Dea Sea which cause lumps of asphalt and gases to escape at the surface of the lake: "(The Dead Sea) is full of asphalt. The asphalt is blown to the surface at irregular intervals from the midst of the deep, and with it rise bubbles, as though the water was boiling; and the surface of the lake, being convex, presents the appearance of a hill. With the asphalt there arises much soot, which, though smoky, is imperceptible to the eye; and it tarnishes copper and silver and any-thing that glistens, even gold; and when their vessels are becoming tarnished the people who live round the lake know that the asphalt is beginning to rise; and they prepare to collect it by means of rafts made of reed. The asphalt is a clod of earth, which at first is liquified by heat, and is blown up to the surface and spreads out; and then again, by reason of the cold water the lake in question has, it changes into a firm, solidified substance, and therefore requires cutting and chopping; and then it floats, because of the nature of the water of the lake... They reach the asphalt on rafts and chop off as much as they can... (after discussing Poseidonius' story on the use of urine to harden the asphalt Strabo continues:) It is reasonable that this behaviour should occur in the middle of the lake, because the source of the fire is at the middle of it; but the bubbling up is irregular, because the movements of the fire, like that of many other subterranean blasts, follow no order known to us. Such, also, are the phenomena at Apollonia in Epeirotis (where burning natural gases appear on the surface near a temple).

Many other evidences show that the country is fiery; for near Mas-sada are to be seen rugged cliffs, that have been scorched, as also, in many places, fissures and ashy soil, and drops of pitch dripping from smooth cliffs and boiling rivers that emit foul odour to a great distance, and ruined settlements here and there, and therefore people believe the oft-repeated assertions of the local inhabitants, that there were once thirteen inhabited cities in that region of which Sodom was the metro-polis, but that a circuit of about sixty stadia of the city escaped un-harmed; and that by reason of earthquakes and of eruptions of fire and hot waters containing asphalt and sulphur, the lake burst its bounds, and rocks were enveloped with fire; and as for the cities, some were swallowed up and others were abandoned by such as were able to escape."

According to Aristotle the winds from the outside and those generated from underground waters by the earth's heat blow through many
passages and shake the earth and at times catch fire and burst out
violently. The ancient philosophers were clever enough to realize the
benefits derived from the outpourings of volcanic material over Sicily,
Campania, Etruria, Latium and other places. Bashan, the ancient grana-
ry of Syria, owed its fertility to such volcanic material the streams from
Mount Hauran carrying water onto the fertile red-brown soil. The
Troad, Lesbos, Lydia and Mysia derive their fertility from the volcanic
"manure" (178): "The whole of Mysia is without trees except the vine,
which produces the Catacecaumite wine, which is in quality inferior
to none of the notable wines. The surface of the plain is covered with
ashes, and the mountainous and rocky country is black, as though
from conflagration... it is not reasonable to suppose that all the country
was burnt all at once by reasons of such disturbances (mythical stories
having been summed up before), but rather by reason of an earth-born
fire, the sources of which have now been exhausted. Three pits are to
be seen, which are called "bellows", and they are forty stadia distant
from each other. Above them lie rugged hills, which are reasonably
supposed to have been heaped up by the hot masses blown forth from
the earth. That such soil should be well adapted to the vine one might
assume from the land of Catana (Sicily), which was heaped with ashes
and now produces excellent wine in great plenty."

Strabo (179) realizes that this "law of compensation" is also opera-
tive round Mount Etna and Pliny points out, that because of it, Thera
and Melos are rightly famous for their wines and exports of alum and
sulphur (180).

In the Aegean a great submarine eruption took place at Thera about
2000 B.C. or may be a little later (181), another one in 196 B.C. and
again in 46. An island emerged near Crete (182) and so did a hill near
Methone (183) which Strabo describes in these words: "And about
Methone in the Mermionic Gulf a mountain seven stadia in height
was cast up in consequence of a fiery eruption, and this mountain was
unapproachable on account of the heat and the smell of sulphur, while
at night it shone to a great distance and was so hot, that the sea boiled
for five stadia and was turbid for even twenty stadia, and was heaped
up with massive broken-up rocks no smaller than towers." The
emergence of such new islands was a common phenomenon in the
Aegean (184).

In Italy we know volcanic rifts in a series running from Padua through Tuscany to Naples and Eastern Sicily. Thus Ischia suffered from volcanic eruptions in 474 B.C. and again in 300 B.C. Campania was severely harrassed in Nero's days and finally in AD 79 (185).

Volcanic action is also reported from the Lipari islands and from Epemeo, an island near Napels, where the inhabitants were scared off and which has since disappeared. The ancients held that the earthquakes and volcanic eruptions in this region had declined in violence after volcanic vents were opened in Etna and the Aeolian islands and the rift at the Sicilian strait was formed (186). As Strabo has it: "Now at the present time that earth about the Strait (of Rhegium), they say is seldom shaken by earthquakes, because the orifices there, through which the fire is blown up and the red-hot masses and the waters are ejected, are open. At that time (when Sicily was torn from Italy), however, the fire that was smouldering beneath the earth, together with the wind, produced violent earthquakes, because the passages to the surface were all blocked up, and the regions thus heavened up yielded at last to the force of the blasts of wind, were rent asunder, and then received the sea that was on either side, both here and between the other islands of the region." The struggle of the enclosed winds to escape caused the earthquakes in this group (187) and shook the earth again in 183 and in 125, attended by a submarine eruption, the emergence of a small island in the sea and changes in the coastline (188). Stromboli, then as now, acted as a lighthouse and weatherglass for sailors. Poseidonius (189) describes such a sunmarine eruption:

"Poseidonius says that within his own recollections, one morning at daybreak about the time of the summer solstice, the sea between Hiera and Eunymus was seen raised to an enormous height, and by a sustained blast remained puffed up for a considerable time, and then subsided; and when those who had the hardihood to sail up to it saw dead fish driven by the current, and some of the men were stricken ill because of the heat and stench, they took flight, one of the boats, however, approaching more closely, lost some of its occupants and barely escaped to Lipara with the rest, who would at times become senseless like epileptics, and then afterwards would recur to their proper reasoning faculties; and many days later mud was seen forming on the surface of the sea, and in many places, smoke, flames and murky fire broke forth, but later the scum had hardened and became as hard as mill-stone...".

Philostratus (190) reports on the Aeolian islands, notably on Dydime the Twins, two severed portions of which have been separated "by the width of a river" and are now linked with a bridge. It was believed that these islands had some subterranean connection with Mount Etna.

We have many testimonies on Mount Etna and Mount Vesuvius and their history. Mount Etna has always drawn the attention of classical scholars. Aeschylus mentions the eruption of 479 B.C. in his Prometheus Vinctus, Thucydides mentions no less than three during the period after the Greeks colonized Sicily, he himself observed that of 425 B.C. Pindar's description in his first Pythian Ode would tend to show that he was a spectator of the eruption of 475. Diodorus (191) knows Etna well, for he lived in Sicily, and Strabo's remarks are correct too (192).

Aulus Gellius (193) blames Virgil for his description of Mount Etna: "Virgil's is full of monstruous inaccuracies", but the poem he refers to is not the work of that great poet. The Latin didactic poem "Aetna" in 644 hexameters is attributed to Virgil (both in the manuscript and by Donatus!) but it was more probably written by Lucilius, the friend to whom Seneca the philosopher wrote his letters, one of which (194) contains this remarkable passage: "I shall have the boldness to ask you to perform another task, to climb Aetna at my special request. Certain naturalists have inferred that the mountain is either wasting away or gradually settling, because sailors used to be able to see it from a greater distance".

The poem (195), written before 79 A.D., scorns the silly myths of Vulcan's forge or imprisoned giants and expounds, none too cleary, that the cause of the eruptions is air imprisoned in the hollows of the earth, which, confined in such narrow spaces, acts like the bellows of a furnace. The nature of the fuel is indicated by the extensive deposits of sulphur and traces of bituminous material, but above all by the "lapis molaris", the lava itself, which fuses more easily than iron. When "its heart" is burnt out by the repeated cookings it becomes "pumex" (pumice). In this poem we also find a description of the "solfatara" between Napels and Cumae (ii, 431—433), well-known to Strabo (196), and the sulphur wells, and it describes the small eruption cone in the middle of the great crater of Etna, also reported by Strabo, the word "crater" hailing from Aristotle. Vitruv has, of course, a good description of lava from the point of view of using it as building material.

The long passage on Etna in Lucretius' De rerum natura was probably inspired by the eruption of 122 B.C. It stresses the relative insignificance of such an eruption, which is due to the winds in the interior of the earth bursting forth. Also the sea must supply the sand and rocks to the interior of the mountain which then throws them out again(197):

"Now what is the reason, that through the jaws of Mount Etna flames sometimes breathe forth in so great a hurricane, I will unfold. For indeed, the flaming storm gathered with no moderate force of destruction and ruled tyrant through the fields of the Sicilians and turned to itself the gaze of neighbouring nations, when they saw all the quarters of the heavens smoke and sparkle, and filled their breasts with shuddering anxiety for what new change nature might be planning.

Herein you must look far and deep and take a wide view to every quarter that you may remember that the sum of things is unfathomable, and see how small, how infinitely small a part of the whole sum is one single heaven, not so large a part as is a single man of the whole earth. And if you have this duly before you and look clearly at it and see clearly, you would cease to wonder at many things. For does any of us wonder, if a man has caught in his limbs a fever gathering with burning heat, or any other painful disease in his members? For a foot swells suddenly, often a sharp pain seizes on the teeth or makes its way right into the eyes: the holy fire breaks out and creeping about the body burns any part which it has seized, and crawls through the limbs, because, as we may be sure, there are seeds of many things, and this earth and heaven have enough disease and malady from which the force of measureless disease might avail to spread about. So, then, we must suppose that out of the infinite all things are supplied to the whole heaven and earth in number enough that on a sudden the earth might be shaken and moved, and a tearing hurricane course over sea and land, the fire of Etna well forth and the heaven aflame. For that comes to pass too, and the quarters of heaven blaze, and there are rain-storms gathering in heavier mass, when by chance the seeds of water have so arranged themselves... "Nay, but the stormy blaze of this fire is exceedingly gigantic". So, too, be sure, is the river which is the greatest seen by a man who has never seen any greater before: so a tree or a man may seem gigantic, and in every kind of thing, the greatest that each man has seen, he always imagines gigantic, and yet all of them together, yea, with heaven and earth and sea besides, are nothing to the whole sum of the universal sum.

But now in which way the flame is suddenly excited and breathes abroad from the vast furnaces of Etna, I will unfold. First of all the nature of the mountain is hollow beneath, resting everywhere on arches of basalt. Moreover, in all the caves there is wind and air. For air be-

comes wind, when it is set in motion and aroused, when it has grown
hot, and as it rages has heated all the rocks and the earth around wherever it touches them, and has struck out from them a fire hot with swift
flames, it rises up and so drives itself forth on high straight through
the mountain's jaws. And so it carries its heat far, and afar it scatters
the ash and rolls on a smoke with thick murky darkness, and all the
while hurls out rocks of marvellous weight; for you must not doubt
that this is the stormy force of air. Moreover, in great part the sea
makes its waves break and suck in its backwash at the roots of that
mountain. From this sea caves stretch underneath right to the lofty
jaws of the mountain. By this path we must admit that wind mingled
with the waves passes in, and that the nature of the case compels it to
rise and pierce deep in from the sea, and then breathe out, and so lift up
the flame and cast up rocks and raise clouds of dust. For on the top-
most peak are craters as the inhabitants name them: what we call jaws
or mouths." The craters are described by Diodorus in these words:

"great wonder there called the Craters which are great hollows in
the earth, not very large in compass but of incredible depth from
whence break out great sparks of fire and burning liquid, as though
from boiling cauldrons. The liquid cast forth resembles so many
streams of fire; but there is no knowing of its nature, for no one hitherto even dared to approach it: for the violent eruption of the fiery
matter is so wonderful, that it seems to be the immediate effect of some
divine power. It smells like brimstone, and the bottomless gulf roars
and makes a most dreadful and horrible noise. And that which is far
more to be wondered at is this, that the river of fire neither flows nor
makes any stay upon the ground, but in a continual motion, with an
amazing force, hurls itself up in the air."

Equally detailed descriptions of Mount Vesuvius are given (198) of
which we reproduce here that by Strabo: "Above these places lie
Mount Vesuvius, which save for its summit, has dwellings all around
on farmlands that are absolutely beautiful. As for the summit, a considerable part of it is flat, but all of it is unfruitful, and looks ash-
coloured, and it shows porelike cavities in masses of rocks that are
soot-coloured on the surface, these masses of rock looking as though
they had been eaten by fire; and hence one might infer that in earlier
times this district was on fire and had craters of fire, and then, because
the fuel gave out, was quenched. Perhaps, too this is the cause of the
fruitfulness of the country all round the mountain; just as at Catana,
it is said, that part of the country which had been covered with ash-

dust from the hot ashes carried up in the air by the fire of Etna made the land suited to the vine; for it contains the substance that fattens both the soil which is burnt out and that which produces the fruits; so then, when it acquired plenty of fat, it was suited to burning out, as is the case with all sulphur-like substances, and then when it had been evaporated and quenched and reduced to ashes, it passed into a state of fruitfulness."

Mount Vesuvius was of course innocent until A.D. 79 but in its neighbourhood Lake Avernus and the Phlegrean Fields, hot springs and gaswells had been noticed (199) as Strabo reminds us in an earlier passage: "Under these mountainous regions (round Vesuvius) there are both hot earth and many springs. And these would not be unless deep down they had huge blazing fires of sulphur, alum and pitch (bitumen). Therefore the fire and vapour of flame within, flowing through the cracks makes the earth light. And the tufa which is found to come out there is free of moisture. Therefore, when three substances formed in like manner by the violence of fire come into one mixture, they suddenly take up water and cohere together." or Vitruvius (200) reports in these words: "Immediately above the city lies the Forum of Hephaestus (now La Solfatara), a plain shut in all around by exceeding-ly hot ridges, in which numerous places have fumaroles that are like chimneys and that have rather a noisome smell; and the plain is full of drifted sulphur."

Silius Italicus has a story about Etna and Vesuvius thundering during the war with Hannibal (201), which is of course incorrect. The first warnings came in A.D. 63 with the big earthquake and then came the destruction of Pompeii and Herculaneam in A.D. 79 (102). Again we have Procopius' description of the eruptions of 472 and 512, which are fairly accurate, but which he must have had from hearsay as he places Vesuvius north of Napels (203).

Preussen (204) had rightly drawn our attention to the fact that the appearance of Mount Vesuvius has changed considerably since Anti-quity. Though a wall-painting at Pompeii shows the mountain with a bare cone in the background of a charming picture of Venus teaching Cupid to fish, Plutarch tells us in the Life of Crassus how the gladia-tors, besieged on this mountain by Clodius, escaped with the help of ropeladders made from wild vines growing on the top. A recently dis-covered picture of Bacchus and Vesuvius (Fig. 2) shows this vegeta-tion. Velleius Paterculus (I) and Florus (III) (205) confirm Plutarch's story, that the crater was then still unbroken. The present Monte

Fig. 2.

Bacchus and Mount Vesuvius (mural painting of a lararium at Pompeii, now in the Museo Nazionale of Napels)

Summa is but a surviving part of it. Dio Cassius gives this very accurate picture of the catastrophe:

"In Campania remarkable and frightful occurences too place, for a great fire suddenly flared up at the very end of the summer (of A.D. 79). It happened in this wise. Mount Vesuvius stands over against Neapolis near the sea and it has inexhaustible fountains of fire. Once it was equally high at all points and the fire rose from the centre of it; for here only the fires have broken out, whereas all the outer parts of the mountain remain even now untouched by fire. Consequently, as the outside is never burned, while the central part is constantly growing brittle and being reduced to ashes, the peaks surrounding the centre retain their original height to this day, but the whole section, that is on fire, having been consumed, has in course of time settled and therefore become concave; thus the entire mountain resembles an amphitheatre — if we may compare great things to small. Its outlying heights support both trees and vines in abundance, but the crater is given over to the fire and sends up smoke day by day and a flame by night; in fact, it gives the impression that quantities of incense of all kinds are being burned in it. This, now, goes on all the time, sometimes to a greater, sometimes to a lesser extent; but often the mountain throws up ashes, whenever there is an extensive settling in the interior, and discharges stones whenever it is rent by a violent blast of air. It also rumbles and roars because its vents are not all grouped together but are narrow and concealed.

Such is Vesuvius and these phenomena usually occur there every year. But all other occurences that take place there in the course of time, however notable, because unusual, they may have seemed to those who on each occasion observed them, nevertheless would be regarded trivial in comparison with what now happened, even if all had been combined into one. Numbers of huge men, quite surpassing any human stature — such creatures, in fact, as the Giants are pictured to be — appeared, now on the mountains, now in the surrounding country, and again in the cities, wandering over earth by day and night and also flitting through the air. After this fearful droughts and sudden and violent earthquakes occurred, so that the whole plain round about seethed and the summits leaped into the air. There were frequent rumblings, some of them subterranean, that resembled thunder, and some on the surface, that sounded like bellowings; the sea also joined in the roar and the sky re-echoed it. Then suddenly a portentuous crash was heard, as if the mountains were tumbling in ruins; and then first huge stones were hurled aloft, rising as high as the very summits, then came a great quantity of fire and endless smoke, so that the whole atmosphere was obscured and the sun was entirely hidden, as if eclipsed. Thus day turned to night and light into darkness. Some thought the Giants were rising again in revolt (for at this time also many of their forms could be discerned in the smoke, and moreover, a sound as of many trumpets was heard), while others believed that the whole universe was being resolved into chaos or fire. Therefore they fled, some from the houses into the streets, others from outside into the houses, now from the sea to the land and now from the land to the sea; for in their excitement they regarded any place where they were not as safer than where they were. While this was going on, an inconceivable quantity of ashes was blown out, which covered both the land and the sea and filled all the air. It wrought much injury of various kinds, as chance befell, to men and farms and cattle, and in particular it destroyed all fish and all birds. Furthermore, it buried two entire cities, Pompeii and Herculaneum, the former place while its population was seated in the theatre. Indeed, the amount of dust, taken all together, was so great that some of it reached Africa and Syria and Egypt, and it also reached Rome, filling the air overhead and darkening the sun. There, too, no little fear was occasioned that lasted several days, since the people did not know and could not imagine what had happened, but, like those close at hand, believed that the whole earth was being turned upside down, that the sun was disappearing into the earth and the earth was being lifted up to the sky. These ashes, now, did the Romans no great harm at the time, though later they brought a terrible pestilence upon them."

Together with this exact geological description of the eruption we should read the moving picture, drawn by the younger Pliny in a letter to his friend Tacitus describing the death of his uncle, the naturalist and encyclopedist Pliny, who died in the catastrophe:

"Your request that I would send you an account of my uncle's end so that you may transmit a more exact relation of it to posterity, deserves my acknowledgements... He was at the time with the fleet under his command at Misenum. On the 24th of August, about one in the afternoon, my mother desired him to observe a cloud of a very unusual size and appearance. He had sunned himself, then taken a cold bath, and after a leisurely luncheon was engaged in study. He immediately called for his shoes and went up an eminence from whence he might best view this very uncommon appearance. It was not at the distance discernable from what mountain this cloud issued, but it was found afterwards to be Vesuvius. I cannot give you a more exact description of its figure than by resembling it to that of a pinetree, for it shot up a great height in the form of a trunk, which extended itself at the top into several branches; because I imagine, a momentary gust of air blew it aloft, and then failing, forsook it; thus causing the cloud to expand laterally as it dissolved, or possibly the downward pressure of its own weight produced this effect. It was at one moment white, at another dark and spotted as if it carried up earth and cinders.

My uncle, true savant as he was, deemed the phenomenon important and worth a nearer view. He ordered a light vessel (liburna) to be got ready and gave me the liberty, if I thought it proper, to attend him. I replied that I would rather study; and, as it happened, he had himself given me a theme for composition. As he was coming out of the house he received a note from Rectina, the wife of Bassus who was in the utmost alarm at the imminent danger (his villa stood just below us and there was no way to escape but by sea); she earnestly entreated him to save her from such deadly peril. He changed his first design and what he began with a philosophical, he pursued with an heroical turn of mind. He ordered large galleys to be launched, and went himself on board one, with the intention of assisting not only Rectina, but many others; for the villas stand extremely thick on that beautiful coast. Hastening to the place from whence the others were flying, he steered his direct course to the point of danger, and with such freedom of fear, as to be able to make and dictate his observations upon the successive motions and figures of that terrific object.

And now cinders, which grew thicker and thicker and hotter the nearer he approached, fell into the ships, then pumice-stones too, with stones blackened, scorched and cracked by fire, then the sea ebbed suddenly from under them, while the shore was blocked up by land-slips from the mountains. After considering a moment whether he should retreat, he said to the captain who was urging that course: "Fortune befriends the brave; carry me to Pomponianus". Pomponianus was then at Stabiae (now Castèl è Mar di Stabia), distant by half the width of the bay (for, as you know, the shore, insensibly curving in its sweep, forms here a receptacle for the sea). He had already embarked his baggage; for though at Stabiae the danger was not yet near, it was in full view, and certain to be extremely near, as soon as it spread; and he resolved to fly as soon as the contrary wind should cease. It was full favourable, however, to carry my uncle to Pomponianus. He embraces,

comforts and encourages his alarmed friend, and in order to soothe the
other's fears by his own concern, desired to be conducted to a bath-
room; and after having bathed, he sat down to supper with great
cheerfulness, or at least (what is equally heroic) with all appearance of it.

In the meanwhile Mount Vesuvius was blazing in several places with
spreading and towering flames, whose refulgent brightness the darkness of the night set in high relief. But my uncle, in order to soothe
apprehensions, kept saying that some fires had been left alight by the
terrified country people, and what they saw were only deserted villas
on fire in the abandoned district. After that he retired to rest, and it is
most certain that his rest was a most genuine slumber; for his breathing, which, as he was pretty fat, was somewhat heavy and sonorous,
was heard by those who attended at his chamber-door. But the court
which led to his appartment now lay so deep under a mixture of pumice-
stones and ashes, that if he had continued longer in his bedroom egress
would have been impossible. On being aroused, he came out, and
returned to Pomponianus and the others, who had sat up all night.
They consulted together whether they should hold out in the house,
or wander about in the open. For the house now tottered under repeated and violent concussions, and seemed to rock to and fro, as if torn
from its foundations. In the open air, on the other hand, they dreaded
the falling pumice-stones light and porous though they were; yet this,
by comparison, seemed the lesser danger of the two; a conclusion
which my uncle arrived at by balancing reasons, and the others by
balancing fears. They tied pillows upon their heads with napkins; and
this was their whole defence against the showers that fell around them
by now.

It was now day everywhere else, but there deeper darkness prevailed
than in the most obscure night; relieved, however, by many torches
and divers illuminations. They thought proper to go down upon the
shore to observe from close at hand if they could possibly put out to
sea, but they found the waves still running extremely high and contrary.
There my uncle having thrown himself down upon a disused sail,
repeatedly called for, and drank, a draught of cold water; soon after,
flames, and a strong smell of sulphur, which was the forerunner of
them, dispersed the rest of the company in flight; him they only
aroused. He raised himself up with the assistence of two of his slaves,
but instantly fell; some unusually gross vapour, as I conjecture, having
blocked his windpipe, which was not only naturally weak and con-
stricted but chronically inflamed. When day dawned again (the third

from that he last beheld) his body was found entire and uninjured, and still fully clothed as in life, its posture that of a sleeping, rather than a dead man.

Meanwhile my mother and I were at Misenum. But this has no connection with history, and your inquiry went no further than concerning my uncle's death, I will therefore put an end to my letter..."

8. *Fossils and evolution*

We have seen that the ancients had observed fossil shells which they took to be proofs that the seas and lakes had formerly risen to the highest levels of the mountain ranges, or that these mountains had become great heights at some later date, but they never suspected that the shell-bearing strata might have been raised by movements of the earths crust to their present elevated position. Herodotus (206) mentions that "there were shells on the hills" of Egypt and Plutarch in his De Iside et Oriside says: "Egypt was once all sea, for which reason at this day it is found to have an abundance of molluscan shells both in its mines and on its mountains". Similar observations can be found in Strabo's Geography (207): "Eratosthenes says further that this question in particular has presented a problem: how does it come about that large quantities of mussel-shells, oyster-shells, scallop-shells and also salt-marshes are found in many places in the interior at a distance of two thousand or three thousand stadia the sea, — for instance in the neighbourhood of the temple of Ammon, and along the road, three thousand stadia in length, that leads to it?" and he quotes from Xanthus' Lydia-ka, written about 450 B.C.: "That far from the sea in Armenia, Matiene, and Lower Phrygia, he himself (Xanthus) had often seen, in many places, stones in the shape of a bivalve, shells of the pecten order, impressions of scallop-shells, and a salt marsh, and therefore was persuaded that these plains were once sea".

Ovid puts a lecture on geology in the mouth of Pythagoras (208) to explain why such sea-shells are found so far inland, but Orosius shrugs his shoulders and says, that, obviously, they had never heard of Noah when referring to a flood because of "stones rough with shells" found on remote mountains.

In some cases the very stones used by the architects contained such fossil shells and they gave rise to strange stories such as that of Strabo (209) on the nummulitic sandstone of Egypt: "There are heaps of stone-chips lying in the front of the pyramids; and among these are found chips that are like lentils both in form and size; and under some of these heaps lie winnowings, as it were, as of half-peeled grains. They say that what was left of the food of the workmen has petrified; and this is not improbable. Indeed, in my home-country (Pontus), in a plain, there is a long hill which is full of lentil-shaped pebbles of porous stone (tufa)". Pausanias too (210) describes a "shelly marble". "The Megarian mussel-stone is very white and softer than other stone, in it throughout are sea-mussels". In various passages from Pliny (211) we find that such stones could suggest wrong ideas by false resemblances.

It is also clear from our documents that such fossils were collected. Suetonius (212) reports that "this own villas, Augustus decorated... with objects noteworthy for their antiquity and rarity; for example at Capreae the monstruous bones of huge sea monsters and wild beasts, called "the bones of the giants" and Pausanias mentions (213) that "at Megalopolis in Arcadia in the sanctuary of Boy Asclepius are also kept bones, too big for those of a human being, about which the story ran that they were those of one of the giants mastered by Hopladamus to fight for Rhea".

This was of course the common explanation given for fossil bones in the days when science had not yet discovered and described the huge prehistoric creatures, with which we are now familiar. The classical tradition survived in patristic literature, for instance Clement (214) mentions "the giants... men of immense bodies, whose bones of enormous size are still shown in some places for confirmation", and Augustine (215) mentions a huge tooth picked up on the African shore as a proof that giants existed before the Flood.

We know that the fossil spines of echinoids (sea urchins), which Dioscorides (216) calls "Ioudaikos lithos", were used in medicine from Egyptian days onwards up to the present day (217). In ancient China (218) fossils were also well-known and used in medicine on a large scale. Towards the end of the fifth century Li Tao-Yuan in the Shui Ching Chu (Commentary on the Waterways Classic) says "In Shih-Yen Shan there are a sort of stone-oysters which look like swallows. Hence the name of the mountain. There are two varieties of these stone shapes, one large and one small, as if they were parents and offspring. During thunderstorms these "stone-swallows" fly about as if they were real swallows. Yet Lo Han said: "Now the stone-swallows do not fly any more". Later authors have many passages on "stone oysters", "conchs" "stone silkworms", "stone crabs" and also "dragon bones" and "dragon teeth". Many fossil animals found during excavation of canals from 133 B.C. onwards are mentioned in terms like "strange bones were found where the serpents and dragons had been".

We also find Theophrastus (219) talking of "fossil ivory which is variegated with white and dark markings" and Diogenes Laertius (220) ascribes to Theophrastus an essay on petrifications, probably containing a systematic treatment of fossils. On the other hand we must remember, that the Greek "oryktos" means "dug up" rather than "fossil" in the modern sense of the word. This is notably clear from Pliny's passage (221) on elephants burying their tusks, evidently a reference to the fossil ivory of mastodonts and the like. This is also evident from a problem, which intrigued many ancient authors, that of the "*fossil fish*", on which Aristotle (222) reports: "In Heraclea in Pontus and in Rhegium they say that some fish are caught by digging, and that these are mostly found in riverside and watery places. When these places dry up they can be caught in certain places on the land, and when the ground still dries more they penetrate into the mud in search of moisture; then when that grows dry they remain in the moisture like those that survive in holes. But when they are dug up before the water comes they move. And they say that in Paphlagonia those fishes which are dug up are bred deep down, and that they are good in quality; although no water is to be seen near by, not any river flowing in, but the earth itself propagates these creatures".

There is no doubt that these "piscis fossilis" refer to "dug-up fish" rather than to real fossil fish. Strabo (223) knows such fish too from the region of the Ruscino: "a short distance above the sea, a marshy district, full of salt-springs, which contains the "dug mullets"; for if one digs only two or three feet and thrusts his trident down into the muddy water, it is possible to spit a fish, that is notable for its size; and it feeds on the mud just like eels do".

Seneca (224) quoting Theophrastus mentions such "fish taken from the earth" in Paphlagonia and again referring to a passage in Pliny says: "In the neighbourhood of Heraclea and Cromna and in many parts of the Black Sea there is one kind (of fish) that frequents the water at the edge of rivers and makes itself caverns in the ground and lies in these, and also in the shore of tidal rivers when left dry by the tide; and consequently they are dug up when the movement of their bodies shows that they are alive". Again we have Athenaeus (225) who reports that "Polybius in the Thirty-Fourth Book of his Histories says that after the Pyrenees as far as Narbo there is a plain traversed by the rivers Illeberis and Roscynus which pass towns of the same name inhabited

by Celts. In this plain are found the so-called underground (oryktous)
fish. The plain has a light soil and a great deal of agrostis grow there.
Under the plants, where the soil consists of sand to a depth of two or
three cubits, the flood-water of the river penetrates, and together with
the water in flood-time certain fish descending in search of food — for
they are very fond of the roots of the agrostis — make all the plain full
of subterranean fish which they catch by digging them up".

Evidently these passages refer to fish burying themselves in a dry
hot summer and reappearing with the first dry weather such as observed by Buchanan (226).

Strangely enough the classical authors have not discussed the process
of *petrification* or *fossilisation* of such vegetable or animal remains as did
the Chinese, who studied it carefully in various cases. The role of the
petrifying springs and waters is recognized in early Chinese encyclope-
dias, e.g. in the early sixth-century Shu I Chi (Records of Strange
Things): "The Yang Chhüan spring is located north of the Thien-Yü
Shan mountain. A clear stream flows forth several dozen yards. Herbs
and pieces of wood placed in the water are all turned to stone, clear
and hard".

From the third century onwards texts refer to trees turning into
stones after three thousand years. In some regions like that in Central
Asia inhabited by the Uighurs a river called Khang-Kan will turn
into blue-coloured stones any piece of wood dropped into it. In 767
the painter Pi Hung made a famous fresco depicting fossilized pine-
trees.

At the end of the ninth century Tu Kuang-Thing in his Lu I Chi
(Records of Strange Things) said: "In a pavillion on the mountain in
Yung-khang Hsien near Wuchow there are what look like rotten fir
trees. But if you break a piece off, you will find that it is not decayed
in the water but a substance changed into stone, which preciously was
not yet transformed in that manner. On examining other pieces in the
water at that place they turn out to be transformations of the same
character. These metamorphoses do not differ from fir-trees as to
branches and bark; they are simply very hard". Shen Kua in 1080
writes: "In recent years there was a landslide on the bank of a large
river in Yung-Ning Kuan near Yenchow. The bank collapsed, opening
a space of several dozens of feet, and under the ground a forest of
bamboo shoots was thus revealed. It contained several hundreds bamboos with their roots and trunks all complete, and all turned to stone.
A high official happened to pass by and took away several, saying that

he would present them to the emperor. Now bamboos do not grow in Yenchow. These were several dozens of feet below the present surface of the ground, and we do not know in what dynasty they could possibly have grown. Perhaps in very ancient times the climate was different so that the place was low, damp, gloomy and suitable for bamboos... These petrified bamboos appeared under the ground, so deep, though they are not produced in that place today".

Some modern authors have traced back our *evolution* theory to a passage from Xenophanes, but unfortunately some of their speculations go far beyond the limits of the original text. Actually the earliest hint of the concept "evolution" can be found in Anaximander's theory of the cosmos, vaguely mentioned by Aristotle (227), but better known from fragments quoted by other authors. Freeman (228) gave an excellent summary of the ideas of Anaximander: "He said that all living creatures arose from the moist element as it was evaporated by the sun. In our cosmos this process is going on; for the moist element is being dried up by the hot, and some day all will be dry. Creation means differentiation of opposites, which are then in a state of strife with each other; now the one, then the other gets the upper hand. When in due time they return to the source, all the differences will be merged in the impartial whole.

These primitive creatures have come into being in the moist element and were covered with prickly wrappings, but as they grew older, they climbed out on the drier part; their wrappings broke off, and they survived only a short time. Mankind, therefore, was originally like a fish, or to put it differently, these fish-like creatures contained within themselves human beings, to which, by bursting asunder, they subsequently gave birth. The reason for thinking that man was originally born from creatures of a different species is that whereas other animals soon find food for themselves, man is the only one requiring a long period of suckling; so that if he had so been made originally, he could not have survived. Hence in the beginning another creature must have nutured the human foetus until it was old enough to look after itself".

The Theophrastean account of this theory has been well preserved by the doxographers (229):

"Living creatures arose from the moist element as it was evaporated by the sun. Man was like another animal, namely, a fish, in the beginning. The first animals were produced in the moisture, each enclosed in a prickly bark. As they advanced in age, they came upon the drier part. When the bark broke off, they survived for a short time.

Further he says that originally man was born from animals of another species. His reason is that while animals quickly find food for themselves, man alone requires a lengthy period of suckling. Hence, had he originally been as he is now, he would never have survived.

He declares that at first human beings arose in the inside of fishes, and having been reared like sharks, and become capable of protecting themselves, they were finally cast ashore and took to land".

These fragments allow us to conclude with Burnet, that Anaximander had a vague idea of what we call "adaptation to environment" and "survival of the fittest", and that he saw that the higher mammals could not represent the original type of animal. But he did not go beyond such hints.

This theory propounded by Anaximander no doubt made a big impression on Xenophanes of Kolophon (c. 530 B.C.) who, as Theophrastus informs us, "heard Anaximander" at some time during his wandering life. The fragment of his writings dealing with "evolution", which is widely quoted, is found in the Philosophumena of Origen, a book now widely held to have been written by his contemporary Hippolytus (230). Actually, it is second-hand evidence for Hippolytus took it from an account of Xenophanes' theory by Theophrastus and it is much less a theory of evolution such as Anaximander gave than an observation and an explanation of fossils. We give here the translation which Bromehead made from the original and published in his "Geology in Embryo": "He (Xenophanes) said that the sea was salt because a large variety of mixed materials flows into it. Further Xenophanes laid down that land and sea were mixed up; the land even thought to be dissolved in the course of time by moisture; he offers as a proof of this that fact that sea-shells (lit. smooth-shelled bivalves) are found in the midst of the earth, even in mountains. Again, that in the stone quarries of Syracuse remains of fish and a certain kind of seal are found; while in Paros in the depths of the rock one finds impressions of sprats (aphye) and in Malta even moulds of all kinds of marine creatures. He says that it follows from this that at one time all these lands were under water. The impression of the fossils has been dried out and consolidated (made costive) in the mud. All human beings were destroyed when the earth has been carried down into the sea and turned to mud. This change takes place for all the worlds".

This passage has often been misquoted (231) and neither Xenophanes not any other classical author worked out in more details the hint given by Anaximander. If Aristotle arranges the different kinds of living beings in a series, his "Ladder of Nature", in which the gradations are easy, this does not mean that he regards these different species as actually related by descent. This applies to geology too. There is no ancient stratigraphy or palaeontology, even if we recognize some modern ideas in chance remarks by ancient authors. To Galen (232) the parts of the body are so well constructed for and marvellously adapted to their functions that nothing better is possible than the divine planner created. A similar static creation was in the mind of St. Basil (233) who held that "all which sprang forth from the earth in the first beginning is kept the same in our time, thanks to the constant reproduction of kind" and "animals do not see their pecularities destroyed or affected by any length of time; their nature, as though it had just been constituted, follows the course of ages forever young".

9. *The origin of minerals and ores*

Modern petrology does not only study the physical and chemical properties of rocks but also their origin taking into account the data derived from geomorphological studies and from structural geology. We are interested to know whether such rocks are igneous, sedimentary or metamorphic rocks. The igneous rocks are formed by extrusive, volcanic action or by intrusive action, i.e. they belong to the masses cooled below the earth's surface now exposed by erosion. Such igneous rocks like lava, granite, etc. may have fine- or coarse-grained structures. The most important sedimentary rocks are conglomerates (formed by the cementing of fragments of older rocks), sandstone, shale (mainly clay), limestone (mainly calcite) or dolomite (mainly magnesite) In the course of the centuries recrystallization or other changes may take place in rocks and form metamorphic rocks like slate, schist, gneiss, marble (metamorphic limestone) or quartzite (mainly quartz and sandstone). The ancients never developed such a classification based on the origin and gradual transformation of rocks, they were interested only in the origin of metals and ores, a subject which would now belong to both economic geology and petrology and the study of which would involve drawing on many other branches of geology too.

The first consistent theory on the origin of rocks is given by Plato (234) in his Timaeus:

"The kinds of water are, primarily, two, the one being the liquid, the other the fusible kind (metal!). Now the liquid kind, inasmuch as it partakes of those small particles of water which are unequal, is mobil both in itself and external force owing to its non-uniformity and the shape of its figure. But the other kind, which is composed of large and uniform particles, is more stable than the first and is heavy, being solidified by its uniformity; but when fire enters and dissolves it, this causes it to abandon its uniformity, and this being lost it partakes more largely in motion; and when it has become mobile it is pushed by the adjacent air and extended upon the earth; and for each of these modifications it has received a descriptive name — "melting" for the disintegration of its masses, and for its extension over the earth "fluidity". Again, since the fire on issuing from the water does not pass into a void but presses on the adjacent air, this in turn compresses the liquid mass which is still mobile into the abodes of the fire and combines it with itself; and the mass, being thus compressed and recovering again its uniformity, because of the departure of the fire, the author of its non-uniformity, returns to the state of self-identity. And this cessation of the fire is termed "cooling" and the combination which follows on its departure "solidification".

Table I

Plato's theory on the formation of ores and metals

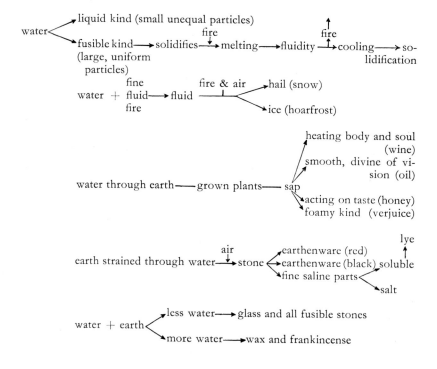

Of all the kinds of water which we have termed "fusible", the densest is produced from the finest and most uniform particles: this is a kind of unique form, tinged with a glittering and yellow hue, even that most precious of possessions, "gold", which has been strained through stones and solidified. And the off-shoot of gold, which is very hard because of its density and black in colour, is called "adamant". And the kind which closely resembles gold in its particles but has more forms than one, and in density is more dense than gold, and partakes of small and fine particles of earth so that it is harder, while it is also lighter owing to it having larger interstices within it, — this particular kind of the bright and solid water, compounded thus is termed "chalkos" (copper or bronze). And the portion of earth that is mixed therewith becomes distinct by itself, when both grow old and separate again each from the other, and then it is named "rust".

And the rest of such phenomena it is no longer difficult to explain in full, if one aims at framing a description that is probable...

Of the species of earth, that which is strained through water becomes a stony substance in the following way. When the water commingling with it is divided in the process of mingling, it changes into the form of air; and when it has become air it rushes up to its own region; but because there was no void space above them, therefore it pressed against the adjacent air; and it, being heavy, when pressed and poured round the mass of earth, crushed it forcibly and compressed it into the spaces from which the new air was ascending. But when thus compressed by the air so as to be indissoluble by water it forms "stone"; of which the fairer sort is that composed of equal and uniform parts and transparent, and the coarser sort the opposite. That kind from which all the moisture has been carried off by the rapidity of fire, and which is more brittle in its composition than the first kind, is the kind to which we have given the name of "earthenware". But sometimes, when moisture is still left in the earth and it has been fused by fire and cooled again, it forms the species which is black in hue. On the other hand, there are two kinds, which, in exactly the same manner, are isolated after the mixture from much of its water, but are composed of the finer parts of earth and are saline: when these have become semi-solid and soluble again by water, one of them is purgative of oil and earth and forms the species we call "lye" (of potash or salpetre) and the other, which blends well with the combinations which affect the sensation of the mouth, is that substance which is customarily termed "beloved of the gods", namely "salt".

As regards the kinds which are blends of these two, and are dissoluble by fire and not by water, their composition is due to the following cause. Fire and air do not melt masses of earth; for inasmuch as their particles are smaller than the interstices of its structure, they have room to pass through without forcible effect and leave the earth undissolved, with the result that it remains unmelted; whereas the particles of water, being larger, must use force to make their way out, and consequently dissolve and melt the earth. Thus the earth when it is not forcibly condensed is dissolved only by water; and when it is condensed is dissolved by fire only, since no entrance is left for anything but fire. Water, again, when most forcibly massed together is dissolved by fire only, but when massed less forcibly both by fire and air, the latter acting by the way of the interstices, and the former by the way of the triangles; but air when forcibly condensed is dissolved by nothing save by way of its elemental triangles, and when unforced is melted down by fire only.

As regards the classes of bodies which are compounds of earth and water, so long as the water occupies the interspaces of earth which are forcibly contracted, the portions of water which approach from without find no entrance, but flow round the whole mass and leave it undissolved. But when portions of fire enter into the interspaces of the water they produce the same effects on water as water does on earth; consequently, they are the sole causes why the compound substance is dissolved and flows. And of these substances those which contain less water than earth the whole kind is known as "glass" and all the species of stone called "fusible", while those which contain more water include all the solidified substances of the type of wax and frankincense".

In his Critias (235) Plato mentions that "Atlantis yielded all the extracted products of the miner's industry, solid and fusible alike", the latter representing the "fusible" metals (ores), which he regards as liquids with a high freezing point, as we can read in the extract from the Timaeus given above.

Aristotle had a theory of his own, though he owes much to his master. For this theory we must again turn to his Meteorologica:

(I. iii) "The substance beneath the motion of the heavens is a kind of matter, having potentially the qualities hot, dry, cold and wet and any consequent upon these... So what is heaviest and coldest, that is earth and water, separate off at the centre round the centre: immediately around them are air and what we are accustomed to call fire, though it is not really fire: for fire is an excess of heat and a sort of boiling. But we must understand that of what we call air the part which immediately surrounds the earth is moist and hot because it is vaporous and contains exhalations from the earth, but that part above is hot and dry". He then argues that clouds will not be formed in the "upper region" of fire, which is sometimes driven inwards by the motion of the heavens.

In the fourth chapter Aristotle then argues that there are two kinds of exhalations which rise from the earth, one vaporous, one hot and dry. The dry and hot exhalation is lighter and rises to the top, forming a sheath of "fire" round the terrestial sphere, the more vaporous exhalation of "air" lying below it.

These passages are important when we consider Aristotle's theory on the formation of ores and minerals for there the two exhalations play their part as they do in meteorology. For according to him (II. iv) the moist, vaporous exhalation produces rain, the dry exhalation wind. In the same way (III. vi) "Exhalation produces two different kinds of body (under the earth's surface), being itself twofold just as it is in the upper regions. For there are, we maintain, two exhalations, one vaporous and one smoky; and there are two corresponding kinds of bodies produced within the earth, substances dug or quarried ("fossiles") and substances mined ("metals", better "ores" or "minerals"). The dry exhalation by the action of its heat produces all the "fossiles", for example, all kinds of stones that are fusible — realgar, ochre, ruddle, sulphur and all other substances of this kind. Most "fossiles" are coloured dust or stone formed of a similar composition, for instance cinnabar. Metals are the product of the vaporous exhalation, and are all fusible or ductile, for example, iron, gold, copper. These are all produced by the enclosure of the vaporous exhalation, particularly within stones, whose dryness compresses it together and soldifies it, just as dew and frost solidify when they have been separated — only metals are produced before the separation has taken place. So they are in a sense water and in another sense not: it was possible for their material to turn into water, but it can no longer do so, nor are they, like tastes, the result of some change of quality in the water already formed. For this is not the way in which copper or gold is produced, but each is the result of the solidification of the exhalation before it turns to water. So all metals are affected by fire and contain earth, for they contain dry exhalation. The only exception is gold, which is not affected by fire".

Aristotle here hints at a theory approaching pneumatolysis. He describes, says Eichholz (236), what happens when the moist, vaporous exhalation (which forms rain, dew, frost and snow) and the dry, smoky kind (which forms stars, thunder, lightning, wind and earthquakes are "imprisoned within parts of the earth". Two substances are formed in the earth, "fossiles" (lit. things dug up) and "metals" (things mined), the latter by the vaporous exhalation, the former by the dry one.

By metals Aristotle means all the substances which are mined and which, unlike the fossiles, are fusible or malleable. Thus iron, gold, copper, silver, tin, lead, etc. are formed by the moist exhalation when it is trapped underground and particularly when it is enclosed in rocks. This would then explain why such metals have to be extracted from ores. This moist exhalation condenses when it comes into contact with the dry rock, and is there congealed into metals by cold. However, as the moist exhalation composing the metals contains an admixture of the dry exhalation, metals can no longer revert to water like "hoar-frost". Their matter was potentially that of water but is so no longer.

The moist exhalation, then, is the material of all metals. Along with portions of the dry exhalation it is trapped underground, where it condenses, particularly if it comes into contact with rocks, and then hardens probably through cold. Metals are not formed like dew or hoar-frost, still less like savours. Because the metals contain a variable percentage of earth (the greatest in iron, the least in gold), they cannot revert to water, and for the same reason they are, with the exception of gold, affected by fire.

The fire and the heat needed to form the "fossiles" is supplied by the dry exhalation. Together they reduce the earth to the consistency of fine ash and perhaps cause it to take on bright colours (though this is not quite clear from the text). Those of the fossiles which are stones must furthermore have been hardened by this heat. The dry exhalation is therefore the efficient and not the material cause of the "fossiles".

The latter view is corroborated by Theophrastus de Lap. par. 50, where he discusses a group of mineral earths (ochre), ruddle and real-gar) and mentions that *all* are products of the dry exhalation but "only *some* show clear evidence of having been burnt".

Much later G. Agricola in his De Ortu and Causis Subterraneorum iii, p. 508, when discussing Aristotle's theory in the light of his own practical experience, corroborates this view.

Among the "fossile" Aristotle includes realgar (sandarache) and red ochre (ruddle) (miltos). In the Assyrian terminology sandarache may also represent the yellow sulphide, orpiment. The word miltos is used in the same sense as Aristotle by Herodotus and Dioscorides, but

Pliny (237) also uses it for red lead and later authors apply it as a magical and secret name for blood.

Chinese philosophers developed a concept "chhi", which runs parallel to the exhalations of Aristotle. The preface to chapter 8 of the Pen Tshao Kang Mu (which can be traced back to the second century B.C.) opens: "Stone is the kernel of the chhi and the bone of the earth. In large masses it forms rock and cliffs, in small particles it forms sand and dust. Its seminal essence (ching) becomes gold and jade; its poisonous principle becomes arsenolite (yü) and arsenious acid (phi). When the chhi becomes congealed, it forms cinnabar and green vitriol. When the chhi undergoes transformation, it becomes liquid and gives rise to alums and to mercury. Its changes are manifold for that which is soft can become hard, as in the case of milky brine which sets to rock-salt; and that which moves can become immovable, as in the case of the petrification of herbs, trees, or even of flying and creeping animals, which once had animation, yet turn into that which has it not. Again, when thunder or thunderbolts turn to stones, there is a transformation of the formless into that which has form...".

Theophrastus based his ideas on those of Plato and Aristotle, but he definitely rejects certain points made by this teachers. We find his theory on the origin and nature of mineral substances in the opening paragraph of his essay On Stones:

"Of the substances formed in the ground, some are made of water and some of earth. The metals obtained by mining, such as silver, gold and so on, come from water; from earth come stones, including the more precious kinds, and also the types of earth that are unusual because of the colour, smoothness, density, or any other quality. As metals have been discussed in another place, let us now speak about the stones.

In general we must consider all of them formed from some pure and homogeneous matter as a result of a conflux or percolation, or because the matter has been separated in some other way, as has been explained above. For perhaps some are produced in one of these ways, and others in the other way, and some in a different manner. Hence they gain their smoothness, density, brightness, transparency, and other qualities, and the more uniform and pure each of them is, the more do these qualities appear. In general, the qualities are produced according to the accuracy with which the stones are formed and solidified.

Some things are solidified through heat, others through cold. And probably there is nothing to prevent some kinds of stones being formed by either of these two methods, although it would seem that all types of earth are produced by fire, since things become solid or melt as the result of opposite forces. There are more pecularities in stones; for most of the differences in types of earth concern colour, tenacity, smoothness, density, and so on, but in other respects the differences are rare".

This passage shows that Theophrastus is inclined to follow Plato's concept of the two kinds of "water" rather than Aristotle's complex and none too clear theory of the formation of minerals from the two exhalations. He also tends to approach modern mineralogical theories of crystallisation from magmatic or acqueous solutions. He agrees with Aristotle (238), that crystallisation is due to dry heat (evaporation of a solution) or cold (cooling a molten substance). He also supports Aristotle's opinion that all earthy substances were "born by fire", which is clear to anyone observing the formation of ashes; and he agrees that sometimes earths can be softened or dispersed by water; as the master laid down in the following passages (239):

"So of the things which solidify owing to cold or hot, those that dissolve are dissolved by the opposite property: for those that solidify owing to dry heat are dissolved by water, by moist cold, while those that solidify owing to cold are dissolved by fire, that is by beat".

"Anything which is earthy and has pores larger than the particles of water and harder than water can be softened by water... in earth the pores alternate and the effect differs according to which set of pores the water enters".

In Pliny (240) we find random allusions to a theory regarding the formation of transparent and semi-transparent stones, which is discussed by Eichholz (241) and Nock (242). According to this theory, which appears to have been developed by Poseidonius, the raw material of such stones was water. In the second book (52, 1—4) of Diodorus' History we read what was probably Poseidonius' original view on such problems:

"In these countries (Egypt, Lybia, India, Ethiopia) are generated... also outcroppings of every kind of precious stones which are unusual in colour and resplendent brilliancy. For the rock-crystals, so we are informed, are composed of pure water which has been hardened, not by the action of cold, but by the influence of a divine fire (volcanic action?), and for this reason they are never subject to corruption and take on many hues when they are breathed upon. For instance the smaragdi (emeralds?) and beryls as they are called, which are found in the shafts of copper mines, receive their colour by having been dipped and bound together in a bath of sulphur, and the "gold-stones" (topaz?), they say, are produced by a smoky exhalation due to the heat of the sun, thereby get the colour they have. For this reason what is called "false gold", we are told, is fabricated by mortal fire, made by man by dipping the rock crystals in it. And as for the natural qualities of the dark-red stones (such as carbuncles, rubies and garnets), it is the influence of light, as it is compressed to a greater or lesser degree in them when they are hardening, they say, which accounts for their differences".

Poseidonius holds that the water, possibly impregnated by earthy particles, was compacted either by the cold in the atmosphere or by one or other of the two exhalations described by Aristotle. The colours were imparted to coloured stones by the dry exhalation, which also hardened them. It seems that the theory as a whole was unknown or only imperfectly known to Pliny. Neither does Seneca give us any integrated opinion on this subject. In refuting the thesis of Thales in his Naturales Quaestiones, that the earth floats on water, Seneca (243) says that the Egyptians recognized a male and a female form of each of the four elements. Thus the wind is male, the inactive cloud female; sea-water is male, all other water female; fire is male when burning with a flame, but female in all other cases; earth is male when hard as in stone and rocks, but female if workable and cultivated. He then continues to explain that nature has organized the earth like a human body and that there are channels, comparable with veins and arteries, through which water and air circulate. Also like the human body, the earth contains "many types of liquids indispensable to life as well as a variety of humours". The earth being like a living organism, its parts and the liquids therein mature and ripen (XV—3). "Maturity hardens them. Hence the much-appreciated mines whence human avarice draws its gold and silver; others loose their liquid state and petrify. Earth and water, putrifying, give rise to certain substance, for instance bitumen and similar liquids... As regards the stone which resembles ice, its Greek name (krystallos) indicates how it is formed. They apply this term to the transparent stone as well as to the ice out of which some believe it is formed. Rain water contains extremely few terrestial elements. When it hardens, the persistence of cold condenses it more and more, until, after complete elimination of the air it contains, it is completely condensed to its proper matter and from a liquid turns into a stone..."

The exhalations are also indicated in the following passage from Lucretius (244), where he describes the formation of earth, sky, sun and other heavenly bodies: "Yea, verily, first of all the several bodies of earth, because they were heavy and interlaced met together in the middle, and all took up the lowest places; and the more they met and interlaced the more did they squeeze out those which were to make sea, stars, sun and moon, and the walls of the great world. For all these are of smoother and rounder seeds, and of much smaller particles than earth.

"And so, bursting out from the quarter of the earth through its looseknit openings, first of all the fiery ether rose up and, being so light, carried off with it many fires, in no far different wise than we often see now, when first the golden morning light of the radiant sun reddens over the grass bejewelled with dew, and pools and ever-running streams give off a mist, yea, even as the earth from time to time is seen to steam; and when all these gathered together as they move upwards on high, clouds with body now formed weave a webb beneath the sky". Further lines now discuss the creation of or world by the segregation of the right kinds of atoms.

The theory of the exhalations was the point of departure for later ideas on the generation of metals in the earth. The alchemists, seeking to accelerate this natural process in their laboratories pounced upon it, and much older ideas, such as the natural growth of metals in mines, the astral influences on the generation of metals, etc. are introduced into it.

Thus Proclus, in his Commentary on the Timaeus, tells us that: "Natural gold, silver and each metal, like other substances, are engendered in the earth under the influence of the celestial gods and their effluvia. The Sun produces gold, the Moon silver, Saturn lead; and Mars iron". We can compare this with an ancient Babylonian cuneiform text from the British Museum (CT XX. 49.1.36) in which Anu is said to make silver, Enlil gold and Ea copper. This ancient Babylonian belief permeates all later theories on the generation of metals throughout the Middle Ages into much later generations.

Certain passages in classical authors (245) suggest a belief (which again goes back to pre-classical times) that metals grow in the earth and thus supplement deposits, which would have been exhausted long ago by men's depradations. Servius, commenting on a passage by Virgil, says that this happens on the isle of Elba, and Strabo says that "the diggings which have been mined are in time filled up again as is said to be the case with the ledges of rocks in Rhodes, the marble-rock in Paros and, according to Cleitarchus, the salt-rock in India."

The exhalation theory was converted into the mercury-sulphur theory by the Arabian alchemists and philosophers, but one of them was the first to attack the pretensions of the alchemists. This is what Avicenna (246) has to say on their claims: "There is little doubt that, by alchemy, the adepts can contrive solidifications in which the qualities of the solidifications of mercury (one of the exhalations) by the sulphurs (the other exhalation) are perceptible to the senses, though the alchemical qualities are not identical in principle or in perfection with the natural ones, but merely bear a resemblance and relationship to them. Hence the belief arises that their natural formation takes place in this way or in some similar way, though alchemy falls short of nature in this respect, and, in spite of great effort, cannot overtake her.

As to the claims of the alchemists, it must be clearly understood that it is not in their power to bring about the true change of species. They can, however, produce excellent imitations, dyeing the red metal white so that it closely resembles silver, or dyeing it yellow so that it closely resembles gold".

For further details on these later theories, the mercury-sulphur theory of the Arab philosophers, the theory of the "Petrifying Seed", and the later one of the "Lapidifying Juice" we must needs refer the reader to the works of Adams and others already mentioned before (2).

Neither are we concerned with such apocryphal information as contained in writings such as the Book of Enoch which speaks of "seven mountains of magnificent stones" (XVIII, XXIV) and "there mine eyes saw all the hidden things of heaven that shall be, an iron mountain, and one of copper, and one of silver, and one of gold, and one of soft metal, and one of lead". The silver and the soft metal come from the earth, lead and tin are produced by a fountain in which an angel stands (LXV, 7—8).

The natural generation of metals and the gradual transformation of baser metals into silver and gold by the forces of nature, this much older doctrine, so strongly advocated by the medieval alchemists, can also be found in the writings of Li Shih-Chen (twelfth century), who says: "It is said in the Ho Ting Hsin Shu (New Book of Poisonous Substances) that copper, gold and silver have a common root and origin. That which obtains the chhi of the purple Yang produced green matter and after two hundred years this becomes stone; in the midst of this the copper grows. It is because its chhi possesses a Yang nature, that it is hard and tough".

Such passages can easily be matched with medieval speculations such as this quotation from Vincent of Beauvais' Speculum Naturale (247) of c. 1250: "Gold is produced in the earth with the aid of strong solar heat, by a brilliant mercury united to a clear and red sulphur, concocted for more than 100 years... White mercury, fixed with the virtue of incombustible white sulphur, engenders in mines a matter which fusion changes into silver... Tin is generated by a clear mercury and a white and clear sulphur concocted for a short time subterraneously. If the concoction is very prolonged, it becomes silver".

In a lost Chinese book, the Thien Shu (c. 445) it was stated that "the most precious things in the world are stored in the innermost regions of all. For example there is orpiment. After a thousand years it changes into realgar. After another thousand years the realgar becomes transformed into yellow gold." Indeed such Chinese speculations seem to go back to the philosopher Tsou Yen and his school (c. 350 B.C.) and they must have been developed independently from the pre-Socratic philosophers or Aristotle as Needham rightly claims.

The Chinese did observe various typical *geological formations* such as modern geomorphology studies and their artists depicted them (248) as some symbolical meaning became attached to them in poetry.

No such early attempts at structural geology or geomorphology are found in classical documents, though the practical miners have often shown to be well-acquainted with the regional stratigraphy as they opened new shafts at fairly large distances from each other to reach the same geological horizon, even if the lode did not outcrop. On the other hand there are many instances where they failed to show such practical observation and experience. Only in the case of the Cyprian copper mines do Pliny, Galen and Dioscorides (249) mention the same phenomenon of the decomposition of copper ores, of which Pliny gives this description:

"Chalcitis, "copper-stone", is the name of an ore, that from which copper also, besides cadmea, is obtained by smelting. It differs from cadmea because the latter is quarried above ground, from rocks exposed to the air, whereas chalcitis is obtained from underground rocks and also because chalcitis becomes friable immediately, being of a soft nature, so as to have the appearance of congealed down. There is another difference in that chalcitis contains three kinds of mineral, copper, misy and sori, each of which we shall describe in its place. The approved variety of chalcitis is honey-coloured, and streaked with fine veins and is friable and not stony. It is also thought to be more useful when fresh, as when old it turns into sori... the best sori (from Egypt, Spain, Africa and Cyprus) is that which has the most punguent odour, and which when ground takes a greasy, black colour and becomes spongy. It is a substance that goes against the stomach so violently that with some people the mere smell of it causes vomiting... misy, though got from the mineral chalcitis it is part of its substance and separated from it by force,... its marks being that when broken it sparkles like gold, and when ground it has a sandy appearance, without earth, like chalcitis".

Chalcitis, sory and misy were identified with copper glance, copper pyrites and marcasite and their decomposition products, most of them defying precise definition and identification, according to Bailey (250), who studied Pliny's text carefully. This is one of the few metamorphoses of ores or minerals mentioned by the ancients.

10. Classification of minerals and ores

Mineralogy was the only field of geology to which the preclassical civilisations contributed materially (251). After some earlier attempts by Boston to determine the meaning of certain Akkadian terms for minerals (1914—1916), V. Scheil published a late-Babylonian tablet from Uruk with a word-list of stones and objects of stone, beginning with the words "ZÁ: abnû (stone)", giving the Akkadian equivalents of Sumerian words denoting these stones (1918). His work was continued by R. Campbell Thompson, to whom we owe the complete edition of these word-lists.

Both the Egyptians and the Sumerians had compiled onomastica or word-lists, notably the Sumerians because they derived omens from astronomical, meteorological and other phenomena such as the form of the liver or entrails of the animals sacrified in the temples. The various natural phenomena and the omens to be read from them were carefully recorded in long series of cuneiform tablets. At the same time the natural phenomena, plants, animals, rocks, etc. were carefully observed, grouped and classified. Thus we possess the records of hundreds of years of careful and patient observation of nature and its scholarly tabulation on thousands of tablets. The scribes, who compiled these onomastica, took a great pride in a careful edition of their texts, hence we read at the end of such series: "He has not drawn it up inaccurately nor edited it incorrectly (1500 B.C.)" or "He has not drawn up it inaccurately nor does he withhold incorrectly" (500 B.C.).

In judging such lists we must remember, that ancient Sumer (southern Mesopotamia) is singularly jejeune of minerals and Assyria or the upper Euphrates region fared little better. Only in the mountainous regions, too often in the hands of enemies, the mineral resources were really rich. The basis of the Sumerian classification was formed by the complex of outward appearance and characteristics. The agglutinative nature of the Sumerian language facilitated the choice of a stem-word as the group-name to which a prefix or a suffix was added to mark the individual characteristics of the supposed member of this group of phenomena or things.

This results in something very much like the nomenclature used in modern organic chemistry, where "alcohol" stands for all specimens of a certain group of compounds, and embodies certain common

Table II

Iron and the iron-oxydes

Sumerian	Accadian	English
AN-BAR	parzillu	iron ("heaven-metal")
ZID-ZID-AN-BAR		powder of iron
ᶻᵃAN-BAR		iron stone, iron ore
ᶻᵃKA		iron ore, red ochre
ᶻᵃKA. GÍG		black ochre
ᶻᵃKA. SIG₇		yellow ochre
ᶻᵃKA. PAR		white ochre, spathic iron ore
ᶻᵃKA. GI. NA	ᶻᵃšàdânu	haematite (heavy iron ore)
ᶻᵃKA. GI. NA. DIB. BA	ᶻᵃšadânu ṣabitu	magnetite ("grasping iron ore")
ᶻᵃKA. GI. NA. TIL. LA	ᵃᵃšadânu balṭu	ferrum vivum, lodestone
ᶻᵃBIL	ᶻᵃpindu	pyrites, fire stone
	ᶻᵃmarhaši	marcasite
ᶻᵃTU	ᶻᵃiârahu	iron sesquioxyde

Table III

The white minerals

Sumerian	Accadian	English	Hardness Moh's scale
ᶻᵃPAR		white siliceous sand	
ᶻᵃPAR.AŠ		alabaster (hard white stone)	2
ᶻᵃPAR.AŠ.AŠ.		chalcedony (very hard white stone)	7
ᶻᵃZA.ṬU.PAR.AŠ.	ᶻᵃparûtu	calcite (hard white stone, effervescing under acid)	3
ᶻᵃZA.ṬU.PAR.AŠ.AŠ.		aragonite, magnesite, white marble (very hard white stone, effervescing under acid)	3.5—4.0

characteristics, whereas the individual members of such a group are distinguished by the prefixes "methyl-", "aethyl-", "butyl-", "propyl-", "amyl-", etc., thus turning a name like "methyl-alcohol" into a well-defined label of a certain chemical compound. In the same way all the names of stones in these Sumerian lists are preceded by the "ideogram" na_4(ZÁ), abnû to indicate that this word denote a certain stone or rock.

If we look at Table II we find that the lists of iron-oxydes has the word ^{za}Ka, iron ore or oxyde, in common as the stem to which a number of suffixes are added to denote the members of the family and the same holds good for table III where ^{za}PAR, white stone, is the name common to all. The most frequent characteristic is the *colour*: red stones being called DIR (sâmu), GUG (sându) or HUŠ (russu); blue ones ZA. GÌN (uknû), green or yellow ones both SIG₇ (arku), white with the word BABBAR (pisû), and GÌG (salmu) for black ones. But other suffixes denote further properties such as "sublimate" (IM-KAL), "hardness" (AŠ: hard, AŠ. AŠ: very hard), "effervescent with vinegar" (^{za}ZA-ṬU) (hence carbonates!); and also something about weight, brittleness, fibrous or crumbling nature. "Washed" means a salt or material prepared by leaching. In the case of precious stones and gems we find indications of their form: ^{za}IGI: (spherical) "eye-stone"; ^{za}NUNUZ: "egg-stone" (an ovoid bead) or TAG-GAZ: "cut stone". In certain cases the projected use may determine the name of a stone.

Some 120 of these stones proved to be useful minerals and also aids to the physicians or the magicians, leaving some 60 more "stones" to complete the Assyrian minerals found in these lists by Campbell Thompson. Table IV gives another example of such a grouping of mineral substances (in this case the bituminous substances) believed to belong together. The appropriateness of the terms used here has been discussed in the first volume of these series.

These lists survived because when centuries later the Semitic Assyrians and Babylonians conquered and ruled the country and subdued the Sumerian population they translated these lists in their own Semitic language (Akkadian). Such bilingual lists often had a third column giving the correct pronounciation of the Sumerian original (this "Latin for religious texts and hymns" being by now a dead language) or other philological notes, as the lists were by then used as dictionaries. No less than 8% of the 25.000 tablets of the Royal Library of Niniveh, now in the British Museum, consist of such lists.

A similar classification was achieved in ancient China (252), it was

Table IV

Bituminous Substances

Sumerian	Accadian	English	Greek
ESIR	naptu	bitumen in general	naphtha
IÀ-GIŠ-ESIR	šaman - iddî	oil of bitumen	
IÀ-KUR-RA	šaman - šadî	mountain oil	
ESIR-NE	—	burning natural gas	
ESIR-È (UD-DU)-A		bitumen, "seepage - bitumen"	
A-GAR-GAR-(AN)-(dingir)-ID	kupru	crude natural bitumen	
ESIR - LAH (UD, PAR)	iddù	white-bitumen, natural bitumen	
ESIR-(-A-BA-AL)-HURSAG	iddù, amaru	"mountain bitumen", rockasphalt	
ESIR-IGI (-ENGUR)	kupru	"eye - bitumen", refined rockasphalt	
ESIR	kupru	"coating bitumen"	
ESIR-Ê-A	iddù, kupru	"house - bitumen", mastic	
ESIR - GUL - GUL		"irrigation - bitumen", mastic	maltha
ESIR-APIN		"plough - bitumen", mastic	pissasphaltos
ESIR - ŠUB - BA		bituminous coating	
ŠE - LI - UD	kukru, kirkiranu	wood - tar pitch	

Table V.

Radicals used by the Chinese to classify minerals

Pictogram	Radical	Stands for:
(pictogram)	shih	stones and rocks
(pictogram)	chin	metals and alloys
(pictogram)	yû	precious stones

also due to the pecularities of the Chinese language and the script, which in its original phase consisted of pictograms. Thus we find the radical "shih" for all stones and rocks (Table V), which sign in its most ancient pictographical form seems to represent a man sheltering in a cave. The radical "chin", used for all the metals and alloys seems to picture a mine with a cover over the shaft and two lumps of ore. The radical "yü" standing for jade and all kinds of precious stones, may represent a girdle pendant composed of several pieces of jade.

The radical "tan" (red), a picture of a skeleton with a spot of magic red applied to it, originally meaning cinnabar, was later also used for red minerals in general. The radical "sha" (picturing small particles of rock) denotes all "sands"; "hui" the ashes; "fên" (finely divided ricemeal) all powders; "shuang" all white "frosts"; "thang" all "sugars" and "chih" or "kao" (lit fats) all greasy and soapy clays or soapstone.

Here too a grouping of rocks and minerals according to their external characteristics and other properties like fusibility, etc. as far as known. Such information can be found in the ancient pharmacopoeias (pên tshao), which certainly go back to Han date (e.g. the first century B.C. when the Shen Nung Pên Tshao Ching (The Pharmacopoeia of the Heavenly Husbandman) was compiled, which describes 46 stones and which has been incorporated in later pharmacopoeias.

Returning to the Mesopotamian scene we should remember, that contacts with the Greek world date back to about 750 B.C. and that these two civilisations were very closely allied after the conquests of Alexander the Great and the establishment of several Hellenistic King-doms after his death. The foundation of the Museion of Alexandria and that of the university of Seleucia in Syria by Seleucus Nicator led to a revival and study of the ancient Sumerian and Assyrian knowledge, notably in the Seleucid kingdom. We should also remember that the last cuneiform tablets were writen in the last decade of the first century B.C. and that the Neo-Babylonian temple-schools stood in close con-tact with the Hellenistic centres of learning.

Hence it is clear that Greek information on many minerals was derived from the East. Campbell Thompson has pointed out that the Greek and later names of some twenty minerals and half a dozen rocks have a direct Babylonian ancestry, as will be clear from the following list:

Akkadian	*Greek*	*English*
ḫurašu	chrysos	gold
AŠ.MUR	smyris	emery
burallu	beryllos	beryl
(i)aš(s)pû	iaspis	jasper
kibaltu	?	cobalt(?)
muṣû	misy	copper pyrites
nitiru	nitron	natron, natural soda
sându	sandyx	red(stone)
uḳnu	kyanos, hyakithos	blue stone, lapis lazuli
algamišu	amethystos	amethyst
barraḳtu	smaragdos	emerald
ešmarû	?	émail
aban kašari	kiseris	pumice
pîlu, parûtu	poros	calcite, limestone
gaṣṣu	gypsos	gypsum
sându marḫaši(tu)	sandrisitae	aventurine
immanakku	ammokonia	white (calcareous) and used for glassmaking

Most of these names occur as early as the fourth century in Greek texts.

Books on minerals and rocks are very scarce in classical literature, most of the fragments we possess dealing with supposed magical properties rather than with a systematic study of these materials. Thus a De Lapidibus ascribed to Aristotle is not an essay by the master as Wellmann proved, but rather a compilation of the (mostly imaginary) properties of stones like the works of Bolos Demokritos, Anaxilaos of Larissa and Xenocrates of Aphrodisias. It was probably written around AD 600 in Syriac. We also have fragments of a work by Nicias on petrology, but the outstanding book on these matters was written by Theophrastus (253), which is now available in the excellent translation and edition by Caley and Richards. The introduction of this work, which we were kindly allowed to quote here in extenso, gives an excellent summary of the importance of this work by Theophrastus.

The editors are of the opinion that "apart from a few obvious gaps and the rather abrupt ending, there is no real evidence that the treatise in its present form is not a separate, fairly complete work. Its brevity is apparently the basis of most of the suppositions that the text we have is a mere fragment; but if due considerations are given to the nature of the treatise and to the extent of ancient mineralogical knowledge as shown by other sources, it will be seen that it covers the field indicated by its title in an adequate manner, even though it may not be complete.

Without being a purely descriptive or a purely philosophical work, the treatise seems to be an attempt to classify mineral substances on the basis of Aristotelian principles, and a number of specific examples are used, mainly for purposes of illustration, without the intention of giving extended descriptions. It may be inferred that Theophrastus mentions only a small proportion of the mineral products known to him and his contemporaries; for Pliny, though he draws largely on Greek authors, some older than Theophrastus, mentions ten times as many rocks and minerals. Those mentioned by Theophrastus appear to be introduced mainly to illustrate in a general way contrasting behaviour and distinctive differences in stones and earths, and he may not have intended to catalogue the numerous varieties that were known at the time. This would explain why he describes relatively few mineral substances in detail, and why he pays so little attention to certain common and highly useful ones about which a good deal must have been known even in his day.

From the historical standpoint the treatise is of special interest because it represents, so far as we know, the first attempt to study mineral substances in a systematic way. For this purpose, Theophrastus divides them into two classes, stones and earths, the discussion of the latter being confined to the second and smaller portion of the treatise.

Though few in number, the concise accounts of ancient chemical processes included in this division are of no little importance for the history of chemical technology. At first glance, the structure of the treatise may seem to be loose or even disconnected, but on closer examination it will be readily apparent that this is not so. From the very beginning Theophrastus proceeds in a systematic way to develop the subject under discussion, proceeding regularly from the general to the particular, foreshadowing what is to come and making easy transitions from one phase of the general subject to the other. Though his whole method of treatment is logical enough, the classification or system resulting from it, being grounded on superficial appearance and behaviour rather than upon any concept of chemical composition, necessarily has marked limitations. Nevertheless from a scientific standpoint this little treatise is much better than the other ancient and medieval works on minerals that are known to us. Pliny, for example, though he treats the subject far more extensively, does so in a much less critical and systematic fashion.

The comparative freedom of the treatise On Stones from fable and magic should be especially noted, for many works in this field written centuries later, particularly the medieval lapidaries, dwell largely upon the fancied magical or curative powers of precious stones. In fact, for almost two thousand years this treatise by Theophrastus remained the most rational and systematic attempt at a study of mineral substances."

Not only does this essay contain some of the data which the Greeks derived from the East, but it also proves that the Greek miners, quarrymen, jewellers and those working stones had a practical knowledge of mineralogy on which Theophrastus was able to draw. The characteristics used by him to distinguish the minerals and rocks discussed are "power of acting", "being subject to action", fusibility, combustibility, petrifying power, attraction, capability of testing gold and silver, "giving birth to young" (geodes), workability (with iron tools), colour, hardness, softness, smoothness and dyeing power. We will return to a discussion of these properties later on. Pliny mentions one Sotacus (c. 300 B.C.) who wrote an On Stones, and many authors whose name we know through him only without a hint of what they studied in particular.

The Romans never improved on this essay by Theophrastus, indeed they did not contribute to the development of geology and devoted their energy to surveying, prospecting and mining rather than to the theoretical basis which should guide such mining efforts. Thus Pliny's contributions to mineralogy are anecdotical rather than scientific. The thirty-seventh book of his Natural History, devoted to gemstones is a curious mixture of magic, folklore and practical data. It is now available in a more modern translation (254) than Ball used (255). The latter's notes on early historical and archaeological data can be used only after careful checking though his information on the later history of gems is very useful.

Pliny was of course first of all an encyclopedist, and though he gives a number of tests for gems and earth (256), his work is worthless from the point of view of mineralogy. He followed the later Hellenistic trend of magico-religious speculation, which did not make metals, rocks and minerals objects for clear and cool observation but tended to consider them to be the bearers of certain inner, abstract ideas and powers, which fitted into their theories. Such speculations came to overlay the foundations of observation which men like Theophrastus had laid down. The magical trend continues in the late-Hellenistic, Byzantine and medieval lapidaries. The older Babylonian texts on which these lapidaries are based still show a clear distinction between the observed facts and the speculations on magical properties, in the same way as their medical texts have this sharp distinction between diagnosis, treatment and ritual, which Campbell Thompson so aptly called "the bedside manner of the Assyrian doctor".

Mineralogy suffered severely from this amalgamation of the scientific trend to classify and study minerals with the magical lapidary. There is no need to discuss here these many lapidaries and their strange theories (257). Only in a few of these there is some real attempt at a scientific classification, e.g. in Albertus Magnus' De Mineralibus (260), Alfonso X's Lapidarium (1278), Camillus Leonardus' Speculum lapidum (1502). De Boodt's Gemmarum et Lapidum Historia (1609) has already profited from Agricola's systematic mineral classification of minerals based on observed physical properties (258) in his De Natura Fossilium of 1546. The outline of his classification of "inanimate subterranean bodies" in this:

1. Fluids and Vapours
2. Fossils

	Earths		Harsh (Lean) (salt, alum, chrysocolla)
	Congealed Juices	Unctuous	Inflammable (sulphur, bitumen, orpiment) Non-inflammable
3. Simple (Non-composite) Minerals	Stones		Stones (magnet, haematite, aetites, etc.) Gems Marbles (marble, basalt, alabaster, ophite) Rocks (sandstone, limestone)
	Metals		

4. Mixed Non-Composite Minerals   (constituents separated by fire only: galena, siderite, arsenopyrite)

5. Composite Minerals   (visible constituents) (galena associated with pyrite; quartz and native gold, etc.)

Agricola uses the following physical properties in arranging the minerals and rocks: colour, weight, transparency, lustre, taste, odour, form, texture, hardness, friability, smoothness, solubility, brittleness, cleavage and combustibility. Though his efforts were doomed to failure as he adhered to the Peripatetic theory of the four elements, his is the first modern book on geology on which the classification of a narrower field like gems could be based by de Boodt, without ressort to ficticious magical properties. Wilsdorf has correctly pointed out (258a) that Agricola owed much to the detailed and correct descriptions of minerals in the works of such classical pharmacists and physicians as Dioscorides and Galen.

We now return to the various characteristics on which the ancients based their identification and classification. *Colour* was of course an obvious choice but a dangerous one. In Greek or Latin the word for "emerald" may denote almost every green mineral, emerald, the paler beryl, peridot, malachite, serpentine, amazone stone, green quartz (prase), jasper and green porphyry. Diodorus tells us that an image of Jupiter was decorated with emeralds, a statement distorted by later authors into a fable that it was cut from an emerald. Also archaeologists have often given wrong descriptions of the materials antiquities were made of, thus purple and white agate has been called fluorspar. Again one has to be very careful and suspicious about the terms used by ancient authors. Pliny and Theophrastus sometimes include lapis lazuli in the term "sapphirus", our sapphire being called "hyakinthus" when Solinus says (259): "When put in the mouth it is colder than other stones (a familiar test of stones against glass!). For engraving upon it is by no means adopted is as much as it defies all grinding; it is not, however, entirely invincible since it is engraved upon and cut into shape by means of a diamond". Some names have changed their meaning completely. The Egyptians of the eighteenth dynasty already used peridot from St. John's island in the Red Sea for their jewelry, but both Diodorus and Pliny call the island and the stone "topaz"!

The principle of determining the *specific gravity* was of course well-known. Vitruvius (260) tells the story of Archimedes and the gold crown of King Hiero of Syracuse to illustrate this: "He then let down the crown itself (after having done the test with two masses of the same weight as the crown, one of gold and the other of silver) into the vase after filling the vase with water and found that more water flowed into the space left by the crown than into the space left by a mass of gold of the same weight". Thus he charges the contracting jeweller of having mixed silver with the gold used for the crown.

Though relative weights of certain materials such as amber are mentioned, specific gravity is not determined regularly before the Arabic period. The *streak* was known to be a distinctive property, it is described in a De Coloribus ascribed to Aristotle (261) but more likely by one of the pupils of the Peripatetic school. This passage runs thus:

"Some kinds of stones show different colours, like..., for though black they draw white lines, because they are originally composed of small elements which are thick and black, and by the dyeing process which takes place when they are made, all passages through which the dyeing passes are coloured, so that a different appearance is given to the colour. But what is rubbed off from them is no longer golden in appearance, nor bronze, nor has it any such tinge, but it is entirely black, because by the rubbing the passages through which the dyeing takes place are broken up, but originally they are of the same colour. For when the former colour is dissipated, we see the colour which naturally belongs to them; and so they all appear black. But in the process of rubbing each of them to a homogeneous and smooth surface, as in treating on a touchstone, they loose their blackness, and recover their colour, the dye showing through when there is contact and continuity".

The streak is of course intimately related to the history of the touchstone, the basanos, Lydian stone or Lydit, which Theophrastus mentions in sections 45—47 of his essay. Its use may date back to the seventh century B.C., when it supplanted the evidence obtained by the cupellation of gold and silver admixed with baser metals. It could not have the delicacy of the modern methods with the touchstone, since the ancients did not know nitric acid and aqua regia, but the descriptions are none too clear and it seems that neither Theophrastus nor Pliny had any personal experience of this test used by jewellers and metal-merchants.

We have seen that the Assyrians had an *"acid-test"*, their strongest acid being vinegar, which allowed them to recognize carbonates by the effervescence of the stone touched by the acid. We also have mentioned their" *"hardness-scale"*, the term AŠ actually meaning "resistance to scratching", their standard probably being corundum, a material which the classical authors could have used as a standard too, though they sometimes compare stones with emery, spinel, etc. when discussing their hardness. As it appears they had no fixed scale of hardness yet. They mention an "adamas", a general term for very hard minerals (262), which are difficult to define. In a passage of Manilius one is inclined to say that diamonds were meant, but the diamond is not generally known in Antiquity and Pliny applies the word "adamas" to at least six different stones, some of which are Indian or obtained from Arabia. But without optical instruments or chemical reagents how could anyone today identify the constituents of say the gem-gravel of Ceylon? They might recognize such stones as water-worn as did Maecenas in an elegy, written about AD 8, saying: "Even the beryl surpasses the common sands which the wave tosses about along with it". Thus the Indian "adamas" may be the sapphire rather than the diamond.

The *form of crystals* was to some slight extent a diagnostic. Pliny (263) mentions the "six-angled" shape of rock-crystal "though the faces are not exactly of the same shape but the sides between each edge are so absolutely smooth and even that no lapidary in the world could make the faces as flat and polished". Theophrastus uses the "hexagonal shape" to define his "anthrax", which was probably a spinel. It seems rather strange that the Greeks, who were gifted mathematicians, particularly interested in geometrical forms, never used this crystalline aspect of the minerals as a standard for classifying them.

The *magnetic* properties of certain stones are mentioned and the lodestone was of course well-known. Euripides seems to have been the first to use the word "magnetis", the usual term being "Heraclean stone" as Plato (264) assures us. Theophrastus says that the lodestone is rare as are all stones which possess the power of attraction like amber (265) and Lucretius later tried to explain its action with the help of his corpuscular theory (266).

The ancients also knew that certain stones could be stained. Indeed some of the tricks used in the German agate-industry were used by the Assyrians, who have the technical term "záŠIM.SIG₇, suruppu ša abni", e.g. the dyeing of a stone.

Some of the other properties mentioned do not seem very scientific to us, but when the ancients speak of "*birth-stones*", they mean geodes, stones which contain crystal-lined cavities. Theophrastus mentions that rock-crystal, amethyst and sardion (both sard and carnelian) are often found when certain stones are broken to look to cavities in which fine crystals grow (267). These were the stones which the Assyrians called "záPEŠ₄, aban erî", the pregnant stones!

In the next paragraph Theophrastus mentions *male and female* stones "And for one type of sardion, which is translucent and of a redder colour, is called the female, and the other, which is translucent and darker, is called the male. And it is the same with the varieties of the lyngourion, for the female is more transparent and yellow than the other. Also, one kind of kyanos is called male and the other female, and the male is the darker of the two". This distinction is already made by the Assyrian geologists who describe salt, black (impure) saltpetre, alum, lapis lazuli, misy and pumice as "male" or "female". It is doubtful whether the latter rule can be applied here that the darker stone is considered to be male. The Assyrian botanists use the same distinction "male" and "female" for plants. The "sex" of frankincense depends on the shape of the gum being like testicles or breasts, the usual distinction being hardness in the case of minerals. Pliny' (268) declares that "in each kind (of carbunculus or sarda) the more brilliant are called male and those that shine with a fainter light are called "female". On a similar basis (269) he recognizes male and female herbs.

This curious distinction of sex in precious stones and other minerals was apparently not connected with any theories about their origin, or even with the belief that certain stones have the power to generate others, such as we find in ancient Chinese lore quoted by Li Shih-Chen in the twelfth century: "Orpiment is formed on the Yin side of mountains, therefore it is called "female yellow". The Thu Hsiu Pên Tshao (Earth's Mansions Pharmacopoeia) tells us that if the petrifying chhi of the Yang is not sufficient a female mineral is formed; if it is sufficient a male is formed. They take fivehundred years to consolidate and form minerals. During this time they react ("carry out the role of husband and wife") which is why they are called male and female".

Theophrastus, for instance, relates sex in stones to transparency and colour only, assigning the male sex to the kind that is darker in colour. Generally speaking this holds for other ancient authors too, who apply the term male to indicate a certain characteristic property being more pronounced in the type of mineral they are discussing. Varying the grammatical gender of the words "lithos" and "petros" has no meaning in Theophrastus or Galen, the latter saying (270): "And again they speak of stone in the feminine, not of stone in the masculine... At any rate custom is purposely to interchange the names and to adopt both methods of describing everything of that sort, which some people argue about so unprofitably; for I show that in fact the clearness of interpretation is not harmed at all, whichever way one describes them".

Again we hear of *stones growing in plants*. This may include the tabashir, an opaline material found in the joints of the bamboo and held in esteem for certain imaginary medical properties in the Far East. The Greek papyri mention this tabasios or tabasi which is said to be found on an Indian island and used to "make precious stones by dyeing". It may be the "petrified reed not very different in nature from coral" mentioned by Theophrastus (271).

In the same passage he mentions, what the ancients call a *stone growing in the water*, coral "which grows like a stone, is red in colour and rounded like a root, and it grows in the sea". Probably all classical references are to the precious red coral, Corallium nobile, which species is practically confined to the Mediterranean Sea. It was not used as an ornament, but as an amulet for childern only and as a medicine. Theophrastus does not decide whether this is a stone growing in the water or a living being, but to Dioscorides it seemed to be a plant (272). He says: "But coral (which some call lithodendron) seems to be a sea plant, which hardens when it is drawn out of the deep, being out of the sea and, as it were, dipped into the air flowing around us. Great store of it is found in the Promontory which is called Pachynum, by Syracuse, but the best is that which is red in colour and like sandarach or sandyx, also easy to pound and having a smell resembling that of little seaweeds throughout, but still having many branches and imitating little shrubs like cinnamon. But the stony type, which has a rough colour and which is hollow and loose, is considered worthless." To Pliny it is either a plant or an animal which hardens as soon as it is withdrawn from the waters. Ovid (273) tells us that "the fresh weed twigs" on which Perseus placed the head of Medusa after releasing Andromeda, absorbed the poison of the monster and "take on strange stiffness in their stems and leaves. Even till this day the same nature remained in corals so that they harden when exposed to the air and what was a pliant twig beneath the sea turned to stone above" for the sea-nymphs tested the wonder on more twigs and scattering them in the sea caused coral to grow.

Another such category of stones were the *stones which fall from the air*. Meteoric iron was well-known to both the Egyptians and the Sumerians, as their words for iron (bi3-n-pt: heaven-metal)) (AN-BAR: heaven metal) show. We have plenty evidence that meteorites (betyli, see Pliny (174)) were known, we need only quote the New Testament on the "image of Diana of the Ephesians which fell down from Jupiter" (275). However, Pliny is incredulous about the gem "glossopetra" supposed to fall from the sky during an eclipse of the moon (276), resembling a man's tongue and said to be invaluable in selenomancy (277). Pliny (278) also mentions other stones like "ombria, ceraunia and brontea" falling from the heavens in storms, rain showers and with lightning. Philostratus (279) disbelieves such stories: "They (the lovers) will accept from the impostors and quaks a box of stones which they wear, some of the bits of stones having come from the depth of the earth and others from the moon and the stars" and we need not extend our discussion with such tales which fill the lapidaries and books on magic up to the present day.

BIBLIOGRAPHY

1. SCHIEFERDECKER, A. A. G., (edit.), *Geological Nomenclature* (Royal
   Geological and Mining Society of the Netherlands) (Noorduyn,
   Gorinchem, 1959)
2. GIEKIE, Sir A., *The Founders of Geology* (London, 1897; 2. edit. 1905)
   ZITTEL VON, K. A., *Geschichte der Geologie und Paleontologie* (München,
   1899)
   ADAMS, F. D., *The Birth and Development of Geological Sciences* (Baltimore,
   1938)
   BATEMAN, A. M., *The growth of geological knowledge in the discovery of
   metallic and non-metallic mineral resources* (Cahiers Histoire Mondiale
   vol. II, 1954/55, 979—990)
   BROMEHEAD, C. E. N., *Geology in Embryo* (up to 1600 A.D.) (Proc.
   Geologist's Association vol. LVI, 1945, pags. 89—134)
   EDWARDS, W. N., *Guide to... Early History of Palaeontology* (Brit. Museum
   of Natural History, London, 1931)
   LYELL, C., *Principles of Geology* (7th edit. London, 1847)
   WOODWARD, H. B., *History of Geology* (London, 1911)
3. REITEMEIER, F., *Geschichte des Bergbaus und des Hüttenwesens bei den alten
   Völkern* (Göttingen, 1785)
   SCHWARCZ, JULIUS, *The failure of geological attempts made by the Greeks
   from the earliest ages down to Alexander* (London, 1868)
   LASSAULX, VON E., *Die Geologie der Griechen und Römer* (Abh. Bayer.
   Akad. Wiss. 1852)
   LENZ, H. O., *Mineralogie der alten Griechen und Römer* (Gotha, 1861)
   WHEWELL, W., *History of the Inductive Sciences* (London, 1857)
   HOLMYARD, E. J., and MANDEVILLE, D. C., *Avicennae de Congulatione et
   Conglutatione Lapidum* (Geuthner, Paris, 1927)
   RUSKA, J., *Das Steinbuch des Aristoteles* (Heidelberg, 1912)
   MIELEITNER, K., *Geschichte der Mineralogie im Altertum und im Mittelalter*
   (Fortschritte der Mineralogie... vol. VII, 1922, 427 ff)
   MELY, DE F., *Les Lapidaires de l'Antiquité et du Moyen Age* (Paris 1898/02)
   THORNDIKE, L., *A History of Magic and Experimental Science* (Vol. I)
   (New York, 1923)
   GEIKIE, A., *Love of Nature among the Romans* (London, 1912)
   HILLER, J. E., *Die Minerale der Antike* (Arch. Gesch. Math. Naturw.
   Techn. vol. XIII, 1930, 358 ff)
   WELLMANN, M., *Aristoteles de Lapidibus* (Sitzb. Preuss. Akad. Wiss.
   Stück XI, 1924, 79—82)
   WIEDEMANN, E., *Zur Mineralogie bei den Muslimen* (Arch. Gesch. Na-
   turw. Technik, vol. I, 1909, 208 ff)

BROMEHEAD, C. E. N., *Geology in Embryo* (Proc. Geol. Assoc. vol. LVI, 1945, 89—134)

CHALLINOR, J., *The beginnings of scientific Palaeontology* (Annals of Science vol. VI, 1948, 46—54)

CLARKE, J., *Physical Science in the time of Nero* (London, 1910)

MATHER K. F. & MASON, S. L., *A Sourcebook in Geology* (MacGrw. Hill, New York, 1939)

4. AGRICOLA, GEORGIUS, *De Natura Fossilium* (The Geological Society of America Special Paper no. 63, New York, 1955)

5. GARBOE, A., *The earliest geological Treatise* (1667) by Nicolaus Steno (Macmillan, London, 1958)

6. BURNET, J., *Early Greek Philosophy* (4. edit. Black, London, 1945)

FREEMAN, K., *The Pre-Socratic Philosophers* (Blackwell, Oxford, 1946)

FREEMAN, K., *Ancilla to the Pre-Socratic Philosophers* (Blackwell, Oxford, 1948)

HUXLEY, G. L., *The Early Ionians* (London, 1966)

THOMSON, J. Oliver, *The History of Ancient Geography* (Cambridge Univ. P., 1948)

NINCK, M., *Die Entdeckung von Europa durch die Griechen* (Basel, 1945)

SEMPLE, E. C., *The Geography of the Mediterranean Region* (London, 1932)

CARY, M., *The geographic background of Greek and Roman history* (Oxford, 1949, 22—23)

7. TAYLOR, E. G. R., *Ideas on the Shape, Size and Movements of the Earth* (Hist. Assoc. Pamphlet no. 126, London, 1943)

8. OVID, *Fasti* vi. 269—271

9. ST. AUGUSTINE, *De civitate Dei* xvi. 9

10. STRABO, I. 3. 3. cap. 49

11. ARISTOTLE, *Meteorologica* (transl. H. D. P. Lee, Loeb Classical Library, 1952)

12. CALEY E. R. and RICHARDS, J. F. C., *Theophrastus On Stones* (Ohio State University, Columbus, 1956)

13. STRABO, XIII. i. 54. cap. 609

14. SENECA, *Naturales Quaestiones* (edit. P. Oltramare, Collection Univ. de France, 2 vols., Paris, 1929)

15. OVID, *Metam.* XV

16. DIODOR, IV. 18

17. STRABO, I. iii. 16. cap. 58; Pliny IV. xii. 63; II. xc. 204

18. PLINY, IV. xii. 62

19. STRABO, I. iii. 19. cap. 60; PLINY II. cx—cxii, 204—206

20. PLINY, II. cxii. 206; IV. v

21. THUCYDIDES, II. 86

22. STRABO, VIII. ii. 3. cap. 335

23. PLINY, IV. ii. 6

24. SCYLAX, Periplus 35

25. HERODOTUS, VII. 129

26. SENECA, *Nat. Quaest.* VI. 25; STRABO, VIII. viii. 4. cap. 389

27. PLATO, *Timaios* 20 A — 25 D; PLINY, II. 86—89. 201—203; SENECA, *Nat. Quaest.* VI. 27—30

28. PINDAR, *Olymp. Ode* VII
29. STRABO, I. iii. 3. cap. 49; II. iii. 6. cap. 102
30. ARISTOTLE, *Meteor.* I. 14
31. PLINY, II. lxv. 162; Plutarch *de deo Socr.* 8; Plutarch, *Aem. Paulus* 15. 5—7
32. STRABO, I. iii. 4. 5
33. ARISTOTLE, *de Mundo* V. 25—30; POMPONIUS MELA I. 32
34. TERTULLIAN, *de pallio* cap. 2; APOL. 40
35. ISIDORE, of SEVILLE, *Origines* XIII. 22
36. NEEDHAM, J., *Science and civilisation in China* (Cambridge vol. III, 1959, 598—601)
37. *St. Basil's Hexameron* (edit. SCHENKL, C., *Viena*, 1896, IV. 2—6)
38. PHILOSTRATUS, *Life of Apollonius of Tyana* III. 37
39. SENECA, *Nat. Quaest.* III. 9 & 15; VI. 7. 5; VI. 8
40. ARISTOTLE, *Meteor.* II. i—iii; I. xiii
41. LUCAN, VII. 5; I. 415; X. 258; CICERO, *De Nat. Deor.* II. 15, 40
42. LUCRETIUS, *De Rerum Natura* (edit. C. Bailey, 3 vols. Oxford, 1947) V. 261—272
43. GLOVER, T. R., *Springs of Hellas* (Cambr. Univ. Press, 1945, 1—30)
44. PAUSANIAS, VIII. 18. 4; PLINY, II. 231; XXXI. 26
45. SENECA, *Quaest. Nat.* III. 26; PLATO, *Phaedo* 111c; ARIST. *Meteor.* I. 13; II. 2
46. PAUSANIAS, VIII. 22. 3; STRABO, VIII. viii. 4. cap. 389
47. HERODOTUS, VI. 74; PAUSANIAS, VIII. 17—18
48. CICERO, *De Natura Deor.* III. 17. 43; VIRGIL, *Aeneid* VI. 295—298, 705
49. VIRGIL, *Aeneid* VI. 658
50. VIRGIL, *Aeneid* I. 243—246; PLINY, II. cvi. 226; STRABO, V. i. 8. cap. 214
51. PAUSANIAS, I. 38. 1—2
52. STRABO, XIV, 5. 5. cap. 671
53. PLINY, III. i. 6
54. PAUSANIAS, IX. 30. 8
55. STRABO, XVI. ii. 13. cap. 754
56. PLINY, II. cvi. 227
57. PAUSANIAS, VIII. vii. 2
58. THUCYDIDES, I. 46
59. PLINY, II cvi. 227
60. PAUSANIAS, VIII. 7. 3
61. PLINY, II cvi. 227
62. PLINY, II. ciii. 222; SENECA, *Nat. Quaest.* III. 26; PAUSANIAS, VIII. 14. 1; 23. 2; 44. 3—4; 54. 1—4; VIRGIL, *Eclogue* X. 1—4
63. STRABO, VI. ii. 4. cap. 270—271; POLYBIOS, XII. iv. 3
64. PAUSANIAS, II. 5. 3
65. STRABO, XIV. i. 39. cap. 647
66. STRABO, VI. ii. 4. cap. 272; PAUSANIAS, II. 25. 3
67. ARISTOTLE, *de Mirabilibus* 58
68. PAUSANIAS, X. 32. 7; IV. 36
69. ARISTOTLE, *Meteor.* I. xiv

70. LUCRETIUS, *De Rerum Nat.* V. 488—494
71. PLINY, III. i. 16
72. THUCYDIDES, II. 102
73. STRABO, X. 2. 19. cap. 458; PLINY, II. i. 5
74. STRABO, XII. 8. 17. cap. 579
75. STRABO, V. 1. 5. cap. 212
76. STRABO, I. 38. 8. cap. 53
77. ENOCH POWELL, J., *Das Niltal bei Herodot* (Hermes Vol. 68, 1933, 123—126)
    ENOCH POWELL, J., *Die Quelle des Râ bei Herodot* Hermes vol. 69, 1934, 107—111)
    FRISINGER, H. H., *Early theories on the Nile floods* (Weather, 20, 1965, 7. 206—207)
78. HERODOTUS, II. 10—12
79. ARISTOTLE, *Meteor.* I. xiv. 351b—352a
80. STRABO, I. iii. 10. cap. 52
81. STRABO, I. iii. 13. cap. 56
82. STRABO, I. iii. 17. cap. 58
83. STRABO, I. ii. 29. cap. 36
84. HERODOTUS, II. 5
85. STRABO, XII. 2. 4. cap. 536
86. ARISTOTLE, *Meteor.* I. xiv. II; 1
87. LUDWIG, E., *The Mediterranean* (London, 1943, 20—25)
88. POLYBIUS, IV. 39—40
89. DIODORUS, V. 47. 4—5
90. PLINY, VI. 1
91. STRABO, I. iii. 4—5. cap. 49—51; I. iii. 6. cap. 52
92. PLINY, III. i. 3—4
93. PHILOSTRATUS, *Life of Apollonius of Tyana* IV. xxiv
94. STRABO, IV. i. 7. cap. 182—183; COPISAROW, M., *The Ancient Egyptian, Greek and Hebrew Concepts of the Red Sea* (Vetus Testamentum 12, 1962, 1—13)
95. HERODOTUS, II. 158
96. STRABO, XVII. i. 25. cap. 804
97. PLINY, VI. 145; DIODORUS, I. 33. 9—11
98. STRABO, IV. 1. 7. cap. 182—183
99. POLYBIUS, IV. 70
100. PHILO, *Eternity of the World* xxiii
101. NEEDHAM, J., *Science and Civilisation in China* (Cambridge vol. III, 1959, 603)
102. PLINY, II. 162
103. PLUTARCH, *Aemilius Paulus* XV. 5—7
104. HOLMYARD, E. J., and MANDEVILLE, D. C., *Avicennae De Conglutatione et Congelatione Lapidum* (Geuthner, Paris, 1927)
105. PLATO, *Critias* 111
106. *Trans. American Philological Assoc.* 1927, 199—209
107. GLOVER, T. R., *The Challenge of the Greeks* (Cambr. Univ. Press. 1943, 29—50)

108. PARTSCH, J., *Dünenbeobachtungen im Altertum* (Ber. Ver. Sächs. Ges. Wiss. vol. LVI, 1917, no. 3, 1—27)
109. HERODOTUS, III. 26; STRABO, XVIII. 1. 45. cap. 821
110. STRABO, XV. 2. 6. cap. 722
111. STRABO, XVI. 4. 18. cap. 777
112. PLINY, IV. 5; PAUSANIAS, V. 5. 7; STRABO, XVI. 2. 25. cap. 758; HERODOTUS, II. 11—12
113. DIODORUS, I. 30. 4—7
114. DIODORUS, XVI. 46; XX. 73
115. SENECA, *Nat. Quaest.* VI. i. 26
116. CAMPBELL THOMPSON, R., *A New Record of an Assyrian Earthquake* (Iraq vol. IV, 1937, 186—189); HERMANN, A., *Erdbeben* (Reallex. Antike und Christentum 1962, 1070—1113); James Mellaart in Ill. London News of Febr. 14, 1964
117. RAWLINSON, H. C., *The Cuneiform Inscriptions of Western Asia* vol. III, 61; HASTINGS, *Dictionary of the Bible* vol. I, 634; E. R. LACHEMAN, *An Omen Text from Nuzi* (R. Ass. 34, 1937, 1—8)
118. HERODOTUS, IV. 28
119. ERMAN-GRAPOW, *Wörterbuch der Aegyptischen Sprache* II. 223. 1
120. PHILOSTRATUS, *Life of Apollonius of Tyana* VI. 38
131. PLINY, II. lxxxi. 191
122. HERODOTUS, VII. 129
123. STRABO, XV. 1. 19. cap. 693
124. STRABO, I. 3. 19. cap. 60
125. *Genesis*, XIX. 25; 1 *Ki.* 19. 11; *Isa.* 29. 6; *Job* 9. 5—6; *Amos* 1. 1, 5. 8. *Psalms* 60. 2; 104. 32; *Zechariah*, 14. 4—5; *Math.* 24. 7; 27. 51; *Acts* 16. 26; *Rev.* 6. 12; 8. 5; 11. 13; 16. 18; STRABO, XVI. 2. 44. cap. 764; JOSEPHUS, *Antiquities* IX. 10; XV. 5
126. *Psalms* 114. 3—4
127. *Exod.* 19. 18; *Judges*, 5. 4; 2 *Sam.* 22. 8; *Psalms* 18. 8; 68. 9; 77. 19
128. *Zech.* 14. 5; *Amos* 1. 1
129. *Math.* 27. 51; 28. 2; *Acts* 16. 26
130. SENECA, *Nat. Quaest.* VI. 24. 5; 26. 4; STRABO, I. iii. 16. cap. 58; XVI. ii. 23 & 26. cap. 757—758
131. STRABO, I. iii. 16—19. cap. 58—59; TACITUS, *Annals* II. 47; XII. 50; XIV. 27; PLINY, II. 93. 206; STRABO, XII. viii. 16—18. cap. 578
132. STRABO, XIII. iii. 5. cap. 621
133. STRABO, XIII. iv. 8. cap. 627
134. STRABO, XIII. iv. 10. cap. 628; XIII. iv. 15. cap. 630
135. HERODOTUS, VI. 98; THUCYDIDES, II. 8. 3; PLINY, II. lxxxix. 202
136. DIODORUS, V. 54. 3.
137. THUCYDIDES VIII. 41. 2
138. POLYBIUS, V. 88—90; DIODORUS XXVI. 8
139. STRABO, I. 3. 19—20. cap. 60—61
140. PAUSANIAS, II. 23. 2; IX. 36. 3; THUCYDIDES, III. 87. 4
141. THUCYDIDES, V. 45. 4; 50. 4; III. 89. 2
142. PAUSANIAS, II. 7. 1; DIODORUS, XV. 49; STRABO I. iii. 18. cap. 59; VIII. vii. 2. cap. 384; PAUSANIAS, VII. 24—25; SENECA, VI. 23

143. DIODORUS, XV. 49; STRABO, I. iii. 20. cap. 60; VIII. vii. 2. cap. 384; PAUSANIAS VII. 24—25; SENECA, VI. 23; TACITUS, *Annals* IV. 13

144. HERODOTUS, VIII. 37; STRABO, IX. iii. 8. cap. 421; PAUSANIAS, X. 23. 1—3

145. HERODOTUS, V. 85; STRABO, I. iii. 18. cap. 59; PAUSANIAS II. 34. 1; EURIPIDES, *Hippolytus* (transl. G. MURRAY, 1904, 62—63)

146. PAUSANIAS, II. xxii. 4—5; EURIPIDES, *Iphigenia*; XENOPHON, *Hell.* IV. 7. 4

147. PAUSANIAS, V. 8. 8—9; STRABO, VIII. 5. 7. cap. 367; CICERO, *de Divin.* I. 112; THUCYDIDES, I. 101. 2; VIII. 6. 5; PLUTARCH, *Cimon* XVI; DIODORUS, XV. 66

148. STRABO, IX. 2. 16. cap. 406; IX. 5. 2. cap. 430

149. STRABO, V. 4. 9. cap. 248

150. STRABO, VI. i. 6. cap. 258; VIRGIL, *Aeneid* III. 14

151. PLINY, II. 86. 200

152. STRABO, I. iii. 20. cap. 60

153. LIVY, XXII. 5; PLINY THE YOUNGER, *Epist.* VI. 16. 20

154. ILIAD, XX. 11; ODYSSEY I. 74; PINDAR, *Isthmian Ode* I. 53; III. 37

155. THUCYDIDES, III. 89. 2

156. DIODORUS, V. 47. 3—4

157. HERODOTUS, VII. 129

158. *Acts* XVI. 26

159. HESIOD; STRABO, IX. v. 6. cap. 432

160. STRABO, I. iii. 10. cap. 54

161. PAUSANIAS, VII. 24. 12—25. 4

162. PLINY THE YOUNGER, *Letter to Tacitus* VI. 20

163. LIVY, XXX. 2; XXX. 38; VII. 6

164. STRABO, I. iii. 20. cap. 60

165. COOK, A. B., *Zeus*, vol. III. i. 1—20

166. AULUS GELLIUS, *Attic Nights* II. 28

167. CICERO, *De Divinatione* I. 50

168. AETIUS, III. 15. 3

169. PLINY, II. lxxxi. 191 — xcv. 207

170. SENECA, *Nat. Quaest.* VI. 4

171. LUCRETIUS, *De Rerum Nat.* VI. 535—607

172. NEEDHAM, J., *Science and Civilisation in China*, Vol. III. 1959, 624—629

173. EURIPIDES, *Cycl.* 20; THUCYDIDES, III. 88. 3; VIRGIL, *Aeneid* III. 578—582; VIII, 415; IX. 715; OVID, *Metam.* V. 346—358; PLINY, II. 110, 236; V. 28. 100

174. ILIAD, II. 782; HESIOD, *Theog.* 820—880; PINDAR, *Pythian Ode* I. 30—55; STRABO, V. iv. 9. cap. 248; XIII. iv. 6. cap. 627

175. PHILOSTRATUS, *Apollonius of Tyana* V. 17

175a. MELLAART, JAMES, *Earliest Civilisations of the Near East* (London, 1965, 84)

176. ARISTOTLE, *Meteor.* II. 7—8; STRABO, VI. 2. 8. cap. 274; XII. 8. 18. cap. 579; LUCRETIUS, VI. 701; DIODORUS, V. 74; OVID, *Metam.* XV. 299

177. STRABO, XVI. 2. 42—44. cap. 764

178. STRABO, XIII. 4. 11. cap. 628

179. STRABO, V. 4. 3—4. 8, 9, cap. 242; VI. 2. 3. cap. 269

180. PLINY, XXXV. 50. 174; 52. 184

181. SENECA, *Nat. Quaest.* II. 26; STRABO, I. 3. 16. cap. 57

182. PLINY, II. 89. 203

183. STRABO, I. 3. 18. cap. 59; Ovid, *Metam.* XV. 296—306

184. PLINY, II. 202—203; SOPHOCLES, *Philectetes* 911

185. STRABO, V. iv. 5—9. Cap. 245—249; TACITUS, *Annals* XV. 33—34; SUETONIUS, *Nero* XX; SENECA, *Nat. Quaest.* VI, i & xxvii; TACITUS, *Annals* XV. 22; PLINY, *Epist.* VI, 16 & 20

186. STRABO, VI. i. 6. cap. 258; DIODORUS, V. 1; ODYSSEY X. 1; VIRGIL, *Aeneid* I. 52—78

187. STRABO, VI. ii. cap. 277; PLINY, II. 89. 203

188. STRABO, VI. ii. 8. cap. 276; DIODOR, XIV. 59. 3

189. STRABO, VI. ii. 11. cap. 277

190. PHILOSTRATUS, *Imagines* II. 17

191. DIODORUS, XIV. 42. 4 & 59, 3

192. STRABO, VI. i. 6. cap. 258; VI. ii. 8. cap. 274

193. GELLIUS, AULUS, *Attic Nights* XVII. 10

194. SENECA, *Letter to Lucilius* LXXIX

195. J. W., and DUFF, A. M., *Minor Latin Poets* (Loeb Classical Library, 1935)

196. STRABO, V. iv. 6 cap. 246

197. LUCRETIUS, VI. 639—679; JUSTIN IV. 1. 2—15; SENECA, *Epist.* 79. 2; SERVIUS, *ad Aen.* III. 571

198. DIODORUS, IV. 21; VITRUVUS, II. 6; STRABO, V. 4. 8. cap. 247

199. PLINY, II. cx. 236—238

200. VITRUVIUS II. vi. 1—2

201. SILIUS, ITALICUS, VIII. 655; XVII. 593

202. DIO CASSIUS, LXVI. 21—23

203. PROCOPIUS, VI. iv. 21—30

204. PREUSSE, K., *Ein Wort zur Vesuvgestalt und Vesuvtätigkeit im Altertum* (Klio, vol. XXVII, 1934, 3, 295—310)

205. PLINY, *Epist.* VI. xvi

206. HERODOTUS, II. 12

207. STRABO, I. 3. 4. cap. 49

208. OVID, *Metam.* XV. 66—71; 262—356

209. STRABO, XVII. 1. 34. cap. 808

210. PAUSANIUS I. 44. 6

211. PLINY, XXXVI. 10. 11; XXXVI. 5

212. SUETONIUS, *Augustus* LXXII

213. PAUSANIAS, VIII. 32. 5

214. CLEMENT, *Recognitions* I. 29

215. AUGUSTINE, *Civ. Dei* XV. 9

216. DIOSCORIDES, V. 155

217. ABEL, O., *Die Vorweltlichen Tiere in Märchen, Sage und Aberglaube* (Braun, Karlsruhe, 1923)

ABEL, O., *Vorzeitliche Tierreste im deutschen Brauchtum* (Forschungen und Fortschritte vol. XIII, 1937, 278—279)

30908

MacKinney, L. C., *Animal substances in materia medica* (Hist. J. Medicine, vol. I, 1946, 149—170)

Matiegkova, L., *Tierbestandteile in den altägyptischen Arzneien* (Archiv Orientlaní, vol. 26, 1958, 529—560)

Quenstedt, W., *Verwendung fossiler Wirbeltierreste* (Forschungen und Fortschritte vol. XI, 1935, 115)

218. Needham, J., *Science and Civilisation in China* (Vol. III, Cambridge, 1959, 614—623

219. Theophrastus, *On Stones* 37

220. Diogenes Laertius, V. 2. 42

221. Pliny, VIII. 7

222. Aristotle, *De Mirabilibus Auscult.* 73—74

223. Strabo, IV. 1. 16. cap. 181

224. Seneca, *Nat. Quaest.* III. vi. 5; Pliny, IX. lxxxiii. 176

225. Athenaeus, VIII. 332a

226. Buchanan, J. Y., *Nature, Nov.* 23, 1911

227. Aristotle, *Meteor.* II. i. 353b 5

228. Freeman, K., *The Pre-Socratic Philosophers* (Oxford, 1946, 62—63)

229. Hippolytus, *Refut.* I. 6; Aetius, V. 19. 4; *Ps. Plut. Strom. fr.* 2; Plutarch, *Symp. Quest.* 730 f

230. Origin, *Philosophumena* cap. xiv; Hippolytus, *Refut.* I. 14, 15

231. Eastman, O. R., *Variae auctoritates* (Science, N. S. vol. XX, 1904, 215—217)

232. Galen, *On the use of Faculties* (Kühn's Opera Omnia IV. 360)

233. St. Basil, *Hexameron, Homily* V. 2; IX. 2

234. Plato, *Timaeus* 58 D — 61 C

235. Plato, *Critias* 114 e

236. Eichholz, D., *Aristotle's theory of the formation of metals and minerals* (Class. Quart. vol. 43, 1949, 141—146)

237. Pliny, XXXIII. 115

238. Aristotle, *Meteor.* IV. 6—12

239. Aristotle, *Meteor.* IV. 6. 383a

240. Pliny, XXXVI. 161; XXXVII. 21, 23, 26, 27, 48, 75

241. Eichholz, D. E., *References to a theory on the formation of stones* (Introduction to Vol. X of Pliny's Natural History, Loeb Classical Library, 1962, x—xv)

242. Nock, A. D., (J. Roman Studies vol. XLIX, 1959, 14 ff)

243. Seneca, *Nat. Quaest.* III. xiv. 2; xv. 3; xxv. 12

244. Lucretius, *De Rerum Natura* V. 460—466

245. Pliny, XXXIV. 142; Virgil, *Aeneid* X. 174; Rutilius, *Itiner.* I. 351; Strabo, V. ii. 6. cap. 223—224; Aristotle, *De Mirab.* cap. 93

246. Holmyard, E. J., & Mandeville, D. C., *Avicennae de Congelatione* (Paris, 1927, 41)

247. Vincent of Beauvais, *Speculum Naturale* VIII. 84—85

248. Needham, J., *Science and Civilisation in China* (Cambridge, 1959, vol. III, 592)

249. Pliny, XXXIV. 29—31, 117—123; Dioscorides, V. 115, 117, 119; Galen (Kühn's Opera Omnia vol. XII, 226—229)

250. BAILEY, K. C., *Further Notes on the Historia Naturalis of Pliny* (Hermathena, vol. XXI, 1931, 39—53)
251. AGRICOLA, G. A., *De Natura Fossilium* (*trans.* Bandy, Geol. Soc. America, 1955) (German transl. G. Fraustadt edit., VEB, Verslag. der Wissenschaften, Berlin, 1958)

ADAMS, F. D., *The birth and development of the geological sciences* (Baltimore, 1938)

BAUMGÄRTEL, H., *Vom Bergbüchlein zur Bergakademie* (Freib. Forschungs Hefte D 50, 1965)

BOSON, G., *Alcuni nomi di pietre nelle inscrizioni assiro-babilonesi* (Riv. Studi Orientali vol. VI, 1914, 969—977)

BOSON, G., *I metalli e le pietre nelle inscrizioni sumero-assiro-babilonesi* (Riv. Studi Orientali vol. VII, 1916, 379—420)

CALEY, E. R., and RICHARDS, J. F. C., *Theophrastus On Stones* (Columbus, 1956)

EVANS, J., *Magical Jewels of the Middle Ages* (Oxford, 1922)

EVANS, J., and SERJEANTSON, M. S., *English medieval Lapidaries* (London, 1933)

GARBOE, A., *The earliest geological treatise* (1667) by Nicolaus Steno (Macmillan, London, 1958)

GOBET, *Les anciens minéralogistes de la France* (Paris, 1779, 2 vols.)

GROTH, P., *Entwicklungsgeschichte der mineralogischen Wissenschaften* (Springer, Berlin, 1926)

HILLER, J. E., *Die Minerale der Antike* (Arch. Gesch. Math. Naturw. Technik. vol. XIII, 1930, 358 ff)

JOHNSON, R. P., *Compositiones Variae from Codex* 490 (Urbana (Ill.), 1939)

LENZ, H. O., *Mineralogie der alten Griechen und Römer* (Gotha, 1861)

LEUSCHNER, H., *Streiflichter durch die Geschichte, Verwaltung und Technik des alten Bergbaus* (Metall und Erz, vol. 35, 1938, 104, 163, 314)

MATHER, K. F., & MASON, S. L., *A Sourcebook in Geology* (McGraw Hill, New York, 1939)

METZGER, H., *La genèse de la science des cristaux* (Paris, 1916)

MIETLEITNER, K., *Geschichte der Mineralogie im Altertum und Mittelalter*, (Fortschritte der Mineralogie, etc. vol. VII, 1922, 427 ff)

MULLET, Cl., *Essai sur la minéralogie arabe* (J. asiat. 1868)

MULTHAUF, R., *The beginnings of mineralogical chemistry* (Isis. vol. XLIX, 1958, 50—53)

NIES, W., *Zur Mineralogie des Plinius* (Mainz, 1884)

RUSKA, J., *Die Mineralogie in der arabischen Literatur* (Isis vol. I., 1913, 341—350)

SCHEIL, V., *Vocabulaire de pierres et d'objets en pierre* (Rev. Assyriologie vol. XV, 1918, 115—125)

CAMPBELL THOMPSON R., *A Dictionary of Assyrian Chemistry and Geology* (Oxford, 1936)

CAMPBELL THOMPSON, R., *On some Assyrian Minerals* (J. R. Asiat. Soc. 1933, 885—895)

WELLMANN, M., *Aristotles de Lapidibus* (Sitzb. Preuss. Akad. Wiss., Phil-hist. Kl. vol. XI, 1924, 79—82)

WIEDEMANN, E., *Zur Mineralogie bei den Muslimen* (Arch. Gesch. Naturw. Technik, vol. I, 1909, 208—211)

252. NEEDHAM, J., *Science and Civilisation in China* (Vol. III, Cambridge, 1959, 641—672)

253. CALEY, E. R., & RICHARDS, J. F. C., *Theophrastus On Stones* (Ohio State University, Columbus, 1956)

EICHHOLZ, D. E., *Theophrastus, de Lapidibus* (Clarendon Press, Oxford, 1965)

MULTHAUF, R., *The beginnings of mineralogical chemistry* (Isis vol. XLIX, 1958, 50—53)

ROBINSON, T., *Theophrastus on Fire* (Chymia vol. V, 1959, 51—63)

ROBERTSON, R. H. S., „Perlite" *and palogorskite in Theophrastus* (Class. Rev. 13, 1963, 132)

254. EICHHOLZ, D. E., in Vol. X of *Pliny's Natural History* (Loeb Classical Library, London, 1962)

255. BALL, S. H., *A Roman Book on Precious Stones* (Los Angeles, 1950)

256. PLINY, XVII. 4; XX. 3, 76; XXIX, 12; XXXI, 27; XXXII, 19, 43, 44, 57; XXXIV, 26; XXXVI, 38, 55; XXXVII, 22, 76

257. THORNDIKE, L., *History of Magic and Experimental Science up to the Seventeenth Century* (8 vols., New York, 1929—1958)

258. AGRICOLA, G., *De Natura Fossilium* (trans. M. Bandy, Geol. Soc. of America, 1955)

258a. WILSDORF, H., *Antike Aerzte als Mineralogen und ihr Einflusz auf Georgius Agricola* (Jahrb. Staatl. Mus. Mineralogie Geologie, 1964, 387—400)

259. SOLINUS, XXXIII (Aethiopia)

260. VITRUVIUS, IX. 9—12

261. ARISTOTLE, *De Coloribus* III. 793a, 20—35

262. PLINY, XXXVII. 15; MANILIUS, IV. 296

263. PLINY, XXXVII. 9, 27—29; THEOPHRASTUS, *On Stones* 19

264. PLATO, *Ion* 533 D, E; *Timaeus*, 80 C

265. THEOPHRASTUS, *On Stones* 29

266. LUCRETIUS, *De Rerum Natura* VI. 998—1064

267. THEOPHRASTUS, *On Stones* 30

268. PLINY, XXXVII. 92, 101

269. PLINY, XXV. xviii. 39; XXVII. 125

270. GALEN, *De Simplicium Medicamentorum* IX

271. THEOPHRASTUS, *On Stones* 38; *Hist. Plant.* IV. 11. 13

272. DIOSCORIDES V. 139

273. OVID *Metam.* XV. 416

274. PLINY, XXXVI, li

275. *Acts*. 19. 35

276. PLINY, XXXVI. 59

277. ISIDORE, *Etym.* XVI. 15

278. PLINY, XXXVII. lxv

279. PHILOSTRATUS, *Apollonius of Tyana* VII. 39

CHAPTER II

ANCIENT MINING AND QUARRYING

He putteth forth his hands upon the rocks
He overturneth the mountains by the roots (Job. 28. 9)

1. *Introduction*

Before discussing the general aspects of the development of ancient mining we must needs review a few general points which will help to understand our data on ancient mining.

The terms "mine, mining and mineral" and similar words in French, Italian and Spanish, etc, are said to derive from the Celtic "mein, mainach" (crude metal) and the Cymric "mwyn". The classical term for a mine was "metallon" or "metallum". Philologist have in vain tried to prove that this word goes back to a Semitic or an Indo-European root. It is now, however, generally held with Liddell-Scott, that this word is related to the Greek "metallao", to search (after other things), thence "metalleia", searching for metals, mining and "metallon", mine, quarry (originally perhaps place of searching). It is curious to note that Homer never uses the word metallon but always "metallao". When speaking of gold ores Pliny (1) has a somewhat similar explanation of the word saying: "Wherever one vein is found another is not far to seek. This is the case also with many other ores and seems to be the source of the Greek "metalla" thus giving this word (met'alla) the literal meaning "one after another".

As Mesopotamia, and more particularly its southern part, is practically destitute of building stones and ores, we need not wonder that their language had no words for mining and that such terms were either derived from their original home-country or borrowed from their neighbours in the mountains. Thus the Sumerian word for opening a mine was ba-al, the common term for "to dig" (canals, etc.) The Akkadian term was ḫurru, originally "a hole", the result of digging and hence copper ore was called ṣi-it ḫur-ri, "the product of the mine". The early documents mention silver mines (ḫurrum ša kaspim). Hence the Akkadian term too was derived from the verb "to dig" (ḫerû). To these demonstrations of Limet (1a) one might add that Dossin has suggested that the Sumerian equivalent of the Akkadian ḫurru was ḫabradu, which could be a composite of the Sumerian buru, designating a hole, and that the word for copper (urudu) has originated from the prolonged form burud (copper mine), the cuneiform sign for copper illustrating such a coppermine schemetically, but these speculations still demand further proof.

Though we have a host of publications on individual mines and quarries our general knowledge of the subject is still small even when compared with the relatively meagre facts on the ancient history of metallurgy. This pertains particularly to the details of the evolution of special forms of mining, their tools and methods. Few ancient texts deal with such technicalities. Philosophers, historians and geographers like Aristotle, Herodotus, Strabo, Diodorus and others generally limit their remarks to a general description of some deposit or mine and a few notes on the type of ores or minerals mined there, their characteristics and their uses.

Again, as will be clear after our discussion of ancient mineralogy, ancient mining literature contains many pitfalls for the reader, the terms used, often foreign-sounding and of obscure origin, are not the least of these. The terms for minerals and ores have varied considerably in the course of centuries. We have no book yet discussing the history of such terms. This branch of philology, which is due to yield very important conclusions on the migrations and spread of miners and mining techniques has hardly been tackled yet, for it demands a good deal of technical knowledge of mining apart from a sound training in philology. A few good attempts at collecting and discussing such material have been made (2).

A further difficulty is the lack of proper identification (or terminology) of the specimens shown in museum exhibits or reported in excavation journals, which makes discussion of the subject very difficult and it is apt to lead to wrong ideas about the distribution and use of certain minerals and precious stones in Antiquity. A notable example of this confusion is the history of the pearl which was recently investigated by Bolman (3), who did away with many wrong notions in his book. It is only too little known to archaeologists and museum curators, that sample collections of minerals, ores and stones such as marbles (from the very quarries used by the ancients!) are readily available and allow at least some reasonable identification with simple means (4), should no expert be on hand.

Before discussing ancient mining we must also define such words as rock, mineral and ore, which crop up frequently in our story and which are often used in a very loose way in books on the subject we discuss.

A *rock* or *stone*, strictly speaking, is any naturally formed aggregate or mass of mineral matter, whether coherent or not, constituting an essential and appreciable part of the earth's crust. The vast majority of rocks consist of two or more minerals. Such a *mineral* is a body produced by the processes of inorganic nature and, if formed under favourable conditions, a certain characteristic molecular structure is exhibited in its crystalline form and other physical properties. A mineral must be a homogeneous substance, even when subjected to examination under the microscope; further it must have a definite chemical composition, capable of being expressed by a chemical formula (Dana). Nor all minerals are ores, though all ores are minerals. For an *ore* is a mineral (or mineral aggregate) containing precious or useful metals or metalloids (such as antimony, sulphur, etc.) and which occurs in such quantity, grade and chemical combination as to make extraction commercially profitable. Seeing that profitable extraction is the essential characteristic of an ore, it is clear that it depends on the refining techniques developed during a certain period in history whether a mineral will be considered an ore or not. There were certain minerals like zinc (cobalt, nickel) ores, which were not real ores to the ancients, who did not possess the means of extracting the zinc (cobalt, nickel) from them. In other cases such as iron pyrites, neither in Antiquity nor now is it very profitable to extract the iron from them and they are not iron ores in the strict sense of the word or only low grade ones.

From these definitions it will be clear that the cupriferous sandstone mined by the ancient Egyptians in the Sinai district is a rock, containing several minerals such as the nodules of malachite, chrysocolla and turquoise they were after. The malachite and the chrysocolla were not only minerals as they were used as semi-precious stones but also copper-ores to the Egyptians who extracted copper from them, a process no longer in use now. The turquoise used only as a precious stone was simply a mineral to them.

The earliest traces of mining go back to Palaeolithic times and before discussing details of the mining of stones, minerals and ores in prehistoric and early historic times it is appropriate to give a short survey of the main events during the six or seven millennia under review. The isolated examples of mining in Palaeolithic times expand into mining on a larger scale in certain Neolithic centres. The quest is mainly directed towards *stones for tools*, such as quartzite, flint, jadeit, nephrite and the like and towards the collection of *precious and semi-precious stones*, earth colours, edible earths, etc., the latter category varying according to local habits and beliefs. Certain of these coloured stones were glittering and malleable. During the centuries man used and shaped them other characteristics were discovered, such as the specific metal properties of melting and recovering the original or imposed shape after cooling. When their special metal nature was recognized and metallurgy slowly became a new craft, the gathering of these *native metals*, and their "parents", the rocks and stones from which they could be isolated with the help of fire and charcoal, grew into a new branch of mining, the *mining of ores*. Though considerably later than some other branches of mining, such as flint-mining, it quickly grew to achieve at least the same importance as the older ones.

For in the mean time mining of stones for tools had gone already a long way. Stones such as flint and quartzite had originally been collected and selected on or near the earth's surface for their hardness or flaking and polishing properties as the proper materials for the production of tools and implements. Already in Palaeolithic times certain centres produced flint and exported it over wide areas, a trade increasing materially in Neolithic times. The abrasives used for fashioning stone tools also became an object of trade.

It would seem that the erection of megalithic monuments in different parts of the world had a profound influence on the choice of building materials in classical and preclassical times. Men learnt to apply the lessons learnt in fashioning stone tools to the production of stones from quarries. His flaking and boring techniques and the handling of wedges and hammers were now used to detach stone slabs from the solid walls of quarries to fashion stones for graves, hearths and offering tables. With seemingly primitive tools and methods and the use of abrasives the Egyptians produced as early as 3500 B.C. wonderful art objects in natural stone, vases and statues of hard materials such as granite and diorite. As the Egyptian stone-masons gained experience in quarrying and fashioning stones from their quarries, they applied them more frequently in the construction of mastabas (bank graves) during the early dynastic period until they undertook to erect buildings entirely of natural stone. This was probably due to the initiative of the pharaoh Zoser (2750 B.C.) or more probably still to his vizier and chief architect, Imhotep, worshipped many centuries later as the god of medicine and identified with Asklepios by the Greeks. In the temple-complex encircling the step-pyramid of Sakkarah we see the first wavering efforts to use the natural stone blocks to imitate the earlier architecture, which knew only timber, bundles of reeds and sun-dried bricks as materials and which used slabs of natural stone only as a facing or floor material. Gradually the architect found his way to the forms inherent in natural stone and shapes and builds colonnades and other buildings which might be mistaken for early Greek forms at first sight.

All throughout their history the Egyptians had a lead in natural stone over the Sumerians and their Semitic successors, who found none of the magnificient materials in their alluvial plain and who never did become such prominent architects in natural stone. This is the reason why the Sumerians, Assyrians and Babylonians do not play a part in the history of mining either, their texts reveal a good knowledge of stones and gems and indicate the regions and mines whence they imported their material but they do not tell us about the history of mining techniques and tools. The Egyptians have throughout their history exploited the mines and quarries of the desert along the Nile valley and they transmitted their skill and knowledge to the later Greek and Roman masters of their country.

The coming of the Bronze Age did not stop the mining of stone for tools, for stone implements continued in use side by side with metal tools for many a century. The stone tool had a long history behind it, the techniques for producing it were well developed and efficient. Herig and Kraft have proved that there existed quite a lore of selection of proper material for every type of tool. For each implement requires a stone of definite properties well adapted to the morphology of the tool and its handling. The earlier metal tool had not yet found its true "metal" form and for many centuries stone tools were both better and cheaper for many purposes. As late as the seventh century B.C. the Egyptian army preferred stone arrow-tips to bronze ones and practical archery tests have shown that they penetrated the defensive armour of those days as well and often better than bronze arrow-tips. Then again for other reasons stone implements continued in use in many religious rites and ceremonies, where the use of "later" materials was often strictly forbidden (circumcision, shaving).

The mining of precious and semi-precious stones had little influence on the development of mining techniques as most of them were collected from placers and surface deposits and as far as we know turquoise and a few others were the only gems to be mined or to be collected as by-products of copper-mining and the like. On the other hand the experience gained helped the development of theoretical petrology and mineralogy. The earlier miners looking for these precious stones had no knowledge of their genesis or of the morphology of the strata, where they are found, to guide him to them. Still the search played an important part in early civilisations, as most of these stones were not collected for their aesthetical charms, but because of their supposed magical properties. It is well-known that this belief is far from dead even nowadays and superstitious people will still repeat the ageless fables of the mysterious powers of such stones. Even at the time when they were believed more generally and more sincerely than at present man must have noticed certain outward appearances and properties, certain characteristics of the strata where they were found. These observations are the foundations of the later sciences of geology and mineralogy. In Roman times prospectors knew or believed to recognize certain minerals or rocks which might lead them to the deposits of the minerals they where looking for.

These precious stones were already an object of trade in Neolithic times, when they were carried over enormous distances, probably handed from tribe to tribe to distant countries where there was a demand prompted by the needs and may be the greed of primitive man. The most important of these stones were lapis lazuli, callais, turquoise, and amber, but Red Sea shells like the Spondylus also figure on the list (4a). The gamma of stones known to and appreciated by the ancients differed considerably from ours. At present for instance the diamond accounts for 95% of the value of gems produced, but even in the later eighteenth century this figure was only 50% and it seems that the diamond was unknown before our era. In the history of the production of precious stones Hellenism was a very important era for by establishing direct trade contacts with India the classical world could now gather directly the desired stones from the important deposits of North-Eastern Iran, Afghanistan, India and Ceylon. That is its sources of supplies were doubled or trebled without increasing the number of precious stones known materially, for they were already known to the earlier links in the gem trade, the Sumerians, Assyrians, Arabians and Egyptians. This is evident from the Sumerian/Accadian nomenclature of such stones. It will be an important task of future historians of gemmology, not only to pursue the work started by Beck and Bolman to re-examine the many precious stones in ancient jewelry in our museums, but also to collect the latest archaeological and philological data in order rewrite the history of precious stones in Antiquity.

2. *Prospecting*

Given the lack of scientific geological concepts the early prospectors searching distant countries for flint, precious stones, minerals and ores had little chance of locating good and profitable deposits except in such cases where they could be found on the earth's surface. We are fairly certain that much observational lore was lost when we inspect and compare ancient mines, but we have no clear record of these ancient prospecting methods. Only too often Demas will have tempted them with his "if you will come, with a little pains you may richly provide for yourselves at Lucre Hill".

It is quite certain that prospecting like mining was a chance! "What we caught we left behind, but what we failed to catch we brought with us" is the riddle propounded to Homer by some fishermen who had little luck and had become covered with lice while sitting on the beach. Demetrius of Phaleron had applied this riddle to the capitalists of Attica who had hoped to become rich by their investments in the Attic silvermines but failed. Through the writings of Poseidonius this saying appears in later writings (5) in the form: "What they took up, they did not take, yet what they had they lost".

Of course the ancient prospectors also tried to reduce this element of chance. Pre-Roman mines very often started by working an open-cast deposit, exploring the veins by trenching across them and then having exploited these by trenches along them. Horizontal strata were attacked by pitting, thus for instance Neolithic flint mines consist of pits striking for a definite bed of flints, but often neglecting a suitable one pierced on their way down.

The methods used for locating ores deeper down in the earth remain unknown. It seems that certain colours were considered indicative of other ores, writers like Pliny tell us, that the presence of iron was detected by the red colour. In some cases certain stratigraphical and morphological were properly observed. In Laurium the Greeks sank shafts through the schist to the contact with the limestone at which the galena was mined. In some cases they struck a false contact and the shaft had to be abandoned. However, such practical knowledge does not seem to have been applied outside a rather restricted area. The geological formation of the nearby Ochra district is very much like that of Laurium, yet the ancients were not drawn by its geological similarity to test the Ochra deposits!

Normally a vein-outcrop was followed down by a series of shafts rather than by exploratory galleries lower down the hill, though such galleries do exist when exploration later demanded easy drainage of underground water. It was generally considered cheaper to haul ore

up the shafts than spending much labour in cutting an adit through
sterile rock. In Italy and Spain the Romans (and sometimes the earlier
Iberians or Etruscans) had clear notions of the structure of certain
mines and could follow up the local strata quite well, though compli-
cations such as faulting generally left them dumb-founded. In Central
Italy, at the Capanne Vecchio, Poggio Montierino and Serra Bottini
mines the boundaries of the copper deposits were correctly defined by
shafts. However, when they lost a vein they rarely found it again (6).
On the other hand certain regional experts seem to have been aware of
the importance of igneous rocks like granite, etc. in relation to their
ore deposits, when they cut shafts in or near such rocks where no trace
of such ore was in sight. They also seem to have known that some
metals were apt to occur in what we now call basic rocks and others
in acid rocks. Still the ancients hardly ever found a lost vein due to
the lack of systematic knowledge of ore bodies and their characteristics.

It is certain that the ancient prospector, and notably the Roman
prospector, did not leave the region until he had made a careful field
survey and had taken samples. We will discuss later on an ancient
Egyptian map of the gold mines of the Eastern desert on which deposits were clearly marked. Trenching and stripping the rocks belonged
to his task and in later Republican times also the driving of adits into
the rocky formations.

It is also certain that he had some traditional knowledge about certain key minerals or formations which were to lead him to the desired
deposits. Pliny speaks of the red colour of the earth pointing to iron
ores but he also knows about the concentration of precious metals in
the oxidized outcrops of copper ores in Spain (7). He also mentions
that gold-seekers first remove the "segullum", a bed of sand serving
as an indication, but do not know what they will finds below (8). This
looks like a kind of rule-of-thumb method for discovering high-level
auriferous alluvia such as were worked in Spain and Bosnia. Aethicus
(9) mentions that white pebbles, probably vein material, are sure guides
to gold placers, at least in Britain.

Trenching and stripping the rock were widely used methods when
looking for gold. In Bosnia the prospectors tried to locate the source
of the rich placers by advancing upstream from the alluvium of the
plain to the diluvium of the side-valleys and testing the schist by pitting,
but generally speaking, the gold content of the disseminated pyrites
was too small. Traces of similar methods of exploration are found just

east of Salonica. In several cases they certainly had a good eye for ore. In the Egyptian desert little of value was left in the way of copper or gold. Near Umm Hat the Egyptians tested every blue stain for agentiferous copper, but they seldom sank shafts outside the veins in order to cut them lower down.

In Spain the Romans took little risk and always kept to the ore, though in such cases mines like those at Cerro Muriano show no order or plan. In late Republican times prospecting adits were cut like those at Laurium and Siphnos. Exploratory galleries from the main adit were dug at regular intervals at Sotiel Coronada and Moldova. Many such examples show that the ancients must have had little theoretical knowledge of the oxidized (higher) and the unoxidized (deeper) parts of an ore-body. Pliny mentions that in Spain "the vein of silver nearest to the surface is called "the raw" (crudaria). In early days the excavations used to stop when they found alumen and no further search was made; but recently the discovery of a vein of copper under the alumen has removed all limit to men's hopes (10)". He clearly distinguishes between the gossan, the highly oxidized and leached upper part of the ore body (some 60—100' thick near Rio Tinto), the unoxidized pyritic copper ore down below and the intermediate jarositic earth which was worked for silver (as we shall discuss later on). Pliny's "alumen" may denote ferrous sulphate crystals found near the surface of the main body of copper pyrites down below, which was certainly worked for copper in Roman times. However, gaining more experience they managed to discover most of the copper veins of the Huelva region of Spain and many other provinces. In many cases we do not know what prompted them to attack the ore the way they did. At Linares, the Hannibal shaft was driven in the country rock and the vein was reached by a cross-cut 30 meters in length at a depth of 30 meters. At that point the vein was barren but after 40 meters of drift, minable ore was struck. This was a success, even according to modern standards, but the lack of theoretical knowledge must have made it practically impossible to calculate the paying possibilities of a mine. Pliny (11) describes the complete undermining and collapse of a gold-bearing rocky formation without the certainty of finding gold in larger quantities and certainly ancient mining was more of a chance than modern mining.

In ancient China too (12) the methods used for finding locations of ores and minerals were primarily based on traditional geological lore, the observation of the "lie of the land" and above all on certain coloured key minerals. In the book Kuan Tzu the minister of the emperor Huang

Table VI

Coloured Mineral Substances

English	Sumerian	Accadian	Egyptian	Greek	Latin
Black					
Carbon black, soot	IM-GÍG	(Hebr. ḥeret)	{wbd (I. 297. 9) / dꜣb. t (V. 537. 1) / dꜣb. t (V. 537. 1)	asbole	atramentum
Charcoal	—	pentû	—	anthrakos	carbo
Bitumen	ESIR	iddû, kupru	—	asphaltos	bitumen
Iron oxide, heamatite	^{na_4}KA-GÍG (-DA)	šadanu	b'i3 (I. 438. 11)	aematites?	haematites
Stibium, stibnite	ŠEM-BI-ZI- (-DA)	guḫlu	mśdm. t (II. 153. 8)?	stimmi	
Sulphur (impure)	KI-A-ID	kibritu			
White					
Limestone, chalk	^{na_4}NA. PUR, kak-ku-us	pilu pisû.	inr ḥd (I. 97. 12)	poros	porus
Lime	^{a}ZALÁG (BIR)	{namru, namrûtu	—	konia, gypsos	calx
Gypsum	IM. PAR	gaṣṣu	ḳd (V. 82. 8)	gypsos	gypsum
Ceruse, white lead	^{na_4}NINÍ, ni-ir	hulâlu	ḏḥtj ḥd(?)	psimythion	cerussa
Terra Melia	^{na_4}KA. PAR	—	—	ge melia	Terra Melia
Mercury	IM. KAL. GUG	—	—	hydragyros	argentum vuvim
Yellow					
Ochre	IM-MAL-LI	kalû	sty (III. 488. 3)	ochra	sil
Limonite	^{na_4}KA-SIG$_7$, IM-GUŠKIN	—	?		schistos

Table VI

Coloured Mineral Substances (continued)

English	Sumerian	Accadian	Egyptian	Greek	Latin
Orpiment	šim-saḫar(-guškin)	šêpu, lerû	knit (V. 52. 10)	arrhenicon (arsenicon)	arrhenicum (auripigmentum)
Green					
Malachite	ªNINI-MUŠ-GIR	ªmušgarru	{w3d (I. 267. 3-8) / w3dw3d. t (I. 270. 8)?	chrysoccolla	chrysocolla
Verdigris	URUDU-SUN	šuhtu	w3d (I. 267. 3-8)	{chalkos an-thos, prasitis	aeruca
Blue					
Lapis lazuli	ªZA-GIN	uknû	ḫšbd (III. 334. 1)	{sappheiros / kyanos	sapphirus
Azurite	ªZA-GIN-KUR-RA	tâkiltu	tfrr (V. 300. 2)?	kyanos	cyanus
Copper Carbonate	il-lu A-KAL-URUDU	ḫilu erî	—	armenion	armenium
Red					
Ochre	ªKA, IM-SA₃	šaršerru	{tmš (V. 369. 7) / sšw (III. 481. 13)	{miltos (sphragis)	{sinopis (rubrica)
Red lead	ªZA-TU-BE	sâsu	—	—	sandaraca
Cinnaber	GUG	sându	—	kinnabari	minium
Realgar	—	—	3wt. ib (I. 5. 1)	sandarache	sandaraca

Ti informs his master: "Where there is cinnabar above, yellow gold will be found below. Where there is magnetite above, copper and gold will be found below. Where there is ling shih above, lead, tin and red copper will be found below. Thus it can be seen that the mountains are full of riches. "Lead near the surface is believed to indicate silver below, jade copper ore. The Pên Tshao Shih I (AD 725) states: "Generally one sees those who search for gold dig down into the earth for several feet until they come to a stone called fên tzu shih ("tangle stone") which accompanies the gold. This is always in black lumps, as if charred, and underneath it is the gold-bearing ore, also in lumps, some as large as one's finger, other as small as beans, and coloured a mulberry yellow, when first dug out it is friable."

There are also references to the association of realgar and gold, sulphur and alum, iron pyrites and alum. On the other hand the Chinese also recognize certain connections between vegetation and ores. An interesting passage in the Yu-Yang Tsa Tsu, written by Tuan Chhêng-Shih about AD 800, refers to this geobotanical prospecting in these words: "When in the mountain there is the tshung plant (ciboule onion), then below silver will be found. When in the mountain there is the hsiai plant (a type of shallot), then below gold will be found. When in the mountains there is the chiang plant (ginger), then below copper and tin will be found. If the mountains have precious jade, the branches of the trees all around will be drooping."

In modern times the role of plants as biological concentrators and indicators was first brought out in a classical lecture by the Norvegian geochemist V. M. Goldschmidt in 1937 (13), though the influence of certain rare elements in the soil on the growth of tobacco and the like was already properly recognized. We have no indication that such connections between vegetation and underground mineral deposits were recognized by the inhabitants of the Mediterranean world. However, the bright colours of many mineral substances were well-known to the prospectors (Table VI) and helped to guide them to the deposits and distinguish certain minerals found there.

3. *Preclassical mining*

After the preliminary prospecting had led to promising results the mining proper could be started. In order to understand the achievements of the ancients we must remember that we moderns distinguish two types of mines:

Table VII

Outline of the Evolution of Mining, its Tools, its Methods and its Products

Period	Mining-methods	Mining tools	Stones, precious and semi-precious	Ores and natural stone	Metallurgical methods
Palaeolithic Age	Search for boulders, etc. Open workings, conical pits	Wooden or bone digging stick, horn pick. First stone tools such as hand-axe etc.	Chalcedony, quartz, rockcrystal, serpentine, obsidian, jaspis steatite, amber, jadeite, calcite	Flint and obsidian, later ochre and other natural pigments, emery	
Neolithic Age (-3500 B.C.)	Quarries, stone slabs Open workings, sloping shafts gradually galleries	Stone picks and hammers, chisels and celts	Amethyst, fluorspar, nephrite, jet, turquoise, lapis lazuli, jade, agate.	Granite, diorite Limestone Sandstone	
Predynastic Age (3500-3000 B.C.)	Development of square and round shafts with galleries. Ventilation and chimneys. Propping	Stone picks and first copper tools	Haematite, alabaster, carneol, chrysocolla, malachite, beryl, feldspar	Native metals (gold, silver, iron (meteoric), copper). Copper ores from outcrops. Alabaster, marble, rocksalt	Hammering native metals. Melting and casting of metals, first reduction of copper oxides
Metal Age I (3000-2200 B.C.)	Systematic stripping of outcrops Shafts with staircase(?)	General use of firesetting	Onyx, sardonyx amazonite, azurite, callais	Oxydic and carbonatic copper ores Galena, stibnite,	Silver from galena. Oxidation and reduction with natural blast

				Obsidian, emery	magnetite. Copper. alloyed with lead, antimony and tin
		...with gangue			
Metal Age II (2200-1200 B.C.)	Copper tools become more general	Timbering of shafts(?) Drainage with pails, etc. Wider galleries	Bloodstone, emerald, magnesite, topaze, chrysoprase	Gold-bearing quartz Oxydic iron ores Copper sulphides	Short shaft-furnaces Use of bellows Roasting of sulphidic ores more general
Early Iron Age (1200-500 B.C.)	Iron tools	Drainage adits Large quarries	Sapphire, blue chalcedony, rose quartz, spinels	Limonite, haematite Copper pyrites	Wrought iron "steeled" by case-hardening, quenching and tempering
Late Iron Age (500-50 B.C.)	gradually supersede copper and stone	Mechanical drainage, transport and ventilation	Ruby, moss-agate, zircon, opal, aquamarine, meerschaum, diamond (?)	Magnetite and spathic iron Iron pyrites (?)	Brass from copper and clamaine Higher shaft-furnaces
Roman Empire (50 B.C.-300 A.D.)	tools	Water-wheels, water-screws, etc. more common, deeper mines and large open workings	Aventurine, moon-stone, blue spinel, spinel-ruby, pearl		"Stückofen" Mercury produced

A. *Open-cut mining* (with or without stripping), which embraces:
   a) *quarrying*, the usual way of obtaining natural stone, and
   b) *placer mining*, with such methods as panning, washing, hand-sluicing, dredging and hydraulicking, such as applied to tin-mines and gold-mines.
B. *Underground mining*, embracing:
   a) *breast stoping* (of tabular deposits),
      underhand stoping (veins and larger masses),
   c) *overhand stoping* (steep dipping veins),
   d) *top slicing* (wide veins and masses), and
   e) *caving* (large masses).

In modern mining both methods may be combined to work very large masses of minerals and ores, but such methods were not applied in Antiquity. In the case of underground mining the ore could be attacked by sinking shafts vertically into the soil and tunneling the horizontal levels, drifts and galleries into the ore-bearing strata. This is how mining started, but gradually the ancients preferred driving horizontal adits into the rocky slopes of a valley following the veins rather than sinking shafts, for such adits had the advantage of making drainage and hauling easier.

We have a fairly good knowledge of ancient mining in general (14), yet it is difficult to summarize its development in a few words for the methods used vary from mineral to mineral and from region to region, also our evidence is far from complete as ancient mines when depleted and abandoned, tended to be forgotten and lost. Table VII gives a rough outline of the development of mining in the eastern Mediterranean region, which differs in several details from the developments in Europe.

Again much more evidence might be obtained if experts were called in to study such ancient mines and quarries when found. Still from

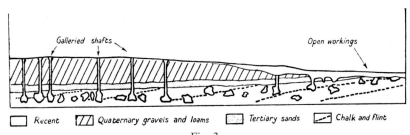

Galleried shafts   Open workings

☐ Recent   ▨ Quaternary gravels and loams   ▨ Tertiary sands   ▨ Chalk and flint

Fig. 3.
Diagrammatic section of the flint mining area at
Spiennes (Hainant, Belgium) (After Cornet et Briart)

those mines and quarries which have been properly studied and described we get the impression that the ancient miners knew the various methods tabulated above and did apply them on their modest scale though their use varies from region to region and what was commonly applied in the ancient Near East may not be found in use in prehistoric Europe until many centuries later.

The depletion of ancient mines referred to above goes for many smaller gold-placers and small veins of minerals exploited locally for a short time only. In the case of larger ore-bodies real depletion was exceptional. Much depended on the variations in such ore-bodies, the decrease of the metal-content of the ore with greater depth or the change of the nature of the ore (say from oxidic ores near the surface to sulphidic ores at greater depths), which necessitated the introduction of new or more intricate refining processes. Mining techniques might be the cause of giving up certain mines, when the known techniques of drainage, ventilation, etc. were insufficient to cope with the local difficulties, but in other cases changes in the market value of the products obtained may have caused man to abandon such mines. Such economic changes, the discovery of new, richer deposits or may be the introduction of cheap slave labour may have been the cause of stopping the work in such mines and such causes are not always traceable. We know from examples in Spain that in war-time mine-shafts were temporarily hidden and covered up and sometimes even destroyed. On the other hand we must handle the lable "depleted" with care for we must remember the great changes in technology in the course of centuries and products mined in earlier periods may have been pushed from the markets by new and totally different products. In the world of gem-mining changes in religion, the death of traditional folklore, immigration and the like must have had a profound influence on mining and trading of precious stones. We must also remember that certain ores, though known, were of no use to the ancients. In ancient mines such ores as wolframite, nickel- and cobalt-ores, zinc-blende and certain lead-ores containing molybdenium were left untouched, for nobody had any use for them at that period.

The mines and quarries mentioned below are given as typical examples of the various periods in the history of mining discussed in the following pages. Further examples will be found in the literature quoted and a more detailed discussion of the ores which play their part in the history of metallurgy as well as the mines they came from will be given in Vols. VIII and IX of these Studies.

The awe in which minerals and precious stones were held by primitive man is still reflected in much later times. The Egyptian "bj3" (I. 436. 1) for "native copper", "metal in general", and "mine" is also used in very early texts for "wonder", "precious" and "astonishing". Even the author of the Book of Enoch (15), who lived shortly after the beginning of our era and gave a Greek translation of a Hebrew and Aramaic original, mentions that the fallen angels not only revealed such magical arts and sciences as botany and pharmacy, but also useful arts such as mining minerals, a tradition confirmed by Tertullian (16).

Stones of different origin were the materials from which *Stone-Age man* shaped his tools and implements and it is useless to speculate how

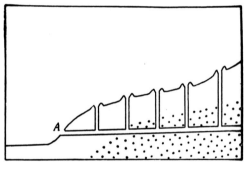

water soaked subsoil

Fig. 4.

Hillside section with a qanât (water-tunnel) and a series of shafts, a technique is evidently based on the older tradition of pitting.

far back men began to pick up such stones to use them or to fashion them into a more useful shape. Flint and obsidian were the most important types of stones collected and mining proper, when surface deposits were mostly exhausted, started as early as 3000 B.C. in Europe and certainly two millennia or more earlier in the Near East (17).

Flint was widely used for tools such as axe-heads, knives, borers, arrow- and spear-heads and such stone tools continued in use in the Near East even in the Iron Age. They were gradually ousted by metal tools, notably by iron tools, when metals became cheaper and of better quality than in the earlier stages of metallurgy.

Flint, a hard and compact form of silica, was plentiful in the deserts along the Nile Valley and in various other regions of the Near East. The usual Egyptian word for flint, "dś" (V. 485. 16) also seems to have been used for the knives and scalpels of the Egyptian physicians. Another term, "bšw" (I. 478. 9) is applied to a special kind of flint. In prehistoric Europe flint was less commonly collected from surface deposits but mostly mined in the form of nodules, which had to be fresh in order to be workable, as flint becomes brittle when it looses too much water. In certain places it is found along the beaches, where

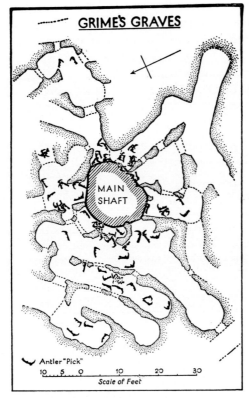

Fig. 5.
Plan of flint pits at Grime's Graves
(After Clark, Prehistoric Europe)

the strata containing these flint nodules are disintegrated by the waves, e.g. in north-eastern Jutland near Snagstrup and also on the east coast of the island of Seeland (Denmark).

From 1866 onwards the ancient European flint mines near Spiennes (Belgium) and other sites have been properly investigated (18). Older generations of naturalists such as Cuvier had believed these shafts to be "geological organs". Much information on this prehistoric flint industry can be gained from the mining and "flint-knapping" of nodules still practised at Brandon (Norfolk) up to the Second World War. Pits were sunk to a depth of 40′ to reach the chalk-stratum which contained the desired flint-nodules. The digging was done with a peculiar one-sided pick, a heavy hammer, a shovel and a short crow-bar. No windlass, pail or ladder was used. The miners ascended and descended by means of a series of foot-holes or "toes" in the chalky side of the shaft.

These chimney-like shafts (Mardellen-Bau, karst-pits) in the limestone were sometimes up to 300′ deep and they usually ended in caverns

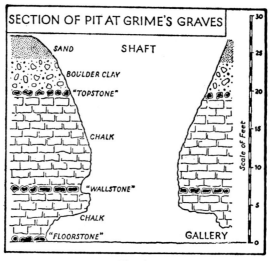

Fig. 6.
Section of flint pits at Grime's Graves
(After Clark, Prehistoric Europe)

from which the flint had been extracted. Such shafts have been found in Wadi el-Cheikh (Egypt), Miskolcz (Hungary), Mauer (near Vienna), Porownia (Poland), near Malmö (Sweden), Jutland (Denmark), Norfolk and Sussex, and in various places in France such as Lumbres (Pas de Calais), Grand Pressigny (near Tours) and other sites in the "départe-ments– of Marne, Charente and Oise. Neolithic underground flint workings were discovered at Campolide near Lisbon. In Spiennes (Belgium) the shafts were found over an area of 3 HA. The shafts are 30′—40′ deep and have a diameter of 2—2½′. The sixth layer of flint from the top in the chalk is the most desirable one and here, at the end of

the shafts, chambers of 6—10′ in diameter and 4—6′ high were excavated
like the bell-pits for coal in the north of England. Sometimes galleries
radiate from this chamber at the bottom of the shaft. Some of the early
mines drain towards a sump-hole near the foot of the shaft. The tools
used were probably flint hammers together with wedges for splitting
the chalk. Such wedges were sometimes made of the metacarpals of
horses, though deer-horn is still used in other quarters. Egyptian
quarrymen knew how to apply the swelling of dry wooden wedges for
splitting off stones.

Galleries radiating from the bottom of the shafts were also found
at Hov (northern Jutland), St. Geertrui (Netherlands), Krzemionki
(Poland), Cissbury and other English sites such as Grimes' Graves on
the Norfolk-Suffolk boundary. Here the early pits were shallow and
without galleries. Bone picks from the long bones of the ox were often
used to extract the flint nodules from the chalk or marl, which sometimes occurs in strata up to one foot thick. In Neolithic times the number of shafts had increased to many hundreds, some up to 330′ deep.
At the bottom of such shafts galleries radiated, which were gradually
transformed into chambers as the desired nodules were extracted on
three sides of the galleries. This technique of connecting the vertical
shafts with horizontal galleries at the bottom of the shafts gave birth
to the qanat, the water-tunnel of the Armenian mountains and finally
to the aqueduct so important in the history of water supply (see Vol. I).

In some cases the flint-mines were merely galleries tunnelled into
the slope of the mountain, e.g. on Monte Tabuto (Sicily) and Isensteiner
Klotz (Baden, Germany).

Obsidian (19), or volcanic glass, is a form of completely fused lava
varying in colour from a completely opaque black to a very rare, perfectly clear and colourless transparency. Recent excavations at Çatal
Hüyük, prove that its story goes back to the seventh millennium B.C.
in Anatolia, and even earlier in the Zagros Mountains. It was no doubt
the "opsianos" or "obsiana" mentioned by various classical authors
(20), on which Pliny (21) has the following rather fantastic story to
tell: "Under the heading glass is included obsiana, named from their
similarity to the stone which Obsius found in Aethiopia. The stone is
very dark in colour, sometimes translucent, but more opaque than
glass, and if a mirror of it is placed upon a wall, shadows rather than
images appear therein. Many use it in jewellery, and we have even seen
it used for solid statues of the emperor Augustus, who was fascinated
by this opaque material, while he himself dedicated four obsian

elephants, as a rare treasure, in the temple of Concord. Moreover, Tiberius Caesar, restored to the people of Heliopolis a sacred image of Menelaus, made in obsian, which had been found amongst the property left by one Sejus, who had been ruler of Egypt. This shows that the material, whose resemblance to glass caused the transference of its name, is really of much earlier origin. Xenocrates is our authority that the obsian stone occurs in the district of Italy called Samnium, in India and in the part of Spain which verges on the ocean. By a colouring process, an artificial obsian glass is prepared..."

There seems no reason to doubt that in most cases the "obsian stone" was real obsidian. The brittleness of this substance would make its use for statues and images very difficult, and it is possible, that in some of the cases mentioned in older texts a black marble was meant. The presence of obsidian in a non-volcanic country must be considered a certain proof of trade with some centre where this volcanic substance occurs naturally. Thus the Egyptian sources for obsidian were probably Nimrud Dagh in the Armenian Mountains, Ala-göz in the Caucasus or Abyssinia. In certain cases the Egyptian "dś" (flint) may refer to obsidian. It is more common in the Ancient Near East in several region. than flint, but the latter material is more widely used in Western Asia Minor and other countries to the West. The Zarzian culture of the Zagros mountains, which possibly came to these regions from the north used obsidian occasionally during Mesolithic times (10.000—9.000 B.C.), which they seem to have obtained from the 1egion North and West of Lake Van, where this material is found abundantly. In proto-Neolithic times it is also used frequently in the Natufian culture of Palestine and Jordan (c. 9.000 B.C.) and such settlements of the Zagros region as Jarmo, Tepe Guran, Tepe Sarab, etc. used mainly flint but also a substantial percentage of obsidian imports for their tools such as knives and sickles, fixing such blades into the wooden handles with bitumen (21 a).

The ceramic cultures of Syria and Palestine seem to have used less obsidian, may be due to difficulties in contacting the obsidian regions during the sixth millenium B.C.

In Anatolia, however, the subsequent settlements of Çatal Hüyük (c. 6500—5650 B.C.), a region with still active volcanoes, seem to have held the monopoly of the obsidian trade with the west of Anatolia, Cyprus and the Levant. Obsidian spearheads in prime condition are frequently found in groups of up to twenty-three specimens buried in a bag below the floor, where they were evidently stored as capital.

In exchange for obsidian the fine tabular flint of Syria was obtained and widely used for daggers and tools. The standard of local technology is amazing and left most of the work of other sites in the Near East far behind. Mirrors of polished obsidian were set in a fine lime plaster to fit neatly into the hand.

The later Halaf Culture, flourishing in the arc of Northern Mesopotamia from the Euphrates to the Greater Zab during the late sixth and fiith millenium B.C., also used obsidian (probably from the Lake Van

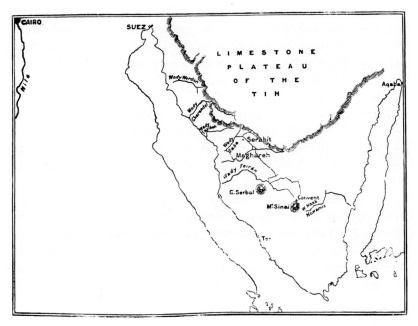

Fig. 7.
Map of the Sinai district (After Petrie)

region) abundantly and produced magnificently cut beads, plaques and vessels from this hard material until it was destroyed by invasion from the south of Mesopotamia. Prehistoric Europe must have depended on Melos, Lipari, Sardinia, Auvergne and the mountains north of Tokay for its obsidian, which does crop up in several prehistoric finds.

However, other useful stones besides these two were mined in prehistoric times. In Neolithic times we find basalt-lava quarries here and there. From the island of Hespriholmen near the south-west coast of Norway a type of "Grünstein" was carried by boat to factories in

Bømlo, situated at the head of a small fjord. Here again the sea served to link quarry, factory and market as in the case of the igneous rock of Penmaenmawr (North Wales), worked on a considerable scale and carried to the coast of Essex and to Wiltshire. In southern England the polished stone celts from rocks of Brittany were frequently used and Olonetz green slate travelled from Eastern Carelia all over the Baltic and Finland. Most of these stones were used for polished blades and axes, used by the neolithic farmers. Other materials like banded flint from eastern Galicia and southern Kielce, from northern Ireland, the Lake District and northern Wales can be shown to have been fashioned in local factories and to have been marketed over wide areas. Another material in demand in prehistoric Europe was serpentine from Janczów (Silesia). The study of archaeological reports proves definitely that Neolithic mining and fashioning of certain stones was a well-developed industry towards 2000 B.C.

With the *Bronze Age* underground mining for different minerals and ores started properly. Generally speaking, *pitting*, the exploration of ore-bodies with the help of shafts at intervals, which were abandoned one after the other as the ore was extracted from the bottom of the shaft, continued in use, for instance at Laurium. The Romans, generally speaking, avoided this method of mining and preferred regular workings. Though the lack of trustworthy reports by experts on ancient mines still impedes writing the true story of *underground mining*, it would seem that the exploitation of ores deposits by means of different levels worked simultaneously became the rule only during the classical period. In Roman mines two to four levels are common enough, though we should not expect a careful, well-planned vertical horizontal arrangement of shafts and levels before the days of Agricola and his contemporaries, e.g. before the sixteenth century. Ancient mines had no wheeled haulage and only drainage adits had to be practically horizontal. Pliny (22) gives a good survey of the types of underground mining used in his days.

However, in the Bronze Age metals such as gold, native copper and tin were still largely obtained by working alluvial deposits or placers. In this period *Egypt* was the gold-land of the Near East and the princes and kings of other country repeatedly mention in their correspondence that "in your country gold is plentiful" when writing to Phraoh. The mineral resources of ancient Egypt have been properly described by modern authorities (23).

Placer-mining in its different forms was quite familiar to the ancients and it developed into the efficient Roman methods of attacking large ore-bodies by *hushing*, by breaking up the softer beds with the help of a strong current of water directed upon them, leading the water and the débris into settling tanks, where the gold-dust and the gold-bearing quartz (24) could be collected. We will discuss the Spanish "arrugiae", so graphically described by Pliny, later on, but in earlier phases the hard stones and rocks were washed and crushed at the site of the placer or at the pit-head in order to avoid transport. Unfortunately most older Egyptian placers have been destroyed by later shafts, as is the case with

Fig. 8.
Entrance to copper mine at Wadi Magareh.

many of the older prehistoric European workings too. Few have been preserved to yield wooden tools, horn picks and the like (e.g. the ancient Cornish tin-workings). In most of these placers we find washing tables (of stone) with cup hollows caused by their use in pounding and crushing larger lumps of ore.

Schürmann gave an excellent description of the Wadi Ballat gold mine where gold was taken from a quartz vein. The rock was mined by fire-setting by groups of 100—200 miners. Around the site the remains of some 100 shelters (2 × 2 M) were found and also large numbers of mill-stones and washing tables with stone rubbers. In most cases, however, such mines were worked at intervals by expeditions sent out from the Nile valley, each reopening tending to obliterate the marks of earlier activity. In most cases the availability of timber and water limited the scope of such workings. In some cases very rich ground was found immediately below the old workings at or about water level, in spite of the fact that the level has fallen apparently at least some feet since the previous exploitation. However, we can say that no outcrop was left untested as the yield of such placers was often very great (25) and we must admire the tenacity of the ancient prospectors (26).

Not only does the Turin Papyrus, dating back to the days of Seti I (1300 B.C.) give a map of the gold mines, which shows the "houses of the miners", but the data given by Schürmann agree with the 400 houses found near Wadi 'Alaki and the over 1300 huts in Wadi Fawakhir as well as the various settlements near the Sinai mines, which we will discuss below.

Though the Egyptians preferred open-cut mining they did drive galleries into the mountains in a few cases. The technique for making such galleries is the same as that used for excavating rock-tombs (27). Notwithstanding the numerous mining activities mining terms had little effect on the Egyptian language. In a song in praise of Thebes we find this city mentioned as "the mother-rock of the towns" (28) and Ptahhotep says that "good speech is more hidden than the emerald, but it may be found with the maid-servants at the grind-stone".

It seems that such mines were not only exploited by the king, but also by temples and private persons (29). The great variety of building stones, minerals and ores produced are not always reflected in the texts or mentioned on the monuments, for these refer to metals and minerals in a more refined form only. Many of the gifts of the "rebellious kings of wretched Palestine and Syria" consisted of copper-ore and metals. The enormous amounts of gold and other metals stored in the temples is obvious from the Papyrus Harris (30), and some twenty titles of gold-workers mentioned in the documents tend to show that there was some classification or difference in social rank apart from specialization. Still we know from modern surveys of the mines and their products (31), that the range is far greater than one would suppose from such official texts or monuments only.

The development of real undergrond mining in order to extract ores in their original position began with the rise of the New Kingdom (about 1600 B.C.) and we find real systematic exploration with shafts and galleries both at Wadi Alaki and in the Sinai peninsula some 300 years later. Copper was obtained in ancient Egypt from Sinai and from mines in the eastern desert, only much later copper ingots are imported from Cyprus, Armenia and other foreign localities.

Copper mining in Sinai (32) became very important after the first attempts to obtain turquoise there during the reign of king Semempses of the first dynasty (c. 3000 B.C.). By the age of the pyramid-builders, the fifth dynasty (c. 2400 B.C.), expeditions went there regularly and the volumes of Breasted's Ancient Records mention the names of the leaders of such expeditions and sometimes of his staff too. The reigns of king Snofru of the fourth dynasty (c. 2700 B.C.), the twelfth dynasty (c. 1700 B.C.) and the eighteenth dynasty (c. 1500 B.C.) were periods of great activity in Sinai. Usually such expeditions number up to 200 persons, but we have records of a few large ones including 8000 persons and 500 pack-animals. They always number soldiers, to protect the workmen from the roaming Arab nomads, and specialists including smelters and smiths apart from the miners proper, for the expedition brought home the turquoise and copper ore or refined copper. Hence the earlier expeditions brought the precious stones (turquoise, etc.) only, later the camps prove that ore was smelted there for the excavations have revealed numbers of crucibles, slags and copper objects. The earlier expeditions worked in the neighbourhood of Wadi Magharah, the New Kingdom miners explored new veins in Serabit al-Khadim.

However, the Egyptians were not the only people to work these copper deposits. Indeed, only recently Rothenberg described copper mines in the Kadesh-Barnea region (Ain el Qudeirat) and proved that the island of Jeziret Fara'un (Jotabe) was not only occupied during the Roman-Byzantine period, but shows signs of occupation during the days of King Solomon (Tenth century B.C.). The latter island not far from Eilath and Ezion Geber may have served to protect the old coastal road into the mining district of southern Sinai and the roads to the western part of this peninsula, where copper was certainly mind during the period of the kings of Judah (Iron Age II) in the desert oasis of Feiran. Concentrations of copper slag were found at Dhahab on the end of the route to the Gulf of Akabah, the western road-head being Markha, where Albright found an ancient Egyptian port dating back to the 15th-13th centuries B. C. Feiran originally bore the name of Paran which may have been the original name in Biblical times for the whole of the Sinai peninsula. Expressions like "wilderness of Sinai" and "wilderness of Zin" are names attached to particular places within the wilderness of Paran.

Such workings by miners from the north, by Roman and Byzantine authorities and by local tribesmen through the ages make it exceedingly difficult to write a detailed story of mining in Sinai and we should remember the words of Černy, who studied the inscriptions of Sinai: "In the face of all this evidence it would be idle to attempt to deny that copper was mined and smelted in the Sinai peninsula probably at an early period. At the same time there is not a scrap of evidence for believing that the miners were Egyptians... Apart from the single inscription which mentions copper as one of the objects of an expedition, we have no proof that the Egyptians ever worked the copper deposits of Sinai on a large scale." It is, however, certain that they worked the copper deposits of the eastern desert, though they should be re-examined in detail.

Barrois has drawn an excellent picture of the difficulties on the path of expeditions trying to reach Serabit al-Khadim by way of the many tortuous and difficult wadi's. On the plateau they found the desired turquoises and small veins and outcrops of copper minerals, haematite and manganese. Remains of a large temple were found in this region, but all over the area there are tablets with inscriptions and remains of huts for workmen. Unfortunately modern prospectors destroyed much evidence in 1903, three years before Sir W. Flinders Petrie conducted the first careful archaeological survey in this region.

Loret showed that the "mfk3. t" (II. 56. 1) of the ancient Egyptians was indeed turquoise. We know that the mining season lasted from January 15th to May 15th to avoid the hot season. However, a stela left by an official, Harrure, mentions that an expedition set out later and found "there is always turquoise in the mountains, but the "skin" does not come in this season. We have heard the like before." As he persevered he succeeded "better than anyone who was there in times of old", the mineral left nothing to be desired, the "skin was good, a treat to the eye, and the product was better than in the accustomed season". This refers to the fact that the Sinai turquoise is rather instable and easily turns from a sky-blue to green or from green to a flat grey and the Egyptians probably looked upon certain of these colours as an indication that the ore was worthwhile or ready for smelting.

At Wadi Maghara the veins of copper are buried below some 50 meters of sandstone. Hence the miners dug small, narrow, horizontal tunnels in the slopes of the wadis to reach this stratum. Then they followed the lode into the mountains enlarging the galleries into chambers, leaving pillars standing to carry the roofs. Sometimes these chambers are interconnected with tunnels and a few mines have vertical shafts leading to such chambers, may be serving as ventilating shafts. Having extracted the ore the miners filled up the galleries with debris if not too sure of the strength of the cover-rock. However, most traces have now been destroyed by Arab miners trying to find more "stones" and many corridors have caved in and destroyed all evidence of the methods of these ancient miners.

The fortified camps and their huts and temples have yielded many heavy stone hammers, pounding stones, stone chisels and wedges as well as flint borers and planing tools. The latter may have been used to extract the pieces of turquoise. Large masses of slags prove that

Fig. 9.
"King Solomon's copper mines" in the desert near Timnah.

extensive local smelting was carried on, though much of the refining was certainly taking place at home in Egypt.

Stelae often mark the mines and describe the work of this or that expedition. Usually they depict the king offering to Hathor, goddess of the mountains of Sinai. Still the mines are not described as possessions of the kings of Egypt and the irregular exploitation may have been caused by the shortage of fire-wood and water. Certainly the expeditions to Sinai were not by far the largest undertakings of this kind in ancient Egypt, for we have records of expeditions to the stone quarries in Wadi Hammamat which are much bigger. Most of these involve a total of 3000—4000 men and during the reign of Ramses IV the High Priest of Ammon sent over 9000 men there to quarry stone, for his records mention that he took 8357 men back and left 900 dead behind, mostly soldiers, and only 140 skilled labour. We have no proof that these miners were slaves. May be war-prisoners or criminals were sometimes used for unskilled jobs in such expeditions, but nowhere in our texts were those "exiled in Nubia" ever condemned to work in mines or quarries! We know that the expeditions to Sinai sometimes included Canaanite "experts" of some kind, who may have been prospectors or itinerant smiths of the Kenite, Edomite or Midianite type, and who became famous for their early attempts to derive an alphabetic script from the Egyptian hieroglyphs. The texts so often quoted to demonstrate the awful fate of political prisoners condemned to work as slave-miners (33) are of Hellenistic date and may apply to that period, but the constantly repeated fable of Egyptian engineering and technology being based on slave labour finds no basis whatsoever in texts and documents or archaeological finds.

The paucity of references to mining in the Old Testament proves that it was of little importance in Bronze Age *Palestine* and even much later. The copper deposits of the Arabah were worked from the Early to the Middle Bronze Age on a small scale, then again by the Edomites or other semi-nomadic tribes of these regions from the 18th century B.C. onwards but fairly intensively during the earlier stages of the Iron Age, though no later than the 11th century B.C. The name "King Solomon's Mines" which clung to these copper mines (of the Western Arabah in particular) is a misnomer as is proved by modern research (34). After a gap starting with the Israelite occupation of these regions more continuous mining starts again by the third century B.C. and particularly some six centuries later. This activity belongs to the story of copper to be discussed in Vol. IX. The type of mining was that used by the Egyptians in Sinai. The selected and washed ores or black copper seem to have been carried to the head of the Gulf of Akabah or other smelting camps and sites where the ores were finally smelted. In one passage only of the Old Testament do we find a clear description of mining activities, Job XXVIII, which Bromehead as a geologist renders thus:

Sulerely there is a mine for silver	And a place for gold which they refine.
Iron is taken out of the earth,	And bronze is molten out of the stone.

Man setteth an end to darkness And searcheth out to the furthest bound the stone of thick darkness and of the shadow of death. He breaketh open a shaft away from where men sojourn;

They are forgotten of the foot that passeth by;	They hang afar from men, they swing to and fro
As for the earth, out of it cometh bread;	And underneath it is turned up by fire.
The stones thereof are the place of sapphires,	And it hath dust of gold
That path no bird of prey knoweth,	Neither hath the falcon's eye seen it.
The lion's whelps have not trodden it,	Nor hath the fierce lion passed thereby.
He putteth forth his hand upon the flinty rock;	He overturneth the mountains by the roots.
He cutteth out passages among the rocks.	And his eyes seeth every precious thing.
He bindeth the streams that they trickel not.	And the thing that it hid bringeth he forth to light.

But apart from the manufacture of salt and the working of these copper mines, which were most of the time in the hands of the enemies of Israel, we have no important mines in the country itself and no pictures connected with mining have been found. Both for metallurgy and for mining the Israelites seem to have had recourse to foreign experts if needed, even for such related projects as the Siloah tunnel constructed at Jerusalem during the reign of King Hiskia (727—699 B.C.) or the metal basins for the Temple.

Like Palestine, *Syria and Mesopotamia* had a few mines and placers of local importance, but their needs for mineral products were amply covered by imports from the Armenian mountains and the Caucasus beyond as well as from India, Oman and *Asia Minor*, which is still a country rich in mineral products. The geology of these districts is not too well known and few authoritative books dealing with these regions have been published (35). In many cases it is not easy to establish to what date certain mines go back nor has a search been made for abandoned mines. In the classical period many mines in this district were famous, some of which were very old and even exhausted by the time such authors as Strabo or Herodotus described them.

This is even more true for our knowledge of early mining in *India* and the Far East. We know that Indian metal mining was well-developed in the days of Alexander the Great. Copper was mined early in various parts of the Daccan. In Râjasthân and in the Western Himalayas, gold-mining yielded good profits and even iron-mining is said to have been started fairly early, but the few data will have to be examined critically, before we can write a sketch of early Indian mining (35a) though it must have been an important industry during the last few centuries B.C. for the Arthaśâstra mentions "superintendents of the mines".

In *Kurdistan*, whence many ores came to Mesopotamia as we know from cuneiform texts, were the famous silver mines of Arghana Maden, the "Alybe in Cappadocia, the birthplace of silver" mentioned by Strabo (36). In Comana Pontica (Tokat) zinc-ores were mined (37) and the Chalybes of Pontus were the earliest iron-smiths (38). In Mysia there were argentiferous lead-ores and the iron of Mount Ida (39). Copper mines near Adramyttium and Pyrrha are recorded by Strabo (40). Gold- and silver-mines are reported in Phrygia, in the Troad and near Abydos (41), the gold placers of the Pactolus were very old (42) as well as the gold mining in the Tmolus Mountains near Sardis (43). Near Smyrna argentiferous lead ores were found and in the neighbourhood of Ephesus there were celebrated cinnabar-mines (44). Caria was famous for its sards, sardonyx, carneole and rock-crystal; Galatia for its crystal and onyx. Cilicia had silver-mines at Zephyrium (Cape Lisan), which is probably the "Tunni" mentioned in Assyrian inscriptions, but copper, lead and iron-ores too were mined in this region.

Cyprus was of course one of the early producers of copper, mining started probably as early as 2500 B.C. and it was already famous in Homeric times. Its importance in the story of copper will be discussed in a later volume (Vol. IX). Later the island figured as a producer of iron ores too.

Modern surveys of these Cyprian mines seems to indicate that neither the Romans nor their predecessors followed any definite plan or system in locating or driving gallaries and stopes into the ore. Much was left to chance and to the judgement of the slaves with probable instructions to mine solely in the better and richer ore. During modern operations cores of reconsolidated ancient waste fillings were often encountered. In some cases the reconsolidation of waste has become so complete as to form a hard rock rib. These ribs have been definitely identified as filling, only after finding particles of foreign matter such as wood, or charcoal remnants of wood, pieces of baskets or occasional iron tools, protected from corrosion by being tightly embedded in impervious clay-waste. Most of the ancient "filling" is in small ribs and not in massive blocks. This indicates that filling was placed in old preexisting galleries as a convenient means of getting rid of it and not as part of a program for supporting the ground in galleries and stopes as in modern practice.

Ventilation must have presented a problem to the ancients and it is quite probable that when the air became too foul and gaseous they merely abandoned working and moved to another site. The Romans had inlet and outlet ways; their galleries however were too small to permit two men to pass each other, particularly if they were carrying a load. The mine at Skouriotissa located on Phougassa hill may have been abandoned for lack of ventilation facilities for "phougass" means "smoke" or "fume" and conditions may have become too unhealthy for work. Even today at Skouriotissa ventilation presents an ever-present and engrossing problem.

The island of *Crete*, though the home of the Dactyles "who discovered both the use of fire and what the metals copper and iron are, as well as the means of working them" (45), did not figure on the list of important early mining districts. Still the island contains various smaller outcrops which may have invited itinerant smiths (such as are mentioned in Linear B inscriptions) to wander and produce some copper, lead and iron for local use. The search for such outcrops and ancient slags may yield results beyond local importance, but it is far from completed. Mosso reported a "prehistoric copper mine" near Chrysocamino, but Mr. Michael Diallinas, an engineer from Heraklion who visited the spot reports that the "mine" is a natural cave, which never contained ore and that there was a slag heap at some distance which points to some short-lived activities of itinerant smiths, which may not date back more than a few centuries only. There is, however a "copper belt" in southern central Crete running East to West, where malachite stained rocks abound in a region important in Minoan times. Still no early copper workings have been traced there yet. The other "copper belt" runs from N. to S. from the region of Chania down to the S. coast and over to Gavdos. In this western part of Crete modern efforts to mine copper have failed, but both these efforts and the destructions wrought by the Germans during the Second World War have destroyed many traces of older mines, still alive in the folk tales and often corroborated with the finds of ancient shafts, lamps, etc. acc. to Diallinas. Galena and barytes supplies ample for local use were found in veins at Ano Vlasamonero and there seems to have been some exploitation of galena at the south-eastern extremity of the island, near Molybdocamino where furnaces are reported on the beach near an ancient and almost submerged settlement called Ampelos, where lead is still pillaged for bird shot and fishing. Iron ores were certainly abundantly available for local production, e.g. 1) specular haematite in the Kera-Lasithi Mts. near ancient Minoan settlements; 2) Limonite in the Sises-Fodele-Rogdia region, with traces of Minoan exploitation in the latter case, but mostly Hellenistic and Roman open-cast mining at Sises (Sisai) and Panormon. Further deposits at Schines (where limonite was actually mined recently) and Rabdoucha have not been investigated for traces of more ancient exploitation, it seems. On the island of *Samos*, which is credited with the invention of casting copper and bronze and that of forging iron statues, copper and iron were indeed mined as well as lead-ores and the "Samian earth" used by potters. *Rhodes* was famous for its manufacture of white lead and copper acetate from lead and copper, but its mining was unimportant.

Early mining in Greece proper will be discussed in our chapter on Greek mining. Here we want to point out that metallurgy, and hence mining too, was definitely practised in the *East Balkan Peninsula* at the end of the Neolithic Period, probably introduced by miners and prospectors moving up from Anatolia and gradually working their way up the Danube valley to initiate the Early Danubian Bronze Age. They smelted gold, copper and tin. In Bulgaria many mines were found (46) dating from the Helladic period and influence from the Aegean and Asia Minor is obvious in the finds. The native Copper Age in the Eastern Balkans was an independent growth, no Danubian influences have been traced there. Copper, gold and silver mining continued in these regions through Roman into modern times.

Further to the West we find Bronze Age mines in Hungary, Austria,

Germany, France, Spain, Portugal and Great Britain. In *Western Hungary* there were copper mines near Velem St. Vid (47), where quartz-lenses containing azurite and malachite were mined and easily broken by fire-setting. Native copper in the Tisza valley probably led to the recognition of the copper ore. About 25 miles away are richer deposits of malachite at Banyá and Vörösvágás. Here were found rubbing stones and pounding stones to crush the ore and to separate the desired copper minerals. At the foot of the mountains antimonite is found. Here cakes of copper contain 1.3—18.1% of antimony. In the same mountain lenses of quartz contain iron carbonate in the form of the easily reducible siderite.

There was an important centre of copper mining at *Mitterberg* (Tirol 45 KM south of Salzburg, which flourished from 1600 B.C. to 800 B.C.

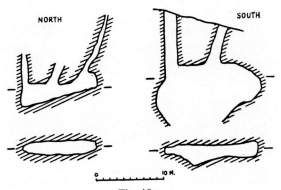

Fig. 10.
Sections of prehistoric coppermines at Viehhofen
(After Kyrle)

but continued its production up to the second century of our era, like the copper mines of the Kelchalpe near Kitzbühel to the west of Mitterberg, but also over 1500 M up in the mountains. The various mines in this part of Tirol have been thoroughly investigated (48).

The ancient copper mines of Mitterberg were rediscovered in 1827 through their extensive slagheaps. The copper of this mine with its slight nickel content supplied the demands of the nearby Bronze Age settlements such as the pile-dwellings at Mondsee. The series of shafts, now marked by firs, the "Bingenzüge", follow the main Josephi gallery over a 1000 M. By fire-setting the surface lode was followed into the mountain to a depth of 70—100 M below the slope. Some stopes were 3—5 M wide and 25—30 M long. The vein of ore was lost at a bifurcation, but it was picked up again by striking left and right of the line of shafts. These works seem later, some of the shafts are still carefully covered up. May be this part of the mine was still working when the invasions or migrations stopped the work, which seems to have been left rather spontaneously.

The cover rocks of Mitterberg were strong and water in the galleries preserved even wooden relics. Some tunnels were so carefully closed that they defied discovery until 1865! The stone hammers, pounding stones and rubbers for crushing or were mostly made of local sandstone obtained by fire-setting. Ventilation was served by sloping galleries or by two or more shafts (1—2 M in diameter) connecting with a single level. Access to the mine was achieved by using notched tree-

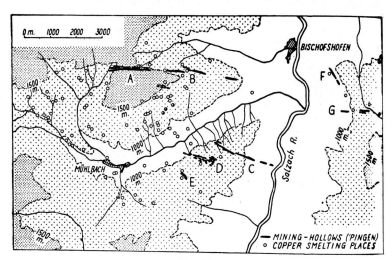

Fig. 11.
Map showing the relationship between mining and smelting
in the Mühlbach- Bischofshofen area, Salzburg
(After Zschokke & Preuschen)

stems. The galleries, up to 100 M in length, were sometimes timbered where the stone was soft, moss and clay being squeezed between the boards. The ore was detached by fire-setting, the water used to disintegrate the heated rock being introduced by launders (throughs) of hollowed half tree-stems and by buckets. Remains of splinter-lights and wood for fire-setting were found at various places in the mine. Miner's lamps all date from the classical period. Most of the tools were cast in bronze. The crushed ore was graded or sieved in wooden riddles with hazel-twigs forming the meshes. Leather bags and wooden troughs served to bring up the ore. The smelting of the ore was very efficient for the slag mostly contains only $\frac{1}{4}\%$ of copper, though some of the slag-heaps may have been resmelted later.

At *Kitzbühel*, where the rock is not a "Grauwacke" but a rather brittle slate, timbering was much more elaborate. In other copper mines in this region (Einödberg, Viehhofen) we find the same disposition. These copper mines were contemporaneous with copper mines of the same type in Wales, Cork (Eire), and Spain. In Eastern Tirol the mining and smelting of pyrites and other copper ores in the valley of the Iser and the region of Matrei seems to date from the early Hallstatt period (600 B.C.) and continued until the days of the Senator Popaius (second century AD) who erected his statue there.

In *Italy* Etruria and the port of Populonia were the centres of early

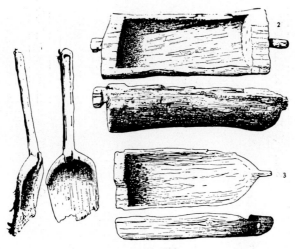

Fig. 12.
Wooden gear from prehistoric salt and copper mines
in the Austrian Alps (After Andrae)

mining activities (49), mostly near Monte Rombolo and Monte Valerio. In Val Temperino smelting furnaces of a type akin to the older pottery kilns were found as well as logs and charcoal. The ore worked was azurite and malachite and in other regions nearby chalcopyrite, blende and galena. Later in the Iron Age Populonia became important as the port where the Elban iron ore was landed to be smelted.

Tin-mining was of course most important in Bronze Age Europe (50). Mostly placers were worked in the way still familiar to Agricola

TABLE VIII

Ancient Terms for various Salts

English	Egyptian	Sumerian	Accadian
		SALT (SODIUM CHLORIDE)	
salt	{ hm3. t (III. 94. 1) { bsn (I. 475.11)?	MUN (ªMUD)	tâbtu (Hebrew melah)* (aban dâme)
(stone of the blood)			
rocksalt, halite	—	MUN-KUR	tâbat šadî
sal gemma	—	MUN-KÙ-GA	tâbtu ellitu
red sal gemma	—	MUN-Ú-MU-UN	tâbat amâni
river salt		MUN-EME-ŠAL-LA (LIM)	tâbat emesalli (salt of fine taste)
deposits of salts		IM-GÚ-EN-NA	hâpu (qadût šikani)
			*Coptic ϩⲙⲟⲩ
		POTASH	
Potash (ashes)	—	ŠIKA-IM-ŠU RIN-NA	iṭranu
		NATRON (NATURAL CARBONATE OF SODA)	
natron	nṭry (II. 366. 8)	(Hebrew nether)	niṭiru, niṭru (Gr. nitron)
sal murale ("dust of the wall")	—	SAḪAR-ÚR	eper assurê
crude natron	ḥsmn (III. 162. 11)	—	—
purified crude natron	ḥsmn wᶜb (III. 163. 1)	—	—
natron from oases	ḥsmn n šḫt (III. 163. 2)	—	—
	{dr-kd (V. 474. 18) ?		
granular natron	{bd (I. 486. 5)	—	—
	ḥḥḥ (I. 471. 15)		

	Egyptian	Sumerian	Akkadian (Hebrew)
natron for purification	{ bsn (I. 475. 11) { św'b (IV. 67. 4)		—
("water (lye) of natron")	mw n ḥsmn (II. 51. 4)		—
NATURAL ALKALI (VEGETABLE)			
vegetable alkali (Salicornia) "horned alkali"	—	ᵘNAGA ᵘNAGA-SI	ᵘuḫûlu (Hebrew: gasûl) ᵘuḫûlu ḳarnânu
plant ashes used as alkali	—		{ ᵘuḫûlu ḳalâti { (Hebrew: kali, borith)
SALTPETRE (POTASSIUM NITRATE)			
nitrate of potash	—	ᶻᵃAN-NE (IZI)	mil'u
SAL AMMONIAC			
sal ammoniac ("sublimate of scrapings")	—	IM-KAL (-LA)	aklu (ḫaṣbu, ḫilṣu)
"soot from dung"	—	SAHAR-SIS	itru, iṭranu
ALUM			
alum	ibnw (I. 63. 8) imrw (I. 87. 19) (?)	IM-SAHAR-ZÁ-KUR-RA	gasbû (Hebrew: eriph) (Coptic ⲱⲃⲉⲛ) annuḫaru kitmu ᵃaban šikkati (ᵘkamun bîni)
white alum (refined?)	—	IM-SAHAR-BABBAR-KUR-RA	
black alum	inr n šn (IV. 501. 3) ?	IM-SAHAR-GE-KUR-RA	
alunite, alum stone ("lichen of the tamarisk")	—	ᵃDÙ-ŠUB-BA	
		—	

and Cancrinus (51). The most important tin-mines were in the mountains on the border of Saxony and Bohemia, the Fichtelgebirge, in certain parts of France such as the departements of Haute Vienne (where tin and gold were often produced together), Creuze, Allier and Morbihan (Bretagne), in Tuscany, in Asturias (northern Spain) and in Cornwall.

In *Spain and Portugal* there were large copper-mines in various sites (52), mainly in the Cerro Muriano, north-east of Cordoba, near Huelva, in Asturias, near Lerida and in the southern Portuguese province of Alemtojo. The copper mines of El Aramo (Asturias) were rediscovered in 1888. Here lodes of copper- and cobalt-ores in limestone have a strength of 30—200 cm. Fire-setting was used to follow the veins into the mountain, the galleries being narrow and polished by the hosts of miners, who crept in and out. Only stone tools were found, hammers weighing up to $9\frac{1}{2}$ Kgr., pounding and rubbing stones, horn picks, etc. but no metal tools have been discovered yet. Apart from splinters, twigs of resinous timber wound with greased strips of skin served as lights. The galleries slope slightly and they are reached by vertical shafts. Many bodies of miners were found here. The mines were probably worked in the early Bronze Age and then again in Roman times. Here again the shafts have been carefully hidden, probably when the work was stopped during an invasion or a war.

Iron Age mining is more or less a continuation of Bronze Age mining, the techniques evolve gradually and there is no significant break, though new and efficient techniques are introduced during the classical period. The great change is that more emphasis is laid on new ores and minerals not mined before on any large scale, such as iron ores and salt. Thus at Burgas (Bulgaria) copper-mining of an opencast, some 50 M long and 40 M deep, with shafts some 8—15 M apart followed a vein of malachite which yielded some 9% of copper, and at Velem St. Vid in Hungary the opencast mining of copper and antimony ores continued right through the Iron Age to produce an antimony-bronze. On the other hand the deeper siderite was now mined and smelted too, this increased the importance of this mining area. We shall find more examples of the quantitative increase of mining activities when we discuss the classical period.

The early salines and salt-deposits and their exploitation have been discussed elsewhere (53). There is no doubt that salt played an important part in Antiquity and the discovery of rock-salt was a valuable one for the economy of the inland population without access to the sea (54). In the Near East and along the coasts of the Mediterranean the production of salt continued along the well-established lines, the elaborate terminology of salt, potash, natron, saltpetre and alum (Table VIII) shows that this production held little mystery to them. Some of these salts like alum (55) were actually mined from opencast deposits as were the salts of the coastal region of the Dead Sea in Galen's days (56).

The type of salt-mine characteristic for the Early Iron Age (57) is found at Hallstatt, Hallein and Hall in Tirol, where rock-salt, together with hard, though masses of anhydrite, is found in Triassic rocks. These mines were rediscovered during the reign of the Empress Elizabeth and reopened in 1311, some say in 1280. The old workings had become filled up with salt muddy water, but they could be recognised by the wooden implements and timbering. The miners called the mountains the "Heidengebirge" as they believed that prehistoric men had mined here. We now know that the Celts have mined salt here from the early first millennium B.C. onwards. Following the veins of salt the miners drove sloping shafts (at an angle of 25—60° to the horizontal) down to depths of 150 M and at places even to 300—350 M. Timbering was used but then the climate was drier and there was less danger of flooding in those days.

When rich masses of salt were encountered, galleries were driven in various directions according to the yield, reaching as far as 390 M. from the adit-mouth and 100 M below the surface. The chambers in the salt were often up to 12 M wide and 1 M high, all carefully timbered. The tools, picks and chisels, were made of bronze and copper, the wooden hafts of the timber of the red beech, larch-wood being used for the timbering. Wooden mallets used for pounding the salt were found together with wooden shovels to load the salt into the leather bags to transport it out of the mine into the valley. No lamps were found, bundles of twigs seem to have served as torches.

Apart from the skeleton of a miner, killed in situ by the fall of the roof, a maple-wood platter used for meals was found, as well as clothing, caps and shoes. There seems to have been no special provision for ventilation and the waste material of the mine has disappeared. The wastage of picks must have been enormous as even today a miner uses up to ten picks (steel!) in an eight-hour shift, but no foundry for recasting the picks was discovered in situ.

4 Greek Mining

Greece was fairly rich in mineral wealth, if we may trust the classical authors, such as Herodotus, Thucydides, Pausanias, Strabo and others. Gold was mined at Siphnos, Thasos, Skapte Hyle, Datum, Crenides, Philippi, Pangaios and perhaps at Laurion. Silver was obtained from Laurion, Siphnos, Pangaios, Damastion (Epirus) and the Bermios-Pieria-Strymon region. Copper was found in Chalkis (Euboea), Delos, Seriphos, Argolis, Sikyon; iron in Euboea, the Tainaron peninsula, Boeotia, Andros, Keos, Kythnos, Gyaros, Seriphos, Melos (where sulphur was dug too); lead obtained from Laurion and Macedonia and coal was known to occur near Olympia, though it was not mined. Much of this information has been confirmed by modern research (58).

Only three authors gave somewhat more details about mining in the Greek homeland, Theophrastus in his work On Stones, Strato (who is said to have written a book on the mining tools and techniques (59)) and Philon, who wrote a book on metals (60), which is lost too.

It would seem that Greece was rather wealthy in gold during the Bronze Age, but that this metal grew rarer during the Iron Age. This gold, containing 8—25% of silver, was probably obtained from small local placers now abandoned. In Macedonia there was some copper production at Sacili and some of the gold-washings seem early, particularly in virgin fields, which were not the most productive in later times. Clement of Alexandria (61) has a curious passage stating that the Noropes, a Paeonian race, now called Noricanes, invented the working of copper and the refining of iron, but this is evidently a mistake and the Alpine copper district and the later Noricum must have been meant.

During the sixth century B.C. the search for gold in Macedonia was started again under Thasian and Athenian influence, encouraged by the expansion of the Macedonian state and its demand for gold. This continued into Roman times. During the Roman Empire there were attempts to produce stream gold in inner Macedonia and the Byzantine emperors looked still further north. The southern mines were worked again by the Slavonic kingdoms and there was great activity here during the reign of the Turks.

Sagui did some research on ancient mines in this region and we will quote some of his remarks on the Lipzada mines near Stageirus, the birth-place of Aristotle, which were known to have been worked in the times of Alexander the Great and which are supposed to have been opened up several centuries earlier. A main vein, some sixty feet thick, known for a length of about ten miles, strikes east-west and dips about 50° south. A great number of veins striking north-south cross this main vein. The deposits consist of manganese minerals at the top, and lower down first calcite with some pyrites and below this sulphides. Gold, silver, lead and a little copper could be obtained from the latter. The ancient miners worked principally the lodes situated at the crossing of the two series of veins, where far the richest ore was found, carrying an average of 15 dwts (23.3 gr.) of gold per Ton and sometimes about 1% of silver.

As a rule the ancient shafts were dug at the crossing of two veins and the lode followed downwards by a long series of somewhat irregular stopes, the country rock being left untouched where it was possible. The miners seem to have had a topographic method of planning the details of the underground working, since it would be impossible otherwise to understand why they made passages between two distant points and through barren rocks. By chisel and hammer they chased a cut about five inches deep and one inch wide along the profile of the tunnel front, and thus were able to cut the remaining rock easily, since one side of the cut was always free. A similar method of working was observed in the Bottino Mines in Italy by Sagui. Passage-ways are frequently so narrow that one wonders how miners of average size could get through, but then the miners of those days lived underground and came out to breathe the fresh air only once a week.

The subterranean abodes are still visible; large abandoned stopes were utilized as kitchens and sleeping chambers, where traces remain of fire-places, and holes still open in the country trock were used as cupboards and lamp-niches.

The ores were lifted by small skips hauled out by a rope, sometimes guided by a wheel placed against the rim of the shaft, but more frequently rubbing against the rock, where deep-graved flutings still show what painful toil this hauling was. Underground waters must have limited the mining under a certain depth. A tunnel, more than a mile long, some 20″ wide and 32″ high with some timbering in frames of three timbers to clear the workings of water is still in existence near Mademilako.

The copper objects, dating back to the earliest periods of Greek history, as well as the copper ingots recovered have different amounts of various impurities and this would go to show that often small local outcrops were worked, traces of which are still visible near Chalcis, Athens, Mycenae and on Seriphos, Paros and Syra. Later much copper must have been imported from the larger copper producers like Cyprus and Asia Minor. The traces of many of these local veins and small mines must have been obliterated until Greek mining started to expand rapidly in the Hellenistic world.

After Alexander the Great the demand for metals rose quickly in the Greece-dominated world. Gold, silver and copper were needed for the abundant and ever-increasing coinage of the time. Most Hellenistic monarchs hoarded gold and silver in the form of ingots or coins, and the temples and private persons followed suit. Copper was in large demand for plate, statues, furniture, toilet articles, tools, instruments and weapons. War, agriculture, transport and navigation absorbed the new metal, iron, in ever-increasing quantities. In many countries like Egypt the Iron Age did not start properly until the Hellenistic period.

The mineral resources of what used to be the Hellenistic world are only partly known and they have been unequally investigated. It is difficult to estimate the activity of the Hellenistic rulers in this field and to judge how many new mines they opened and how many older ones they worked more intensively. However we are certain that they did their best to develop all their mineral resources. The success of Philip II of Macedonia depended on his attempts to increase by prospecting and conquest the output of base and precious metals in his territories and his son Alexander pursued the same policy. He had a special mining engineer and prospector, a "metalleutes" (62), on his staff during his great expedition. This engineer, Gorgus by name, investigated the mineral resources of the kingdom of Sopeithes (near the modern Lahore) and found, besides salt mines, rich veins of silver and gold very primitively exploited by the Indians. He presented his report to Alexander and later published it in book form. No doubt Alexander organized a more systematic exploitation of such mines and Gorgus will not have been the only metalleutes in Alexander's army, who met with success in his prospecting operations.

In Greece there were apparently corporative professional fellowships working for the State in the field of mining, though in other parts of the Hellenistic world native men played a large part in the exploitation of mines. All the existing Greek mines were carefully worked long before the Hellenistic period and some of them, including the silvermines of Laurium, which we will discuss in detail later, were exhausted, very few had proved rich like Laurium. Most Greek cities therefore depended for their supply of metals on imports of ingots and bars of semi-refined metals. In Macedonia the mineral wealth was only just opened up, it was still large and far from being exhausted. King Perseus had much prospecting done and he worked his mines intensively (63). In the days of Philip II the fairly rich silver and gold mines of Chalcidice and the copper mines of Othrys (Thessaly) were newly discovered. The output of the Macedonian mines can be judged from the large booty (gold and silver) taken by the Romans when they conquered the country (64).

The Ptolemies of Egypt showed a similar energy and left little off value in the copper, gold and iron mines of the eastern desert, after abandoning such unprofitable mining as that in Sinai. During the period of their domination in Cyprus, they intensified mining there, and they may have done so in south-western Asia Minor and its silver and iron mines, but we have little data on this point. We know, however, from Strabo (65), that they had access to the iron mines of Cibyra.

It is true, that the Ptolemies worked mainly with condemned and criminals as miners. The pitiful conditions of these miners is given in two largely similar extracts from Agatarchides' lost writings (66), which show that some of the "criminals" working in the mines may have been political prisoners. Agatarchides' statements refer to the Baramia mine, where excavations were not following a regular plan but haphazardly followed the richer portion of the vein. Here and there a pillar is left to support the side, or an occasional stall, packed with deads, erected for the same purpose or as a means of disposing of waste rock. The excavations reach a very hard bottom rock at about 100—200 feet. This is the account of Agatarchides:

"The metal rocks which are called gold-bearing are intensely black, but among them is produced a stone than which nothing is whiter. Of these mountains those which are rugged and have an altogether hard nature they burn with wood; and when they are softened by fire they experiment on them and cut the loosened stone into small pieces with an iron chisel. But the principal work is that of the artificer who is skilled in stones. This man shows to the diggers the track of the metal, and apportions the whole work to the needs of the wretched men in the following manner: Those whole in strength and age break the places where shines the white stone with iron cutting hammers. They use not skill but brute force, and then they drive in the rock many galleries, not straight but branching in all directions, like the roots of a tree, wherever the rock pregnant of gold may diverge. These men thus, with candles bound to their foreheads, cut the rock, the white stone showing the direction for their labours. Placing their bodies in every conceivable position, they throw the fragments to the ground, — not each one according to his strength, but under the eye of the overseer, who never ceases from blows. Then boys, creeping into the galleries dug by the men, collect with great labour the stones, which have been broken off, and carry them out to the mouth of the mine. Next, from these a crowd of old and sickly men take the stone and lay it before the pounders. These are strong men of some thirty years of age, and they strenuously pound the rock with an iron pestle in mortars cut out of stone, and reduce it until the largest piece is no bigger than a pea. Then they measure out to others the pounded stone in the same quantity as they have received it. The next task is performed by women, who, alone, or with their husbands and relations, are placed in enclosures. Several mills are placed together in a line, and standing three together at one handle, filthy and almost naked, the women lay to at the mills until the measure handed to them is completely reduced. And to every one of those who bear this lot death is preferable to life."

On the other hand we have evidence that other mines were worked with statute labour. In Papyrus Flinders Petrie II. 43. 3 (which dates from 241/240 B.C.) Harmachos demands a check-up of his work in the copper-mines of Birket Karûn (Fayyum) by the "architecton" Theodorus in order to prove that he did fulfill his contractual work of his "pleroma" and that his boss Hermogenes demanded extra work from them!

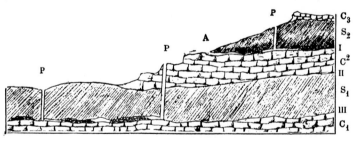

Fig. 13.
The geological strata at Laurium (After Ardaillon)

The Seleucid kingdom was self-sufficient in its early days, though its centre was poor in minerals, but even this situation changed for the worse as they lost almost all the rich mining districts of Asia Minor to local Anatolian kings, the central part becoming part of the Pergamene kingdom, the ring of mining districts from the south-eastern Euxine coast through Armenia to the Caucasus falling in the hands of the Mithridatids of Pontus, who knew how to turn these minerals into wealth. From this mining district we have the cynical report by Strabo on the realgar mines (67) reading: "Mount Sandaracurgium (Mount Realgar) is hollowed out in consequence of the mining done there, since the workmen have excavated great cavities beneath it. The mine used to be worked by publicans, who used as miners the slaves sold in the market because of his crimes; for, in addition to the painfulness of the work, they say that the air in the mines is both deadly and hard to endure on account of the grievous odour of the ore, so that the workmen are doomed to a quick death. What is more, the mine is often left idle because of the unprofitableness of it, since the workmen are not only more than two hundred in number, but are continually spent by disease and death," and also the report by Apollonius Rhodius, who in his Argonautica (68) gives a vivid picture of the "industrialization" in these mining districts of Pontus, the land of the Chalybes "who knew nothing of agriculture and cattle-breeding".

After reading the data on Hellenistic mining the general impression is that the basic process, tools and implements used were all known in the fourth century B.C. at Laurium, improvements being achieved on minor points only in later periods. The essential mining tools like iron gads, picks, hammers, crowbars, spades and hoes had approximately the same form and were used for the same purpose at Laurium and in the Hellenistic, or even the Roman world. The more important later improvements were the machines used for drainage purposes and possibly a more extensive use of optical geodetical instruments of the type of Heron's dioptra for surveying purposes. But the processes of crushing the ore, washing it and even the roasting, smelting and cupellation-furnaces differed little. If it is true that the modern type of bellows with boards and a valve was introduced in the Hellenistic period, it does not seem to have been used extensively, no evidence of it has yet been found in excavations.

When we now turn to the main fount of Hellenistic mining, the *silver mines of Laurium* we have not only a number of detailed and careful studies on both the technical and the social and economic aspects of mining in this district of Attica (69), but also much information from literary, epigraphical and archaeological sources.

The beginnings of the mining at Laurium go back beyond 1500 B.C., but the main period of activity began only in the days of Solon (594/3 B.C.) when the mines were not yet very important. In the days of the Peisistratidae (561—510) the income from the mines begins to figure on the Athenian budget. From this period the irregular, semi-circular shafts, about 2 M in diameter, seem to date. During the Persian wars and after many new, rectangular shafts (from $1.25 \times 1.50 \times 1.40 \times 1.90$ M) were sunk to depths of up to 35 M with galleries striking out at 10 M. depth or lower. The earlier parts of these shafts were sloping, but after a few meters they became vertical. During the Periclean period new shafts sunk sloped $10°$ and penetrated stepwise into the rocks.

During the war between Athens and Sparta Dekeleia, the mining centre, was invested (413 B.C.) and the miners-slaves revolted. After 400 slow recovery took place because of the lack of capital and labour but by 350 Xenophon reports full activity again. The shafts now went down to 110 M. and air shafts (50×80 cm) were now needed to ventilate the mines, may be with fires at the bottom of the shafts to induce upwards draught in such ventilating shafts. The older pillar and stall working had left supporting rock pillars mostly chosen in barren rock or in low-grade ore and packing was used to support the ore. However, a law of 339 B.C. makes it clear that the later miners broke out such pillars to divest them of ore. Galleries were now constructed at the

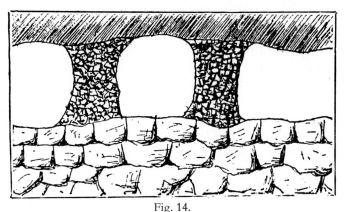

Fig. 14.
The "mesokrineis" of the Laurium mines (After Ardaillon)

50 M level and large spaces were excavated but this could not stop the severe Macedonian competition which made itself felt by the end of the fourth century and the decline of mining at Laurium set in. About 250 B.C. the old slags were reworked to recover lead and silver by more efficient smelting methods then in use.

The revolt of the mining slaves in 102 B.C. put an end to organized mining at Laurium but spurious mining activities continued until the end of the first century of our era. After many centuries work began again in 1864 when the ancient slags were resmelted, first the scoria, then also the "ekbolades" (rejected poor ore) and the "plynites" (residue of ancient washing tables). Then in 1865 new shafts were sunk and iron and zinc ores mined.

Ardaillon has given a detailed picture of the geology of the Laurium region. Three beds of limestone or marble (some of Penthelic quality) are separated by two strata of mica-schist, the whole being here and there transversed by dikes of granite and gabbro. The silver-bearing

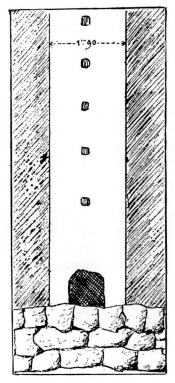

Fig. 15.
Section of a shaft at Laurium showing the ledges for
the rungs of the ladder (After Ardaillon)

galena the miners were after is mostly concentrated at the junctions, more especially at the tops of the lower beds of limestone. At these contacts one usually finds the galena covered by iron ore and resting on zinc ore. The galena (spec. gravity 7. 4—7. 6) is very rich in silver, containing from 1200 to 4000 grams of silver per Ton of ore. The zinc ore is zinc blende (sulphide) and cerussite, or calamine (carbonates), the iron ores found are pyrites and oxides. The third contact zone is the richest, but it was hardly touched by the ancients. The haematite was worked here and there for the manufacture of iron tools and implements used on the spot (Fig. 13).

The earliest workings were open-casts with short practically horizontal tunnels (adits). Then over 2000 shafts connected with galleries were sunk without touching the lower and richer contact-zone, which was not marked by an outcrop and which could only be discovered by inductive geology in the nineteenth century. The ancients used the "follow-your-lode" method common in their days and they did not hesitate to abandon their shafts and galleries if they had given up hope to strike the profitable vein a second time.

The shafts at Laurium had a very regular rectangular section (1. 9 × 1.3 M) but at every 10 M the cross-section is turned some 8—10°, thus giving the shaft a screw-like aspect from the top. These stages seem to depend on the method of access, a series of ladders or notched tree-trunks being fixed to the sides to leave the middle of the shafts free for hauling up the ore with rope and pulley. The deepest shaft is 117.6 M, the limit of mining being the water-table, which is here approximately at sea-level.

At the contact-zones, galleries, (1 M high and 0.75 M wide) were cut. The shafts were sunk in pairs and parallel galleries were driven from them with frequent cross-cuts between such galleries to ensure ventilation. The galleries in some cases run roughly up a dip or slope and this further aids the ventilation. If rich bodies of ore were encountered they were stoped over- and under-hand, e.g. new stopes were made above or below the previous ones. Branch galleries were cut leading to the main roads at the necessary slope to reach the desired spot. From some stopes as much as 100.000 Tons of ore have been taken. In such stopes the "pillar and stall" method was applied, the poorer ore or barren rock being left as pillars, "mesokrineis", to support the roof of the stope. Grooves cut in the side of galleries point to doors used in directing the ventilating air. The draft was ensured by lighting fires under the sloping ventilating shafts. These were sunk to intercept a vertical working shaft but just before their normal junction a horizontal cut was made to be used as a platform for a fire. Pliny also mentions fanning with cloth to improve ventilation. The hammers used had the shape of the modern prospector's hammer, picks with wooden handles, chisels and wedges were found. Each miner seems to have had his lamp, niches to hold them being cut in the face of the rock. We hear from inscriptions that a miner averaged some 4.50 M per month when sinking a shaft. At Laurium timbering was not generally needed, but if so mortise and tenon joints were used between props and lintels.

Mining at Laurium was carried on so intensively that by the time of Strabo the wooded surface of the region had been completely bared to provide timber for the mines and charcoal for the smelting of the ore. Bromehead has pointed out the great resemblance between the evidence obtained at Laurium and Japanese mining as illustrated by several scrolls, dating from the seventeenth century.

5. *Roman Mining*

At the time of its greatest extent the Seleucid kingdom had been the first civilised state to be able to supply all its requirements in metals. In certain cases the enormous cost of land transport made it cheaper to import from abroad, for instance to import tin from the Atlantic seaboard or Bohemia instead of mining it in Drangiana.

The Roman Empire was self-sufficient and more fortunately contained many large rivers and a sea suitable for navigation and commerce. Hence they too could obtain all the metals they wanted and even exported them to peoples outside the Empire, gold to India, silver and copper to Germanic tribes in the north. It is evident from a table which Davies published some thirty years ago (Table IX) that the Romans knew and worked practically all the quarries and mines still in production in the territory of the former Roman Empire. They used the methods their predecessors had evolved and added such innovations as they found in other areas and which they believed suitable. The early Italian adventurers in Spain adopted the native methods readily. In Laurium and Macedonia the Roman contractors, who took over in the second century B.C., found an old tradition of the proper way of exploring and exploiting ore-bodies, with suitable mining tools, crushing and washing machinery and smelting techniques fully developed. Egypt taught them gold prospecting and the treatment of reef gold by pounding, grinding and washing. The Etruscans in the Italian home-land has already developed certain very complicated metallurgical processes like liquation (70).

Bromehead remarks that "the Romans, strange to say, do not appear to have excercized the ingenuity, for which they were famous, in the branch of metallurgy, but everywhere seem to have adopted, with

Table IX

Alphabetical List of the most important Roman Mines in Europe
(after O. Davies, Trans. Inst. Min. Met. 1934)

P = Pre-Roman, of which

    BA = Bronze Age, which ends at different times in different places, but as
    a whole in the last thousand years B.C.;

    IA = Iron Age (pre-Roman).

R = Roman; in Central Europe this implies the first to fourth centuries A.D.,
and does not mean Roman occupation.

M = Post-Roman, normally fourteenth to sixteenth centuries A.D., as little is
known of mining in the Dark Ages, and mines whose principal period of
working was subsequent to the sixteenth century have been specially noted.

Alderley Edge	Cheshire	P	Copper.
Aljustrel	S. Portugal	BA and R	Copper.
Allendale	Durham	M	Lead.
Aramo	N.W. Spain	P and perhaps R	Copper.
Arksib	Algeria	R or M	Lead.
Astoescoria	Basses Pyrénées, France.	Very early R	Copper and silver
Avala	N. Serbia	P	Cinnabar.
Babe	N. Serbia	R and M	Silver.
Ballycastle	Antrim	M	Coal.
Ballydehob	Cork	Supposed to be BA, perhaps as late as M.	Copper. Copper.
Batignano	Tuscany	Ia or M	Copper, silver and lead.
Beauport Park	Sussex	R	Iron.
Beraun	Bohemia	M	Silver.
Bibracte	Nièvre, France	IA	Iron.
Blagaj	N.W. Bosnia	R	Iron.
Bleiburg	Carinthia	M	Lead.
Boicza	Transylvania	R	Gold.
Bottino	Tuscany	IA and M	Lead.
Campiglia Marittima	Tuscany	IA	Copper and silver
Carnon	Cornwall	P	Tin.
Cartagena	S.E. Spain	R and probably IA.	Silver and lead.
Cassandra	GreekMacedonia	Ia and perhaps R	Gold and silver.
Centenillo	S. Spain	R	Silver and lead.
Cerro Muriano	S. Spain	R and probably P	Copper.
Charterhouse	Somerset	R	Lead and silver.
Chitcomb	Sussex	R	Iron.
Come Chaudron	Nièvre, France	IA	Iron.
Cornacchino	Tuscany	P	Cinnabar.
Çorok Su	W. Armenia	R and M	Gold and silver.
Craigy Park	Monmouth	M	Coal.
Crvena Zemlja	Bosnia	R	Gold.
Cythnos	Aegean	R	Iron.
Czebe-Magura	Transylvania	R	Gold.

Dabern	Pomerania	? IA...........	Iron.
Darren	Montgomery ...	? R	Copper.
Denaïra...........	Algeria	R or M	Lead.
Dobrevo..........	Macedonia	M.............	Lead and silver.
Domus Novas	Sardinia	? R	Lead and silver.
Drususkippel......	Hesse	M.............	Iron.
Eisenberg.........	Pfalz	R	Iron.
Sto. Estevão	S. Portugal.....	P (probably BA) and R.	Copper.
Eule	Bohemia	M.............	Gold.
Fichtelgebirge	Bavaria	Probably only M	Tin.
Flumini Maggiori ..	Sardinia	R and M	Perhaps silver or gold.
Friedrichssegen	Hesse	R	Silver and lead.
Friesach	Carinthia.......	M.............	Silver.
Fucinaia	Tuscany	IA	Copper.
Goellheim	Pfalz	? R	Copper.
Gogofau..........	Carmarthen	Probably R.....	Gold.
Gran Cava	Tuscany	IA	Copper and Iron.
Great Doward.....	Monmouth.....	R	Iron.
Grueben..........	Silesia	M.............	Iron.
Hallstatt	Austria	IA	Salt.
Hastenrath	Westphalia	R or M	Lead.
Haya	N. Spain	P and R........	Copper.
Iglesias	S.W. Sardinia...	M.............	Silver and lead.
Jebel Serdj	Tunis	? R	Copper, lead and silver.
Jebel Uenza	Tunis	? M...........	Copper.
Kalavaso	Cyprus	IA and R	Copper.
Karacs	Transylvania ...	R and probably IA.	Gold.
Kayl	Luxemburg	Probably R.....	Iron.
Kenshala	N. Africa	? R	
Korabia	Transylvania ...	R	Gold.
Kremnitz	W. Slovakia	M.............	Gold.
Krinovski Utara ...	S. Russia.......	P	Copper.
Krivoj Rog	S. Russia.......	P	Copper.
St. Laurent le Minier	Gard, France ...	R or M	Lead and silver.
Laurium	Attica, Greece ..	IA and early R	Silver and lead.
Lebertal	H. Rhin, France	M.............	Silver.
Linares	S. Spain	R	Silver and lead.
Lindale	Lancashire	M.............	Iron.
Llanymynech......	Denbigh	R	Copper.
Ludres	Meurthe, France	Probably R.....	Iron.
Luttmersen	Harz, Germany .	IA	Iron.
Macot	Savoie, France ..	Probably R.....	Lead and silver.
Majdanpek........	N.E. Serbia	R and perhaps IA and M.	Copper.
Markirch	H. Rhin, France.	M and perhaps IA.	Silver.
Massa Marittima ...	Tuscany	IA and M	Copper and silve
Maubach	Westphalia	R	? Zinc or lead.

Melle............	Deux Sèvres, France	R and M	Silver and lead.
Minas de Mouros ..	Portugal	R............	Gold.
Mitsero..........	Cyprus	IA and perhaps R	Copper.
Mitterberg........	Austria	BA............	Copper.
Moenchmotschelnitz	Silesia	M............	Iron.
Monte Catini......	Tuscany	M............	Copper.
Monte Rombolo...	Tuscany	P	Tin.
Mraçaj	Bosnia.........	Ia and possibly also M.	Gold.
Muehlhausen......	Harz, Germany .	IA	Iron.
Nantyrarian.......	Montgomery ...	? R	Copper.
Neu-Moldova	Banat..........	R	Copper and perhaps lead.
Nointel..........	Oise, France....	P	Flint.
Ocha.............	Euboea, Aegean	At least mainly M.	Iron, copper and lead.
Palazuelos	S. Spain	R	Silver and lead.
H. Petros	Andros, Aegean	IA	Iron and perhaps copper.
Pimolisa..........	N. Anatolia	R	Arsenic.
Ploermel..........	Morbihan, France	P, probably BA	Tin.
Pongau...........	Salzkammergut .	M and possibly R	Gold.
Posadas...........	S. Spain	R	Silver.
Postenje	W. Serbia	M............	Lead.
Reichenhall	Bavaria	M............	Salt.
Ruda.............	Transylvania ...	R	Gold.
Rudic	Moravia	IA	Iron.
Rudnice	S. Serbia	M............	Silver and lead.
Rudnik	C. Serbia.......	R and M	Silver.
Sana	N. Bosnia	IA, R and M ...	Iron.
Schemnitz	W. Slovakia....	M............	Silver.
Scuriotissa	Cyprus	IA and R	Copper and probably precious metals.
Serra da Vallongo..	N. Portugal	Probably R.....	Gold or silver.
Siedlemin	Posen	IA or early R ...	Iron.
Siedlikowo........	Posen	R	Iron.
Siphnos	Aegean........	IA	Lead, silver and gold.
Soli	Cyprus	IA and R	Copper and copper salts.
Sotiel Coronada....	S. Spain	R	Copper and silver
Srebrenica	E. Bosnia	R and M	Silver and lead.
Tarxdorf.	Silesia	IA	Iron.
Rio Tinto.........	S. Spain	IA and R	Precious metals and copper.
Tireboli	N.E. Anatolia ..	R and M	Copper and silver
Trepça	S. Serbia	M and perhaps R	Silver and lead.
Tuklat............	Bohemia	R	Iron.
Urville	Lorraine	M............	Iron.

Vaulry	H. Vienne, France	P and perhaps R	Tin.
Verespatak........	Transylvania ...	Perhaps IA, R, very probably M.	Gold.
Vulkoj	Transylvania ...	R	Gold.
Zsil	Transylvania ...	R	Gold.

little if any modifications, the furnaces and processes in use by the peoples of the countries they subjugated". This is hardly fair to the Roman mining and metallurgy experts, who have rather neatly adopted well-developed native methods suitable for the local ore, but who can be shown to have introduced methods from elsewhere should this be profitable and needed. The truth is rather that, generally speaking, the Romans were not very deeply interested in mining and metallurgy. Many believed it fit for slaves, prisoners or "damnati" only. Tacitus and Varro argue that it had bad effects on agriculture, the backbone of Italian society and Pliny (71) agrees with these words: "We penetrate into Earth's bowels, and we seek wealth in the abode of the Dead, as though she were not sufficiently kind and fertile, wherever the foot of man is set. But least of all do we search for means of healing, for how few in their digging are inspired by the desire to cure! And yet these she furnished on the surface in the shape of fruits, for she is a bounteous and willing giver of all things that are for our good."

On the other hand copper mines were still being worked between Populonia and Volterra, as well as tin, lead and zinc ores, so that the Etruscan bronze was to some extent a home product. Then "off the city of Tyrrhenia known as Populonium there is an island which men call Aethaleia (Elba). It is about a hundred stades from the coast and received the name it bears from the smoke (aithalos) which lies so thick about it. For the island possesses a great amount of iron-rock, which they quarry in order to smelt and cast and thus secure the iron" (72). Indeed the slag-heaps of Populonia belong to the last four centuries of the Roman Republic, an average of 10.000 Tons of iron ore being treated per year.

Mining in Italy was prohibited by a Senatus consultum, Pliny tells us (73) that it is certainly not due to a lack of ores for "she (Italy) is inferior to no country in abundance of mineral products". This bit of national pride cannot hide the poverty of the Italian ore deposits, mines had already given out in Etruscan days. Probably the Senatus consultum was imposed at the request of the equestrian contractors who took over the Spanish mines. The Senate may also have wished to preserve the Italian supplies in case Spain were ever cut off and the competitive circumstances in Italy must have been bad after the conquest of so many regions where rich ores, some of which had already been exploited earlier, were to be found.

However, the mines in Elba continued in operation and in the north of the peninsula, beyond the river Po, gold mines were worked at Victumulae (near Vercellae) for a while, which the publicans exploited under a provision not to use over 5000 labourers, these were probably the gold mines worked by the Salassi. The gold mines of Spain remained State property and it is quite probable that they alone yielded more silver and gold for Rome during the second part of the second century B.C. than had come from all indemnities and booty collected later during the first century. Italiotes had joined in when the Celts discovered rich placer-gold in Noricum, but they were driven out. However, Rome continued to be the chief market for gold and conquering Noricum later became the producer too.

Mining seems to have been predominantly a state affair in the former Hellenistic kingdoms and in Spain only during the Republic. In Gaul the nobility exploited the mines on their domains freely. In Republican Rome most state-mines were leased to private capitalists, mostly united in corporations. In Spain and Sardinia mines were often worked by slaves but certainly not exclusively and many of those engaged in the mining operations were experts and freemen. In the new provinces like Britain, Noricum, Dalmatia, Pannonia and Dacia exploitation was designed to suit local conditions. Sometimes exploitation was left to "conductores" (Noricum, Dalmatia and Gaul), sometimes to small private persons whose undertakings were checked and taxed by publicans. Quarries were left to "redemptores", who received a fee on the total output, being checked by civil or military authorities. In some cases (Egypt) there was direct state-exploitation with the help of prisoners and slaves. Hence contrary to many general statements, slavery played but a minor part in Roman mining.

Most Roman metallurgical centres had to import their raw materials, mostly from Spain, Gaul and the Danube-region, the mines of the East were of lesser importance except those of gold and silver. The iron ore of Elba was of course still worked on the mainland too. Aquilea in northern Italy became an important centre for the production of arms and agricultural tools importing its pig-iron from Noricum.

In the early Empire the return of the state mines could hardly have been considerable since most of them had been sold. From the times of Tiberius it had been the policy of the emperors to get possession of the mines of precious metals and no doubt they belonged to the imperial treasury by Vespasian's days. It would seem that the Fiscus expected about 50% of the ore in new shafts. Spain remained the most important mining centre from late Republican days to the end of the Empire, the profits being considerable as Pliny and other authors tell us. Trajan in 106 A.D. acquired the profits of the Dacian gold mines. In Noricum and Dalmatia the mines were state-property, they belonged to the Fiscus and the Roman state-contractors or "conductores" who handled these mines resided at Aquilea. The Dacian mines proved as important to the Danube army as the Gallic mines were to the Rhine army during the later Empire.

The most flourishing period of Roman mining was the late Republic and early Empire. During that period new provinces were explored, their gold-placers skimmed and systematic mining operations undertaken. There was a general tendency during the later Empire to make all mines and quarries state property and to lease them to small entrepreneurs, this policy of Hadrian and his successors is also traceable in the "laws of Vipasca", the regulations for certain Spanish mines, which we will discuss further on. Thus there was a tendency of gradual centralization and the spread of homogeneous, systematic exploitation under state control.

However, the lack of personal gradually abolished the state-exploitation of larger mines with slaves and prisoners. The gradually diminishing returns of the gold- and silver-mines of Spain and other provinces forced the state to induce private mining companies or corporations and individuals to do the work by granting them certain privileges. Still the lack of silver and gold in the third century was not due to the exhaustion of the mines, but to the lack of "metallarii". Moreover the decay of civic life and the introduction of compulsory corporations caused a slackening output.

The measures to enforce labour were doomed to failure. In the west the failure of the Empire in the fourth century coincides with the failure of its mining activities. In the east the re-opening of old workings was encouraged like prospecting and officers like the "Comes metallorum per Illyricum" and the "Praepositus metallorum" for the Levant were appointed to supervise mining districts in parts of the Empire.

However, if we now turn to the discussion of some details about mining in the various provinces of the Roman Empire, we must remember that however numerous and rich they were, the mines and quarries were but minor spots on the dominantly agricultural landscape of the Empire and its provinces, as Rostovtzeff rightly claimed.

Sicily held but few rich mines, small lead deposits near Ciancina, north-west of Agrigento were worked (74) and a few unimportant gold and silver mines. In *Roman Africa* some sixty mining sites have been discovered, most of them described by Gsell. These mines were later also exploited by the Arab successors of the Romans. As to the Roman mines in the Near East we are not very well-informed for they have not been sufficiently explored. We have some secondary evidence to the effect that they were controlled and worked by the state.

In *Egypt* the copper ores of the eastern desert and Sinai do not seem to have been mined in Roman days. Documents mention copper ores in the Fayum (75) but no trace of any exploitation has been found there. Gold and iron ores were taken from the eastern desert and the Sudan as well as lead ores from Gebel Rosas and other sites on the Red Sea shores. A tax on lead in the third century A.D. seems to prove that this mining had some importance.

The Egyptian mines and quarries were imperial property and they were worked by imperial agents or leased to contractors. A "metallurch" or a centurion was in charge, "architects" were attached to their staff as technicians. The word "architect" in these texts often stands for our "engineer". Criminals and prisoners of war were assigned to the mines as workmen (76). During the reign of Diocletian work in the mines was imposed as a "liturgy" on peasants, a practice which may have begun earlier. Strikes of such workmen have been reported. The same general conditions applied to salt, nitre and alum deposits. Some gold came down the Nile from Ethiopia, but antimony, silver and tin had to be imported.

We have the impression that such mines and quarries as had been royal domain in *Asia Minor* may have been either neglected or sold into private hands. The quarries of Docimium, for instance, were little worked before Augustus and at that time were in the possession of Agrippa. Publicans worked the realgar mines of Pompeiopolis, the dreadful conditions of which workings we have already mentioned. The gold placers of Astyra, Lampsacus, Atarneus, Mons Bermius, the river Pactolus, Mount Tmolus and Mt. Sipylus, for which Asia Minor had been famous, were now all worked out and abandoned in Roman times, when the gold came from Colchis and Armenia. The silver mines of Pontus were less important than those of Bulgar Maden.

Large quantities of copper still came from Cyprus but also from mines on Mount Ida and Cilicia. Iron was obtained in Pontus, Cappadocia, Troas and Magnesia; lead from Ergasteria, the best producer of modern Turkey. We know that Herod sent half the profits from Cyprus to Rome, this was therefore virtually a concession on shares. Later a procurator was put in charge of the mines.

The *Macedonian mines* were taken over by the Romans in 167 B.C. and the silver mines were placed under the control of the knight's companies in 158 B.C., but it seems that the Macedonian kings had fairly well exhausted them. In Roman Greece Paulus' proclamation closed the silver and gold mines but left those of iron and copper alone. The evidence suggests that some of the profits after 158 went to the local governments. Most of these mines were worked by prisoners of war and slaves.

In the early second century B.C. the *Spanish mines* contributed already heavily to the income of the Roman State. In about 140 B.C. these mines were producing some 9,000,000 denarii worth, the total up to 157 B.C. being estimated to have amounted to some 50,000,000 denarii. The silver mines near New Carthage were at one time employing 40,000 men, they were turned over for exploitation by contract in 179 B.C. When the knight's companies began to operate the Spanish mines they produced an average of 1,000,000 denarii per year, but after a few years this amount had grown to 9,000,000 (140 B.C.) denarii.

Presumably the companies made about the same amount, but when the rich veins of ore gave out, the losses in liquidation were heavy. We will revert to the clever methods of extracting gold reported by Pliny and Strabo later on. The drainage adit of 2,000 M length found at Coto Fortuna confirms the picture of Diodorus, who spoke of "underground rivers diverted" for the purpose of mining. Apart from gold, silver and lead were mined in large quantities and tin was found, mainly in Galicia. Iron ore was obtained over a large area stretching from Baetica through Bilbilis to the coasts of Gallaecia, it was mostly worked locally and exported in the form of arms and cutlery. Cinnabar was mined at Sisapo by publicans.

During the first half of the first century B.C. the Spanish mines seem to have been the chief source of the lead used at Rome, Sulla had confiscated the Spanish silver mines and sold them for ready money. During the principate of Augustus procurators were appointed for the mines and the conquest of the last stronghold of independence in the north-west added to Rome's possession a territory rich in the variety and contents of its precious metals. The Romans worked all the gold-mines of the district known today and it is estimated that their yield per year amounted to some $ 50,000,000 (Frank).

During the reign of the emperor Tiberius a process began (77) which ultimately gave the State the ownership of all mines. The accusation, conviction and execution of Sextius Marius, owner of the mining district Mons Marianus by Tiberius was unjustly attributed to the greed of this emperor. The assignment to the imperial rather than to the senatorial treasury was an act of imperial government policy. But during the later Empire this centralizing tendency was gradually undone. This is evident from the regulations of the Vipasca district, the "Lex Metalli Vipasensis" (78), enacted during the reign of Hadrian. These regulations were definitely meant to encourage and counteract the flagging interest of the small capitalists now prompted to exploit the mines. These documents recall those for the African domain lands but they are even more closely related to the medieval mining organisation. Vespasian is now believed to have formulated this new policy and to have recognised the need of reorganizing the mines. A new regulation, a "lex data", governing the exploitation of each of the various types of mines, was drawn up at Rome. These local rules or "leges" were then sent out to the different provinces to be enforced by the provincial governors. In the Vipasca regulations we see that more skilled labour is now employed in the mines and details for their welfare become very prominent. At Linares arrangements for hot water for the miners's baths were made during the reign of Hadrian, who also laid down times for their use by the women of the community when the men were down below! However, this could not stop the decline of the Spanish mines which set in about 250 A.D. with the gradual disorganisation of the State.

The typical Roman policy of making good use of local tradition in technical matters such as mining is evident from the number of cases in which Hispano-Iberian terms have crept into Roman mining vocabulary (79) such as reported in Pliny's account of the Spanish mines. He mentions the words "balux, balluca" (nuggets), "palae, palages, palacarnas, psalacurnas" (lumps of gold), "gangadia" (tough rocks), "cuniculus" (underground galleries, lit. rabbit warren), "aggans" (washing table) and "arrugiae" (open-cut mining in gold districts, lit. wrinkles) and the Vipasca documents contain such Iberian words as "rutramina, ubertumbus, lausiae, pittaciaria, echolae and ternagus".

Roman Gaul was renowned for its many gold placers, mostly in the Pyrenees, the Cevennes mountains and the Rhine valley. The Romans started to exploit silver mines near Rodez and Gavédan in Aveyron, Toulouse, Ardèche, Hautes Alpes and Vosges. In the days of Tiberius many of these mines were in the hands of the Roman State, but it is not clear whether this is due to the "confiscations" of Tiberius. The Romans also continued the exploitation of the many iron-mines, which had a history going back far beyond the date of occupation of the province of Gaul.

Though the mines of *Roman Britain* were never so important to the Roman world as those of Spain or Dacia, they took a fairly high place among the mining provinces of the empire, and in particular they seem to have been one of the chief sources of a steady flow of silver and lead to Rome. Dated pigs of lead, iron tools and leaden lamps prove that within six years of the occupation of Britain the Romans were mining lead from the Mendip mines (AD 49), which were opened in pre-Roman times. The pigs of lead were found to have been treated with more or less success for the extraction of silver. The production of iron in the Weald started early too, native labour being supplied by trained overseers and foremen. The gold-mines of Dolaucothy in S. Wales were mostly open-cast workings, but there were also adits and shafts reaching to 24 M below sea-level and kept dry with water-raising wheels. An aqueduct, 7 miles long, supplied the necessary water. The tin mines of Cornwall were worked up to the third century, by that time they were under government control. In the Weald and the Forest of Dean there was a local industry using the limonitic iron ores, haematite, clayband iron-stone from coal measures, the Jurassic and other ores being mostly mined on a small scale only.

Coal outcrops were worked more or less systematically in Roman times, more especially in the civilised south-west (Somerset) and in the military north, where coal was regularly used in the frontier-forts. Bromehead (80) has drawn attention to the fact that not only at Charterhouse in the Mendips were engraved signet gems found in the lead-mining centre, but similar trinkets come from the gold-mining area of Dolaucothy. It would seem that in each centre someone connected with the mining engraved gems. The Roman method of dressing ore by pounding and grinding provided a large amount of finely divided, but angular, quartz, which would be an admirable abrasive for such purposes.

After surveying the practical geology of the Romans in Britain

Bromehead concludes that "during the Roman period there is direct and abundant evidence that all the economic metals (tin, copper, lead, iron and gold) were being mined with such obvious exceptions as wolfram. Evidence of pre-Roman mining is usually less direct, but no less certain. During the period of conquest such activities were, naturally, disturbed but by the third and fourth centuries as in the time of Cunobellinus the imports that Britain required to maintain its standard of life which she had set herself were only a marginal fraction of all that she consumed. This also applies to the quarrying of stone, clays, coal, jet, amber, gagates, fluorspar and gems. With the end of the Roman rule there was a real break and the Anglo-Saxon people gradually developed new and separate industries, being neither miners nor metallurgists they had to learn these trades anew and the utilization of stone shows poor technique up to the tenth century when copper, tin and brass are included in a list of imports in the Colloquy of Archbishop Alfric (1006)".

Mining tradition was much more continuous in Central Europe. Petrikovitz has pointed out that the *Limes* was a military frontier protecting the province of Gaul for which the Rhine was a medium of transport over 1200 KM long. Copper, silver-bearing lead, gold, iron and zinc ores were mined, mostly in open-cast workings like the iron mines of the Eiffel. There too the old method of sinking down a shaft to the minerals at the contact of two strata and following up the veins by means of galleries and stopes were applied in the copper-mines of Göllheim and Kordel, at Eisenberg and in the lead-mines of the Eiffel. The ores were usually smelted on the spot and converted into raw or refined metals before transport to the towns or army-depots. Apart from these larger mines there were often small workings on the farms, open-casts worked by the farmers in the neighbourhood in their spare time, probably during the winter months. The tradition of Celtic mining was continued, iron now being needed in ever-increasing quantities. Silver and lead too were in great demand. The migrations of the early centuries of this era depopulated southern Germany and only through water-power moving hammers and tread- and horse-mills applied to drainage such developments were possible again in early medieval times.

We have too few data on the *economics of mining*, a subject worth studying in more detail (81). It is true that, generally speaking, economics were much simpler due to the elasticity of labour-costs, but on the other hand the ancients were well aware of the fact that slave-labour was not as cheap as it seems at first sight. On the other hand the slow means of communication made the markets less sensitive to over-production. As long as a mine was not flooded even uneconomical work could continue until haulage required so much man-power that no food could be obtained for them even by barter. It has been calculated that the Carthagena silver-mines yielded a revenue of 7% so that only the richest ores could be worked. But the cost of machinery and tools was overestimated in this calculation. There was very little machinery, simple wooden constructions mostly, and the tools were locally fashioned or selected pebbles, the metal tools also being made on the spot. The sums mentioned in the classical documents probably refer to the sums paid to the State only and we have no proper information on what the knights' companies actually took, but this must have been attractive enough.

In north-western Spain mining may have been less profitable. Of course the poorer alluvial ores could be worked on a large scale only when slaves were cheap. The lack of machinery increased the amount of labour required for underground work proportionally. Still here the Romans built large aqueducts to supply the required amounts of water and they made elaborate drainage systems or series of water-wheels and Archimedean screws to raise the water. The dimensions of the adits was such as to allow enough space for walking, many adits being wider at the top to allow the passage of men carrying baskets or packs. Though the tools used were small, Pliny mentions the use of battering rams of up to 150 lbs for breaking up the quartz veins.

From the slags and the ingots found near such mines it is clear that with limited markets and production on a scale much smaller than today one could reject ores which we consider worthwhile and stick to working high-class ores only. At Laurium all ores containing less than 10% of lead were generally rejected. In Etruria 4—5% copper ores were not taken. At Minas gold and silver ores, containing 0.0017—0.0018% of gold and 0.025—0.028% of silver and now regarded as high-grade, were neglected. Only vein or lode workings required machinery, organisation and capital and these were inconsistent with free mining. Hence such mines of copper, lead, mercury in veins and large placers of gold and silver were usually worked under state control as at Vipasca or under private companies as at Catulo (Spain). Tin was produced by free miners mostly, iron usually by independent miners and itinerant smelters. Only during the later Empire was iron mining concentrated in certain towns like Beuvray or organized by imperial lessees (Aude, Carinthia). The itinerant smiths produce blooms of iron in the forest furnaces, which were welded together and sold in large blocks to be worked locally by military experts or by smiths in villas, as proved by the many slag-heaps found on their grounds. In the Balkan districts we find nomadic gold-washers ("collegium aurarium"). The "Comes metallorum per Illyricum" allows free placer mining to all in

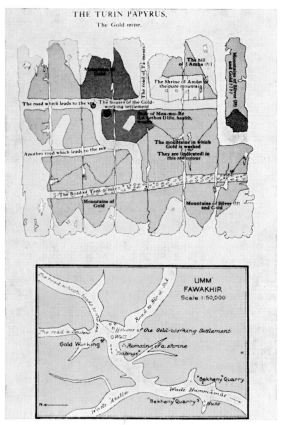

Fig. 16.
The Turin Papyrus; the gold mines of Umm Fawakhir.

365 (82), but later had to impose compulsory working and heriditary profession and domicile (83). As ancient mining involved few over-head costs tonnages of ore-body could be worked for a few pounds of metals only. Only hard rocks to be broken or water flooding a mine set a definite limit to mining in Antiquity.

6. *Ancient Quarrying*

The development of quarrying was closely related to that of mining and so our most detailed information about pre-classical quarrying comes from Egypt (84) rather than from Mesopotamia or other part of the Near East. Both Engelbach, an architect by training who lived for years in Egypt, and Zuber have described Egyptian quarrying in detail. Since Zoser started building in stone the quarries on both sides of the Nile valley were worked, though the earliest stones were natural boulders dressed with tools made of chert, a stone closely allied to flint.

Still granite and other boulders were gradually replaced by building blocks obtained by quarrying. There was a difference between the

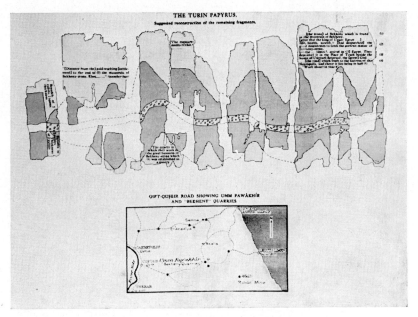

Fig. 17.
The Turin Papyrus. The quarries of Bekhen-stone.

methods used for quarrying such softer sedimentary rocks like limestone and sandstone and for quarrying the thougher igneous rocks like basalt and granite.

Even in early days quarries might be located at some depth underground and nearly horizontal tunnels have been cut into the cliff face to reach the required bed at such sites as Tura and Ma'sara. These tunnels rise slowly upto the quarry face, presumably in order to

Table X – *Soil, Sand and Rock*

English	Egyptian	Coptic	Sumerian	Accadian	
earth, soil	s3ṯw (III. 423. 7)	ечнт			medical use, "stuff of earth"
,,	t3 (V. 214. 3)	то ѳо			medical use
,,	pnś (I. 510. 9)	—			
earth (of Nile)	ḳ3ḥ (V. 12. 9)	каҳ			
silt, loam (of Nile)	3ḥ. t (I. 12. 18)	еιωϩе			
clay, loam	im (I. 78. 2)	оме, оϻι, ᴧ.ме	IM, IMI	ṭiṭṭû	
clay (potters)	śjn (IV. 37. 11)		GIRAS	kerṣu	
sand	{s'j (IV. 419. 22)				
	{s' (IV. 419. 23)				
sand (for building)	nš (II. 338. 6)				
grain of sand	nš, nš3 (II. 338. 16)				
gravel, rubble	'r (I. 208. 11), also	ᴧ̀			
	ḥm' (III. 282. 6)				
stone, rock	imj t3 (I. 75. 18)	—			
stone	inr (I. 97. 11)	ωне, ωнι	ZA(NA$_4$)	abnu	
hard-(building) stone	rwḏ. t (II. 412. 14)				
solid, hard stone	'3. t rwḏ. t (II. 412. 18)				
,,	inr n rwḏ. t (II. 413. 1)				
(sculptor) stone	'3. t (I. 165. 13)				
(waterfree) stone	nḥ3 n inr (II. 291. 1)				
(mountain) stone	{ḥ3. t (III. 360. 15) {ḥ. t (III. 359. 6)				
very hard (mill) stone	bnw. t (I. 458. 12)				
ore (general)	bj3 (I. 438. 8)				

facilitate the transport of the blocks. The face is kept vertical and blocks of rock were removed by cutting and hammering out a recess near the roof about half a metre high and of the same width as the blocks to be removed. On such a shelf a man could squat to cut narrow trenches some 10—12 cm wide along the three vertical sides of the block. The base was then detached by inserting wedges of wood between to thin plates of metal ("feathers") or such wooden wedges as could be made to exert pressure by wetting this wood. The next block could be removed directly below the first until the ground level of the quarry was reached and the process was then started again. In underground quarries such faces are upto 6 metres high but in open-air quarries their height might attain double or triple this value. The extraction of blocks from the faces of solid rock required metal tools, though stone tools may have played their part when the blocks of stone were dressed on the building side and finishing, polishing and incision of inscriptions and figures followed. All tools used seem to have been made of copper and bronze, they had to be recast and resharpened constantly. Engelbach found close analogies between the methods used in ancient Egypt and those of France in his days, the picks, stone-mason's hammers, mortice chisels, etc. left their marks on stones and in quarries, which differ hardly in shape and size from those of modern tools.

In the case of harder rocks of the granite, diorite and quartzite type other methods had to be used which can be studied in such cases where for one reason or another the work had to be abandoned before completion as for instance the granite quarry of Aswan where an incompleted granite obelisk can been studied. The partially weathered surface rock was broken by fire-setting, and the burnt and crumbled granite removed and pounded with boulders or hammers made from such stones like dolerite balls show on rammers with a diameter of 12—30 cm, weighing an average of 5.5 K., such as Engelbach found.

Thus a flat surface of fresh rock was prepared. Sometimes (like at Aswan) this meant removing the surface rock to a considerable depth in order to set out for the preparation of really flawless blocks. The outline of such a block was marked by shallow grooves and red or black paint and small trenches were pounded out to ascertain how far cracks or fissures penetrated into the rock. At Aswan the original size of the monument seems to have been modified at least three times in order to avoid cracking of the obelisk along fissures when lifting it. A separating trench was cut all along the proposed obelisk, 70—75 cm wide, and at least twice as deep.

Table XI

The building stones of the Ancient Near East

Egyptian			Sumerian	Accadian
Limestone				
inr ḥḏ	(I. 97. 12)	("the white stone")	na₄NA. PUR	pîlu pişû
ʾjn	(I. 191. 4) }	("the "beautiful" from the Tura Quarries")	na₄ZA. ṬU	ᵃallalu, ellalu
ʾnw	(I. 191. 1) }			
Alabaster				
ʾnḫ	(I. 204. 10)		na₄(GIŠ)ŠIR(GAL)	gišširgallu
bj. t	(I. 433. 11)		na₄PAR	parrû, parûtu
šš	(IV. 540. 10)			
šš. t	(IV. 541. 6)			
Sandstone				
inr ḥḏ n rwḏ. t	(I. 97. 13)	("enduring")	na₄ŠAM	ašammu
inr ḥḏ nfr n				
rwḏ. t	(II. 413. 2)	(coarse granular reddish-brown quartzite sand-		
bjз. t	(I. 438. 16)	stone from Gebel Ahmar)		
Serpentine				
w3ḏ	(I. 267. 7)	(from Lower Egypt)	na₄MUŠ. GIR	mušgarru
Breccia				
tíi33t?			—	túr.min-na. banda

			ⁿᵃ⁴AD. BAR ⁿᵃ⁴GA. ŠUR. RA	kašurrû
nmḥt	(II. 268. 1)?			
Diorite-gneiss				
mnt. t	(II. 91. 10)	("chephren diorite")	ⁿᵃ⁴ESUG, ESI	ešu, ušu
ibhty	(I. 64. 1)?			
Granite				
m3ṯ	(II. 34. 3)	(from Elephantine)		
m3ṯ rwḏ. t inr km	(II. 412. 17)	("hard granite")		
'3. t rwḏ. t	(I. 97. 15)	("black granite")	AN. ŠE. TIR	ašnan
inr(n) 3bw	(I. 165. 19)	("black hard") ?		
Felspar				
nšm. t	(II. 339. 19)			
nšn	(II. 340. 10)?			
Graywacke				
bḫn	(I. 471. 1)	(dark hard graywacke from Hammâmât and Elephantine)	(Gr. basanites)	
Quartzite				
bi3t	(I. 438. 16)	(red crystalline quartzite sandstone from Gebel Ahmar)		
nmtt	(II. 272. 2), nmti (II. 272. 1)	white quartzite		

This was achieved by pounding with dolerite balls, removing a thin layer of rock some cms. thick at a time. The work was executed so regularly that the side of the trench shows a regular corrugated surface, each groove corresponding to the width of rock cut by a dolerite ball. Such large blocks could not be undercut by wedging, this was carried out by hammering tunnels underneath the monument, in what must have been exceedingly cramped positions. The undercut tunnels were probably filled with stacks of rubble to hold the block in position, while the intervening rock was also removed.

Indeed Somers Clarke gave a description of the methods used by Courtney Clifton in 1895, when he brought Italian granite workers to the quarries in Aswan. They cut "holes" with steel points and a six-pound hammer, about 3—4″ deep and 3—4″ apart along a shallow groove indicating the line where the holes had to be sunk. Into the holes thus prepared plugs were hammered with a hand hammer. It was also found that blocks up to ten Tons could be easily moved with the help of wooden rollers, crowbars and a few screw-jacks. Though the Egyptians did not possess the last-named tool they shifted large blocks with simple tools in the same way as still practised in many eastern countries. The monoliths used for obelisks were 20—50 M long, those erected for Queen Hatshepsut at Karnak were 30 M long and weighed 390 Tons a piece. The architect Sen-mut reports that their extraction in the quarry including the finishing and polishing took seven months! Pliny (85) even mentions obelisks 63 and 73 M high, but those at Karnak range from 28—48 M only. Anthes rightly pointed out that it would be interesting to compare the methods used by Egyptian sculptors with those used in the quarries to finish stone monuments and art objects fashioned there.

The oldest geological map we have is that of the quarry of "Bekhen stone" (graywacke or mica-schist) shown in the Turin papyrus (86) dating back to the reign of King Seti I (1312—1292 B.C.). We have here preserved for us a geological map showing schist, granite and, crossing both, strips of "head" or "coombe deposits" with notes on the mines and quarries drawn 3500 years ago. It is the ancestor of the earliest geological maps, which were all drawn for economic purposes! Table X will show that the Egyptians had a very varied nomenclature for different types of soil, sand and rock with which they could make notes on maps such as the Turin one. This map shows a long road or wadi, called "the road of Tent-p-mer", which had a branch-road leading to the gold-mines and a continuation "leading to the sea". This was supposed to represent the Wadi Hammamat and the wadi before the branch-road would then be the Wadi 'Atalla, the gold-mines being those at Umm Fawakhir. This supposition is now properly proved by investigation on the spot, the remains of the huts for miners indicated on the map have been properly traced and described.

We have good information on the quarries and building stones of ancient Egypt (87), the nomenclature of these stones being known in many details (Table XI). The most important types of stone used were:

Limestone, carbonate of lime with different impurities, was used for building, statues, etc. It forms the main substance of the hills bordering the Nile valley up to Esna. Limestone quarries were found at Ţura, El Ma'ṣara (south of El-Ma'âdi), El Gabalein, Abydos, Qâw, Beni Hassan en El-'Amarna. In these quarries limestone blocks were sometimes handled in the same way as the Aswan granite obelisks. The stones were taken out in regular lifts and galleries were made in the best quality limestone. Cracks were avoided and a layer of stone on both sides of such cracks was left standing. The limestone was worked with copper-blade saws fed with sand or saws set with emery teeth were used. For carving tubular drills were used, the stone dressing being illustrated in detail in the Sakkarah tomb-paintings. *Marble*, a cristalline limestone which takes a high polish, was taken from the eastern desert. In predynastic times small vases were fashioned from it, then after a gap of time marble statues reappear during the XVIIIth dynasty (c. 1500 B.C.).

Dolomite and dolomitic limestone from the eastern desert was sometimes used for stone bowls and small stone objects. *Alabaster*, crystalline calcium carbonate or calcite, was used both for small objects and for building purposes. The mines at Hat-nub date back to the third dynasty, others were located in Sinai, Helwân and Wadi Asyûṭi.

Sandstone (88), quartz sand cemented by clay, carbonate of lime, oxide of iron and silica, was used from the earliest period onwards. It was applied in a few buildings of XIth dynasty date, but it became the main building material during the XVIIIth dynasty. It was mined at Gebel el-Silsila, south of Kom Ombo, at Sirâg and at Qirṭâs in Nubia. South of Esna sandstone is the country-rock of the Nile valley replacing the limestone of the north. *Quartzite*, the hard, compressed form of sandstone was used for building in the Pyramid Age but later for sarcophagi and monuments only. Its most ancient quarry was in the Red Mountain near Cairo.

Serpentine, a hydrated silicate of magnesium, is a hard rock with marks not unlike the skin of a serpent. It was sometimes carved in predynastic times like *Steatite*, a serpentine with a different state of hydration, which later became popular for the manufacture of scarabs and statuettes. It was quarried near Aswân, Gebel Fatîri, Bîr Gûlân (north of Ras Benas) on the Red Sea coast. *Breccia*, a mixture of rocks, fragments of one colour being embedded in a matrix of another, was occasionally used in predynastic and Late Egyptian times. A red-and-white variety was found in the western desert, a green one in Wadi Hammamat. This was

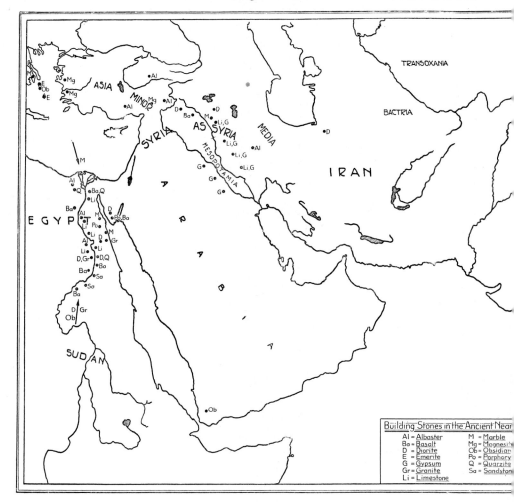

Fig. 18.
The building-stone quarries of the Ancient Near East.

the kind of stone that served for the pavement of the procession-road "Aibur Shabu" at Babylon, whence it was brought from the northern mountains. *Gypsum*, calcium sulphate, was occasionally used for vases, it was fairly common in the Fayyum, on the Red Sea coast and in the Maryût region of the Delta. *Selenite*, a transparent form of gypsum, was the material from which slabs were made to be used as window-panes (89) like slabs of alabaster. This use was unknown in ancient Egypt, but began in Roman times.

Basalt, the black, heavy composite rock, was the common material for vases, temple pavements and sarcophagi (90). It was mined early in the Fayyûm and later in Abu Za'bal, Bilbeis, Kirdâsâ and Aswân too. *Dolerite*, a coarse-grained granite, was used for stone bowls and pound-

Fig. 19.
View of the Aswan Obelisk, showing the grooves made by stone hammers in order to separate this block of stone (After Engelbach)

ing stones. It was mined near El Quṣeir on the Red Sea coast, Gebel Abu Dukhkhân, Wadi el-Hammamat and Wadi el-'Allâqi in Nubia. In Mesopotamia diorite was an important material, which was imported from beyond the Persian Gulf via Magan. A variant of basalt, the *basalt-lava* of Mayen in the Rhine-valley played an important part as a material for pounders and rubbing stones in Central Europe since Neolithic times. It may have been somewhat less popular during the Bronze and Early Iron Age when tools were rather inadequate for dressing it, but it became the material for mill-stones in the Later Iron Age and continued to function until well in Roman times, being used in all the towns and Limes-fortresses. A foundered shipment of such mill-stones was recovered near Straatsburg in 1911.

Diorite, white and greenish felspar and black hornblende, banded and speckled, was mostly used for statues, stone bowls and small objects (91). The "Chephren diorite" came from Nubia, 80 KM west of Tushka, other forms from all over Egypt. *Granite* (92), a crystalline mixture of quartz, felspar and mica, ranges in colour from pink and grey to black. The grey variety was *Syenite* from Aswân and Wadi Hammamat. It was used for building, statues and small objects. *Schist* and tuff, finely divided volcanic material, often with foliated structure, or graywacke is the "bhn (bekhen) stone" of Wadi Hammamat. This hard, dark building stone, Sethe argued (93), gave its name to basalt by way of the Hebrew "bashan" and the Greek "basan" and "basanites", like the Tura quarries, called "r-3w" (elongated mouth, because of the series of rooms and corridors) and the Tura region, "t3-r-3w" (region of "r-3w") became Troia to the Greeks, like they called Egyptian cities Thebes and Babylon and the Tura limestone "Troian stone"!

Porphyry, an igneous rock with conspicuously coloured crystals embedded in the ground mass, was mainly quarried in Roman times (94). The Imperial Porphyry (porfiro rosso antico) quarries at Gebel Abu Dukhkhân in the eastern desert were re-discovered by Burton in 1822. It is also found in other parts of the same desert and near Aswân. The purple variety is a special variety of the more general grey tuff of the region, the Romans quarried it to ship it down the Nile Valley. The quarry at the top of a hill shows a working face 25 M in height, the stone conveyed 96 miles overland to the river Nile. In the eastern desert there were also the Mons Claudianus quarries in hornblende granite, which may have been started by Claudius to employ the Jewish prisoners. A pillar on the site measures 18 × 2.6 M. A number of Egyptian building stones are still unidentified (Table XII).

Unfortunately both modern and ancient literature give us much information on the Greek building stones used in various buildings such as Parian marble, Penthelic marble, Egyptian porphyry, etc., but we do know little on the technical side of *Greek quarrying* (95). Frazer gave an excellent description of the Pentelicon quarries (96) but few technical details on the methods used there in Antiquity. In fact we know that there were "technites" in charge of the operations in the quarries, more often than not non-citizens and largely ignored in ancient literature. We know that there must have been great activity in these quarries, notably during the Hellenistic period, when there was an increasing demand for stone for the many new public buildings erected in the Greek cities in the homeland and abroad. Still we must realize that even this increased quarrying was still on a much more limited scale than during the Roman period. In Egypt, for instance, the richer quarries of rare porphyry and other stones were first opened by the Romans.

In the Greek homeland Paros yielded white statuary marble, Naxos a greyish marble and Mount Hymettos the sandstone for general use. The huge limestone quarries of Syracuse, where production reached its limit during the reign of Hiero II (269—216 B.C.), have a rockface of 27 M high and 2000 M long. Here over 40,000,000 M³ of stone were extracted, mostly by the 7000 Athenian prisoners of the fateful war of 413 B.C. Pausanias (97) waxes lyrical over the green porphyry (verde antico) quarries of Crocaea: "As you go down to the sea towards

Table XII

Unidentified Egyptian minerals and rocks

i33	kind of natural stone	(I. 27. 8)
'n(w)	,, ,, ,, (limestone?)	(I. 189. 18)
wtšj	white stone from Elephantine	(I. 381. 8)
bhs	stone used by sculptors	(I. 469. 12)
r'gs	stone from Elephantine	(II. 403. 6)
tmḥj	Stone from Nubia (species of red ochre?)	(V. 369. 4)
knm. t	stone from the Oases used for statues	(V. 133. 9)
śnn	mineral used in pharmacy (expensive)	(IV. 166. 9)
śhr. t	,, ,, ,, ,, (serpentine?)	(IV. 208. 16)
śhw. t	(identical with śhr. t?)	(IV. 207. 10)
śhrr	(,, ,, ,,)	(IV. 209. 4)
m3d	mineral used in pharmacy (pumice)	(II. 35. 2)
gśfn	,, ,, ,, ,, (black eye-paint?)	(V. 206. 9)
hsg	material for unguent vases	(III. 169. 8)
idbw	material for manufacture of amulets	(I. 153. 11)
bḳs 'nḫ	rare stone for amulets (magnetite?)	(V. 18. 1)
prḏn	mineral from Elephantine	(I. 533. 5)
sn. t	,, ,, ,, (ochreous earth?)	(III. 458. 5)
śsm. t	mineral from Nubia and Syria	(IV. 539. 1)
iśmr	,, ,, ,, ,, ,,	(I. 132. 18)
smr	,, ,, ,, ,, ,,	(IV. 139. 11)
škr	mineral from Nubia	(IV. 550. 6)
ḥkn	,, ,, ,, (red stone?)	(III. 180. 14)
ḥtś	,, ,, ,, (carnelian?)	(III. 203. 11)

Gythium you come to a village called Crocae and a quarry. It is not a continuous stretch of rock, but the stones they dig out are shaped like river pebbles; they are hard to work, but when worked sanctuaries of the gods might be adorned with them, while they are especially adapted for beautifying swimming-baths and fountains", which Pliny (98) describes as the "green Lacedaemonian marble which is brighter than any other marble". The strata there are very disrupted and it is difficult to find larger pieces, but the "verde antico" was very popular at Rome and even as far as Syria. Pausanias (99) describes a terrace of "porinos lithos" a conglomerate and Aristotle is credited with the following description of a "pyrimachos lithos", a fire-resisting stone used in lining metal-lurgical furnaces, probably a dolomite (100): "It is said that the origin of the Chalybian and Amisian iron is most extraordinary. For it grows,

Fig. 20.
Egyptian stone-cutters at work (After Quibell, Hierakonpolis)

so they say, from the sand which is borne down by the rivers. Some say that they simply wash the residue which is left after the first washing and heat it, and that they put into it a stone which is called fire-proof and there is much of this in the district. This iron is much superior to all other kinds. If it were not burned in a furnace, it would not apparent-ly be very different from silver. They say that it alone is not liable to rust, but that there is not much of it."

Strabo mentions most of the well-known marble quarries such as those of Cappadocia (101): "the river Melas makes the stone quarries hard to work, though otherwise easy to work; for there are ledges of flat stones from which the Mazaceni obtain an abundant supply of stone for their buildings, but when the slabs are concealed by the waters they are hard to obtain", or those of the "synnadic marble" (102): "And beyond Synnada in Phrygia is Docimaea, a village, and also the quarry of "synnadic" marble (so the Romans call it, though the natives call it "Docimite" or "Docimaean"). At first the quarry yielded only stones of small sizes, but on account of the extravagance of the modern Romans great monolithic pillars are taken from it, which in their variety of colours are nearly like the albastrite variety; so that, although transportation of such heavy burdens to the sea is difficult, still both pillars and slabs, remarkable for their size and beauty, are conveyed to Rome", but we are not given any technical details about their extraction and it seems that modern research should be carried out on the spot to find out what the analogies and differences between Egyptian and Greek quarrying really were.

We are better informed about *Roman quarrying* (103), more particularly through the excellent volumes written by Miss Marion Blake.

Fig. 21.
Relief of a votive altar found at St. Martin-am-Bacher near quarries, showing a miner working at the rock-face with hammer and gad.

Generally speaking, the blocks were extracted in approximately the size in which they were to be used, there seems to have been no standardization. The chief implement was a kind of pickaxe with a broad cutting axe, such as illustrated in the Carrara quarries and on other Roman monuments. Most stones were roughly shaped at the quarry and it would seem that the methods at present in use at Carrara do not differ much from those of the Roman quarrymen. The surface-treatment varied from case to case as the quarry-stones were of course used in various types of constructions. The quarries seem to have been chosen, as far as possible, near rivers which allowed proper and cheap transport by water to Rome, where there were special wharves and yards for the handling of such stones such as those for taking care of marble near the later Pons Aelius. It is well-known that the emperor Augustus prided himself of having transformed Rome from a city of bricks into a city of marble but of course most marbles were used for dressing (104).

Travertine was among the hard stones used at an early period and hard and durable basalt served as slabs for pavements, when the earlier gravel roads were being converted into good roads by Appius Claudius and his successors. Many ancient authors mention this "lapis silex" for use on the main roads (105), for instance Livy: "the censors (174 B.C.) first of all let contracts for paving the streets of the City with flint, and for laying the bases of roads outside the City with gravel and constructing footpaths along their edges", and Procopius: "For all the stone (for the Appian Way), which is mill-stone (basalt) and hard by nature, quarried in another place and brought there. And after working these stones until they were smooth and flat, and cutting them to a polygonal shape, he fastened them together without putting concrete or anything else between them."

The Carrara quarries near Luna were exploited to a large scale (106) and Strabo tells us, that "the (Carrara) quarries of marble, both white and mottled blueish-grey marble, are so numerous and of such quality (for they yield monolithic slabs and columns) that the material for most of the superior works of art in Rome and in the rest of the cities are supplied therefrom; and indeed, the marble is easy to export, since the quarries lie above the sea and near it, and since the Tiber in its turn takes up the cargo from the sea and conveys it to Rome".

They were certainly worked from 100 B.C. onwards, and 80-Tons blocks were used in Trajan's column. Serpentine was obtained from the quarry near Gytheion in Laconia (107). The quarries of the other provinces, except Egypt and Asia Minor, mostly served local demands. Thus the granite quarry in the Odenwald mostly supplied Rhenish towns. Here a pillar was found, 30' long and tapering from 5'1" to 4'1". In the terrace wall of the Temple of Jupiter at Baalbek three blocks of limestone measuring 63—64 × 13 × 13 feet have been used, the largest blocks ever to be used in building. In the quarries, still attached to its base, was found another block, measuring 68 × 14 × 14 feet, which corresponds to a weight of roughly 1500 Tons! In the basalt-lava quarries holes were made with picks at distances of 5—6 cm, then iron wedges were driven in to split off the blocks from the quarry face.

The coloured "marbles" and other stones, mentioned by so many authors (108), were mostly sawn in thin slabs to be used as a "veneer". This was done with copper saws, like those of the ancient Egyptians.

In the Greek palace of Tyrins a copper blade with square emery teeth, about 1.60 M long, was found. For harder rocks toothless blades were used with emery, grains of which were soon embedded in the copper. Such were the saws, sometimes driven by water-power during the Later Empire, of which Ausonius (109) says (though Lynn White and others hold this to be a later interpolation): "and that other (the Ruwar), as he turns his mill-stones (of corn-mills) in furious revolutions and drives shrieking saws through smooth blocks of marble, hears from either bank a ceaseless din". These were the saws on the banks of the Erubris (Ruwar), which enters the Moselle just below Trier, working by the end of the fourth century. But such saws were also mentioned by Vitruvius and Pliny (110), the latter discussing a kind of "steatite" found in Belgium in these words: "In the province of Belgic Gaul a white stone is said to be cut with a saw, just like wood, only even more easily, so as to serve as ordinary roof tiles and as rain tiles (imbrices) or, if so desired, as the kind of roofing known as "peacock-style". Pliny adds that the coarser the sand used in sawing the more subsequent polishing is required, for which he recommends pumice.

Vitruvius has a long passage on the quality of various building stones and materials (111), such as the pozzolana found in the neighbourhood of Baiae and round Mount Vesuvius, which, when mixed with lime and rubble, forms an hyraulic cement-concrete. This passage seems to indicate that certain stones were subjected to some kind of weathering in or near the quarries, for "now these are found to be of unequal and unlike virtue. For some are soft... others are medium... some are hard like lava... stone which is indeed cut like wood with a toothed saw. But all these quarries which are of soft stone have this advantage: when stones are taken from these quarries they are easily handled in working, and if they are in covered places, they sustain their burden, but if they are in open and exposed places, they combine with ice and hoar-frost, are turned to powder and are dissolved: along the sea-coast, also, being weathered by the brine, they crumble and are dissolved and do not endure the heat. Travertine and all stones which are of the same kind, withstand injury from heavy loads and from storms, but from fire they cannot be safe; as soon as they are touched by it they crack and break up. And the reason is that by the nature of their composition they have little moisture and also not much of earth, but much air and fire. Therefore there is less moisture and earth in these, then also the fire, when the air has been expelled by the contact and violence of the heat, following far within and seizing upon the empty spaces of the fissures, seethes and produces, from its own substance similar bodies... When we have to build, let the stone be got out two years before, not in winter but in summer, and let it lie and stay in exposed places. Those stones, however, which in the two years suffer damage by weathering, are to be thrown into the foundations. Those which are not faulty are tested by Nature, and can endure when use in building above ground."

In Roman Africa there was the most important marble quarry of Simitthus, yielding the "giallo antico", which had been the property of the Numidian kings, then public property in Roman times but finally managed by a procurator. Roman Egypt was an even more important producer of building materials for the Roman architect, being the source of alabaster, breccia, dolerite, granite, gypsum, limestone, marble, quartzite, sandstone, schist, serpentine and steatite. Pliny (112) informs us that several of these were being quarried under Augustus and Tiberius. The emperor Claudius started working the hornblende-granite of Mons Claudianus in the eastern desert with Jewish prisoners. It was called the "granite of the forum" because it was used in Trajan's Forum. He also opened the quarries of Imperial Porphyry in the Dukh-khan range east of Assyut. Septimius Severus opened a quarry near Syene, producing the red granite called "syenite" by Pliny. Other quarries worked to a large scale under Roman rule were Mons Porphyrites, Mons Berenicies, Kalâbsche, Gebel Silsile (sandstone), El-Hosch, El-Kab, Gebel Tûch (limestone), Lycopolis, Tanis, Oxyrhynchus and Hibeh. These quarries are discussed in detail by Fitzler.

In Syria there were the large quarries at Baalbek near Damascus, already mentioned before, and most extensively worked during the reign of Antonius Pius (138—161). In Roman Asia Minor most of the older quarries were being worked under Roman supervision. We have some information on the organization of the quarries of Docimium (113). The blocks in the quarry were properly marked with the date, the person in charge of the section, the engineer in charge of the cutting and the subdivision under him, like those of the Great Pyramid of Cheops. Some blocks have indications to show that an inspector rejected them, but those approved went to the central office at Synnada and were consigned to their eventual destination. It appears that the imperial quarries of Asia Minor were worked directly by imperial officials, freedmen and slaves without intervention of contractors.

BIBLIOGRAPHY

1. PLINY, XXXIII. 96
1a. LIMET, H., *Le travail du métal au pays de Sumer* (Paris 1960);
DOSSIN, G., *Le nom du cuivre en sumérien* (Bull. Class. Lett. Accad. R.
de Belgique, 5e sér. XXXVIII, 1952, 433)
2. ARKELL, W. J., and TOMKEIEFF, S. I., *English Rock Terms* (Oxf. Univ.
Press, 1953)
KIRKHAM, N., *Derbyshire lead mining glossary* (Cave Research Group
Publication no. 2, Leaminton Spa, 1949)
TAUBE, E., *Mining terms of obscure origin* (Scient. Monthly vol. LVIII,
1944, 454—456)
3. BOLMAN, J., *The mystery of the pearl* (Leiden 1941)
4. YOUNG, W. J., *Latomus* vol. XI, 1952, 465 ff.
HAWKINS, A. C., *The Book of Minerals* (New York, 1935)
4a. LAMBERG-KARLOVSKY, C. C., *Amber and faience* (Antiquity XXXVII,
1963, 301—302)
5. STRABO, III. 2. 9; ATHENAEUS, VI. 233 e; DIODORUS V. 37. 1
6. SIMONIN, *Annales des Mines* vol. V, 14, 1858, 557; BARTELS, *Verh. Berl.
Ges. f. Anthrop.* 1896, 292
7. PLINY, XXXIII. 31. 98
8. PLINY, XXXIII. 21. 73; XXXIV. 21. 67
9. AETHICUS, *Cosmog.* xxv
10. PLINY, XXXIII. 31. 98
11. PLINY, XXXIII. 21. 73
12. NEEDHAM, J., *Science and Civilisation in China* (vol. III, Cambridge, 1959,
673—680)
13. GOLDSCHMIDT, V. M., *The principles of distribution of chemical elements
in minerals and rocks* (J. Chem. Soc. 1937, 655)
14. ADAMS, F. D., *Origin and Nature of Ore Deposits, an historical study* (Bull.
Geol. Soc. America vol. XXXV, 1934, 375—424)
ANDRÉE, J., *Bergbau in der Vorzeit* (Leipzig, 1922)
BROMEHEAD, C. E. N., *The evidence for ancient mining* (Geogr. J. vol. 96,
1940, 101—120)
CLINE, W., *Mining and Metallurgy in Negro Africa* (Geuthner, Paris, 1937)
FREISE, FR., *Geschichte der Bergbau- und Hüttentechnik* (Leipzig, 1908,
vol. I)
GROSS, H., *Erzbergbau, Hüttentechnik und Metallhandel* (Erlangen, 1934,
vol. I)
HAUPT, P., *Philological and Archaeological Studies* (mercury) (Amer. J.
Philol. vol. 45, 1924, 238—259)
HECKER, R., *Der steinzeitliche Mensch als Versteinerungssammler* (Natur
und Volk, vol. 64, 1935, 515)

LAUFFER, S., *Bergmännische Kunst der Antiken Welt* (In: H. Winckelmann, *Der Bergbau in der Kunst*, Glückauf Verlag, Essen, 1958)

MICHNA, H. K., *Wie unsere urzeitlichen Vorfahren sich die Kenntnisse des Bergbaus erwarben* (Natur und Kult. vol. 29, 1932, 165—171)

PARET, O., *Bergbau auf Metalle im Altertum* (Aus der Heimat, vol. XLV, 1932, 305—316)

PITTARD, J. J., *La recherche et l'exploitation des mines au Moyen Age* (Revue Polytechn. vol. XXXV, 1933, 2451—2453, 2459—2461)

READ, T. T., *Historical aspects of mining and metallurgical engineering* (J. Eng. Education, vol. XXIV, 1933, 229)

REITEMEYER, J. F., *Geschichte des Bergbaus und des Hüttenwesens bei den alten Völkern* (Göttingen, 1785)

RICKARD, T. A., *Man and Metals* (2 vols., Macmillan, New York, 1931)

ROSENFELD, A., *The Inorganic Materials of Antiquity* (London, 1965)

TAUBE, E., *Mining Terms of obscure origin* (Scient. Monthly vol. 58, 1944, 454—6)

TREPTOW, E., *Der altjapanische Bergbau und Hüttenbetrieb dargestellt auf Rollbildern* (Jahrb. Berg-, Hüttenwesen Sachsen, 1904)

TREPTOW, E., *Der älteste Bergbau und seine Hilfsmittel* (Beitr. Gesch. Techn. Ind. vol. VIII, 1918, 155 ff)

TREPTOW, E., *Bergmännische Kunst* (Beitr. Gesch. Techn. Ind. vol. XII, 1922)

WILSDORF, H., *Bergleute und Hüttenmänner im Altertum* (*Berlin*, Freiberg. Forsch. Hefte, 1952, Serie D. 1)

WITCOMBE, W. H., *All about mining, the story of mining from the earliest times* (New York, 1938)

SZABÓ, GEORGE, *Prehistoric and aboriginal mining in America, a preliminary bibliography* (Archaeologia Austriaca, vol. 29., 1961, 38—56)

15. CHARLES, R. H., *The Book of Enoch* (Oxford, 1893)
16. TERTULIAN, *De cultu feminarum* I, 2
17. ANDRÉE, J., *Bergbau in der Vorzeit* (Kabitsch, Berlin, 1922)

BROMEHEAD, C. E. N., *The evidence for ancient mining* (Geogr. J. vol. 96, 1940, 101)

BROMEHEAD, C. E. N., *Practical Geology in Ancient Britain* (Proc. Geol. Assoc. London, vol. 58., 1947, 345; vol. 59, 1948, 65)

BROMEHEAD, C. E. N., *Mining and Quarrying* (History of Technology, edit. Singer, vol. I, 1954, 558—571)

CLARK, G., and ST. PIGOTT, *The Age of the British Flint Mines* (Antiquity, vol. 7, 1933, 65 ff)

HAWKES, C. F. C., *The Prehistoric Foundations of Europe to the Mycenean Age* (Methuen, London, 1940)

CLARK, J. D. G., *Prehistoric Europe* (Methuen, London, 1952)

HECKER, R., *Der steinzeitliche Mensch als Versteinerungssammler* (Natur und Volk vol. 64, 1935, 515 ff)

HÖRTER, P., *Der Kreis Mayen in ur- und vorgeschichtlicher Zeit* (Mayen, 1928)

MOREY, J. E., and SABINE, P. A., *A petrographical review of the porcellanite axes of N. E. Ireland* (Ulster J. Archaeol. 3rd. ser. vol. 15, 1952, 56)

MORTON, F., *Der älteste vorgeschichtliche Bergbau* (Kali vol. 34, 1940, 7—8)

QUIRING, H., *Die Schächte, Stollen und Abbauräume der Steinzeit und des Altertums* (Z. f. Berg-, Hütten- Salinenwesen vol. 80, 1932, B 274 ff)

QUIRING, H., *Der älteste Bergbauschacht* (Forschungen und Fortschritte vol. VIII, 1932, 389—390)

SALIN, Ed., *Sur un pic de cerf trouvé à Grand* (Vosges) (Rev. Etud. Anc. XV, 1964, 155—166)

SANDERS, W., *The Use of the Deer-horn Pick in Mining Operations of the Ancients* (Archaeologia vol. 62, 1910, 101 ff)

WARREN, S. H., *The Neolithic Axes of Graig Lwyd, Penmainmawr*) (Archaelogia Cambrensis vol. 77, 7th ser., 2, 1922, 1 ff)

18. ALLCHIN, Br., *The Stone-Tipped Arrow* (Phoenix, London, 1966)

BECKER, C. J., *Flint Mining in Neolithic Denmark* (Antiquity vol. XXXIII, 1959, 87—92)

BARNES, A. S., *The difference between natural and human flaking on prehistoric flint implements* (Amer. Anthrop. vol. 41, 1939, 99—112)

BAUMGÄRTEL, E., *The flint quarries of Wadi Sheykh* (Ancient Egypt 1930, 103—8)

BAYER, J., *Neolithisches Feuersteinbergwerk nächst Mauer bei Wien* (Forsch. und Fortschritte vol. VI, 1930, 273)

BENFIELD, E., *Purbeck Shop, a stoneworker's story of stone* (Cambr. Univ Press, 1940)

CREUTZE, E. and MORIARTY, J., *Inferences on the use of San Diego percussion-flaked artifacts* (Amer. Antiquity 29 (1963), 82—89)

CLARKE, R., *The Flintknapping Industry at Brandon* (Antiquity vol. IX, 1935, 38—56)

CLARK, G., and ST. PIGGOTT, *The age of the British flint mines* (Antiquity vol. VII, 1933, 166)

CLARK, J. G. D., *The Mesolithic Age in Britain* (London, 1932, Append. VI)

HILLEBRAND, I., *Neuere Ausgrabungen auf dem Avasberg bei Miscolcz in Ungarn* (*Eiszeit und Urgeschichte* vol. VI, 1929, 136)

HURST, V. J., & KELLY A. R., *Patination of Cultural Flints* (In: New Roads to Yesterday, Thames and Hudson, Londen, 1966, 517—530)

JAHN, M., *Der älteste Bergbau in Europa* (Abh. Sächs. Akad. Wiss., phil.-hist. Kl. Band 52, Heft 2, Berlin, 1960)

KNOWLES, SIR FRANCIS H. S., *Stone-worker's Progress, a study in stone implements* (Oxf. Univ. Press, 1953)

LAUER, J. PH., & DEBONO, F., *Techniques de façonnage des croissants de silex utilisés dans l'enceinte de Zóser à Saqqarah* (Ann. Serv. Antiq. Egypte vol. L, 1950)

MATHIASSEN, TH., *Flinthandel in Stenaldern* (Fra Nationalmuseets Arbjedsmark 1934, 18)

ORSI, P., *Miniere de selce e sepolcri eneolitici a Monte Tabuto e Monteracello presso Comiso* (Siracusa) (Bull. di Palet. ital. 1889, 165—206)

ROEDER, J., *Zur Lavaindustrie von Mayen und Volvic* (Auvergne) (Germania vol. XXXI, 1953, 24—27)

SCHNITTGER, *Die prähistorischen Feuersteingruben bei Kvarnby und Sallerup in Schonen* (Präh. Z. 1900, 163)

SMITH, RALPH E. L., *The Solutrean Culture* (Scient. Amer. CCXI, 1964, 86—94)

VIANA, A., & ZBYSZEWSKI, G., *Exploracoes Prehistoricas de silex em Campolide* (Anais de Fac. de Cien. de Porto vol. XXXIII)

WIEGERS, FR., *Das Ende des Eolithenproblems* (*Forschungen und Fortschritte* vol. 26, 1950, 49—50)

VIGNARD, E., *Les stations de taille de la plaine n.e. de Kom Ombo* (Bull. Soc. préh. France, vol. 53, 1956, 588—598)

19. MULLER, H., *La question de l'obsidienne* (*Revue Etud, Anc.* 1914, 91—94)

SKUTIL, J., *Prähistorische Obsidianwerkstätten in der Ostslowakei* (*Forsch. und Fortschritte* vol. XIII, 1937, 352—353)

SÜDHOFF, K., *Der Obsidianhandel in der Aegais und Kos* (*Die Naturwissenschaften* vol. XV, 1927, 235—337)

WAINWRIGHT, G. A., *Obsidian* (Ancient Egypt 1927, 77—93)

20. FORBES, R. J., *Studies in Ancient Technology* (Vol. V, Leiden, 1965, 187—188)

21. PLINY, XXXVI. 67. 196

21a. MELLAART, JAMES, *Earliest Civilisations of the Near East* (London, 1965, 16, 20, 32, 50, 58, 71, 80, 83, 84, 85, 105, 124)

22. PLINY, XXXVII. 66—77

23. BALL, J., *Contributions to the geography of Egypt* (Cairo, 1939)

BARROIS, A., *Aux mines du Sinai* (*Revue biblique* vol. 39, 1930, 578—589)

BLANCKENHORN, M., *Aegypten* (*Handbuch der regionalen Geologie*, vol. VII, Heidelberg, 1921)

DAY, E., *Geology of the Lebanon, and of Syria, Palestine and neighbouring countries* (London, 1934)

HUME, F., *Geology of Egypt* (3 vols., Cairo, 1931—1937)

TOLL, M., *The Mining resources of Syria* (*Engineering and Mining* J. vol. 112, 1921, 851)

24. BREIDENBACH, H., *Das Goldvorkommen im nördlichen Spanien* (Z. f. prakt. Geol. 1893, 16 & 49)

DE LAUNAY, L., *L'or dans le monde* (*Colin*, Paris, 1907, 89 ff)

SCHÜRMANN, H. M. E., *Alter Bergbau im Wadi Ballat* (*Geologie en Mijnbouw N. S.* vol. XIV, 4, 1952, 113—114)

BROMEHEAD, C. E. N., *Ancient Mining Process as illustrated by a Japanese Scroll* (*Antiquity* vol. XVI, 1942, 193—207)

25. ARISTOTLE, *de Mirab. Ausc.* 45; DIODOR, III. 45

26. *The gold resources of Egypt* (In: *Gold resources of the World*; XVth *Int. Geological Congres*, South Africa, 1929, no. 11)

27. BRUNNER, H., *Die Anlage der ägyptischen Felsgräber* (Glückstadt, 1936)

28. MORENZ, S., *Aegypten und die altorphische Kosmogonie* (*Schubart-Festschrift*, Leipzig, 1949, 100)

29. GUNN, B., and GARDINER, A., *The Temple of Wadi Abâd* (J. Egypt. Arch. vol. 4, 1917, 241—250)

GRIFFITH, J., *The Nauri decret* (L. Egypt. Arch. vol. 13, 1927, 193—207)

30. SCHAEDEL, *Die Listen des grossen Papyrus Harris* (Glückstadt, 1935)

31. LUCAS, A., *Ancient Egyptian Materials and Industries* (London, 1962)

32. BARROIS, A., *Aux mines du Sinai* (*Rev. biblique* vol. 39, 1930, 578—598)

BLAKE, R. P., *The Egyptian Mines on the Sinai peninsula* (In: M. Rostovtzeff, *The Social and Economic History of the Hellenistic World*, Oxford, 1941, Vol. III, 1633—1635)

DAVEY, J. G., *Turquoise in the Sinai Peninsula* (Trans. R. Geol. Soc. Cornwall, vol. 16, 1928, 42)

DAVIES, O., *Bronze Age mining round the Aegean* (*Nature* vol. 130, 1932, 985)

HARRIS, J. R., *Lexicographical Studies in Ancient Egyptian Minerals* (Berlin, 1961)

ROTHENBERG, BENO, *God's Wilderness, discoveries in Sinai* (London, 1961)

SIR FLINDERS PETRIE, W. M., *Researches in Sinai* (*Murray*, London, 1906)

GLUECK, NELSON, *The Other Side of Jordan* (New Haven, 1945, 50)

ČERNÝ, J., *Semites in Egyptian Mining Expeditions to Sinai* (*Archiv Orientalni*, vol. VII, 1935, 384—389)

JÉQUIER, G., *Précis Historique des mines du Sinai* (In: J. de Morgan, *Préhistoire orientale* Vol. II, 1926, 239—247)

MURRAY, G. W., *A New Empire Copper Mine in Wadi Araba* (Ann. Serv. Arch. Egypte, vol. 51, 1951, 217—218)

WEILL, R., *Les mots bi3, cuivre, métaux, mine, carrière, transport, blocs, merveille et leurs déterminatifs* (*Revue d'Egyptol.* vol. III, 1938, 69)

33. DIODOR, III. 12—14

34. GLUECK, N., *The Other Side of Jordan* (New Haven, 1940)

GLUECK, N., *Rivers in the Desert* (New York, 1959)

FORBES, R. J., *King Solomon's Copper Mines* (*Technion Yearbook* vol. 14, 1957, 43—47; 135—137)

BEN-ARIEH, Y., *Caves and ruins in the Beth Govrin area* (Israel Explor. J. XII, 1962, 47—61)

ROTHENBERG, B., *Ancient Copper Industries in the Western Arabah, Part I* (Pal. Expl. Quart. Jan./June 1962, 5—71)

ROTHENBERG, B., & LUPU, A. N., *Excavations at Timna* (Bull. Mus. Haaretz, Tel Aviv no. 7 June 1965, 19—28)

KIND, H. D., *Antike Kupfergewinnung zwischen Rotem und Totem Meer* (ZDPV 81, 1965, 56—73)

35. FREISE, FR., *Die Gewinnung nutzbarer Mineralien in Kleinasien während des Altertums* (*Z. f. prakt. Geol.*, 1906, 277—284)

FREISE, FR., *Geographische Verbreitung und wirtschaftliche Entwicklung des Bergbaus in Vorderasien und Mittelasien während des Altertums* (*Z. f. prakt. Geol.* 1907, 101—117)

ST. PRZEWORSKI, *Die Metallindustrie Anatoliens* (Leiden, 1939)

HANCAR, FR., *Urgeschichte Kaukasiens von den Anfängen seiner Besiedlung bis in die Zeit seiner frühen Metallurgie* (Wien, 1937)

MONGAIT, A. L., *Archaeology in the U.S.S.R.* (*Pelican Books*, London, 1961)

REFIK, A., *Osmanli devrinde Türkiye madenleri* (Ankara, 1931)

DAVIES, O., *The Copper Mines of Cyprus* (Ann. Brit. School Athens vol. XXX, 1932, 74)

35a. BASHAM, A. L., *The Wonder that was India*, p. 226; Ill. London News Sept. 1, 1962, pp. 322 ff.

DUNN, J. A., *The mineral deposits of Eastern Singhbhum...* (MGSI LXIX, 1937, 54 ff)

ALLCHIN, F. R., JESHO V, 1962, 195—211

SINGH, S. D., JESHO V, 1962, 214

GOETZ, H., *Building and sculpture techniques in India* (Archaeology 15, 1962, 252—261; 16 (1963), 47—53)

36. STRABO, XII. 3

37. ARISTOTLE, *De Mirab. Auscult.* 62

38. STRABO, XII. 3. 19. cap. 549; APOLLONIUS RHOD. 1007

39. PLINY, XXXVI. 16. 127

40. STRABO, XIII. 1. 51. cap. 607

41. XENOPHON, *Hell.* IV. 8. 37

42. HERODOTUS, I. 93; V. 101

43. HERODOTUS, V. 101

44. ISIDORUS, *Origin.* 19. 17; PLINY, XXXIV. 106; VITRUV VII. 8. 1

45. DIODOR, V. 64. 5

46. GAUL, J. H., *Possibilities of prehistoric metallurgy in the East Balkans* (Amer. J. Arch. 1942, 400—409)

47. VON MISKE, K., *Bergbau, Verhüttung und Metallbearbeitungswerkzeuge aus Velem St. Veit* (Westungarn) (*Wiener. Präh. Z.* vol. XVI. 1929, 81—94)

48. FRANZ, L., *Vorgeschichtliches Leben in den Alpen* (Wien, 1929)

HELL, M., *Der Götschberg bei Bischofshofen in Salzburg und seine Beziehung zum Beginn des alpinen Kupferbergbaus* (*Wiener Präh. Z.* vol. 14, 1927, 8—23)

HRADIL, G., *Der Geitschacht am Röhrerbühel in Tirol* (*Bl. f. Gesch. Techn.* vol. I, 1932, 81—91)

KRÜGER, H. PH. K., *Bergbau der Metallzeit* (*De Gruyter*, Berlin, 1931)

KLOSE, O., *Die zeitliche Stellung des prähistorischen Kupferbergbaues in den Ostalpen* (*Mitt. Anthrop. Ges.* Wien, vol. 61, 1931, 137)

KYRLE, G., *Der prähistorische Bergbau in den Salzburger Alpen* (*Oesterr. Kunsttopographie* vol. XVII, 1918)

KYRLE, G., *Die zeitliche Stellung der prähistorischen Kupfergruben auf dem Mitterberg bei Bischofshofen* (*Mitt. Wiener Anthrop. Ges.* 1912, 196 f)

KYRLE, G., *Die Gold-, Silber-, Blei- und Kupfer-gewinnung in urgeschichtlicher Zeit in den Oesterr. Alpen* (*Bl. Gesch. Technik* 1932, Heft 1, 63)

PAŠALIČ, E., *L'exploitation des mines dans l'antiquité en Bosnie-Herzégovine* (Galsnik, Serajevo, N. S. vol. IX, 1954, 47—75)

PARET, O., *Bergbau auf Metalle im Altertum* (*Aus der Heimat* vol. XLV, 1932, 305)

PITTIONI, R., *Neue Ergebnisse der österr. Bergbauforschung* (*Forschungen und Fortschritte* vol. XIV, 1938, 67—68)

PITTIONI, R., & PREUSSCHEN, E., *Osttiroler Bergbaufragen* (*Festschrift Egger*, Klagenfurt 1953, vol. II, 64—75)

PITTIONI, R., *Zum gegenwartigen Stand der Urgeschichte des Kupferbergwesens* (Sibrium vol. IV, 1958/9, 83—96)

VON SRBIK, R., *Ueberblick des Bergbaus von Tirol und Vorarlberg* (Innsbrück, 1929)

VOGL, K., *Bergbau und vorgeschichtlichen Funde um Kitzbühel* (Tirol) (*Wiener Präh. Z.* vol. XVI, 1929, 34—39)

ZSCHOKKE, K., und PREUSSCHEN, E., *Das urzeitliche Bergbaugebiet von Mühlbach-Bischofshofen* (*Anthrop. Ges.*, Wien, 1932)

49. ACHIARDI, G. D., *L'industria mineraria e metallurgica in Toscana al tempo degli Etruschi* (*Studi Etruschi* vol. I, 1927, 411 ff)

MINTO, A., *L'antica industria mineraria in Etruria ed il porto di Populonia* (*Studi Etrusche* vol. XXIII, 1954, 291—319)

BADII, G., *Le antiche miniere del Massetano* (*Studi Etruschi* vol. V, 1931, 455 ff)

RELLINI, U., *Miniere e forni preistorichi* (*Riv. di Antropol.* vol. 25, 1922/3, 155)

SAGUI, C. L., *Primary and secondary ores of the Bottino mines, Italy* (J. Econ. Geology, vol. XIX, 1924, no. 6)

50. CHAMPAUD, CL., *L'exploitation antique de cassitérite* (Notices Archeol. amor. 1957, 46—96)

SIEBER, S., *Zinnseifen* (Urania, vol. 18, 1955, 232—237)

BORLACE, C., *Historical Sketch of the tin trade in Cornwall* (Plymouth, 1874)

DAUBRÉE, *Aperçu historique de l'exploitation des mines métalliques dans la Gaule* (*Rev. Archéol.* 1881)

ENDERLEIN, G., *Sächsische Zinnbergwerke* (Abh. Ber. Dtsches Museum, vol. III, 1931, 127—152)

SCHUHMACHER, H., *Übersicht über die nutzbaren Bodenschätze Spaniens* (Leipzig, 1926)

STEPHENS, F. J., *General notes on ancient mining in Cornwall* (95. Report R. Cornwall Polt. Soc. 1928, 162)

STEPHENS, F. J., *The ancient mining districts of Cornwall* (Rep. R. Cornwall Polyt. Soc., N. S. vol. VII, 1932, 159—178)

51. CANCRINUS, *Beschreibung der vorzüglichsten Bergwercke* (Frankfurt, 1767)

52. VASSEUR, *Une mine de cuivre exploitée à l'age du bronze* (Anthrop. 22, 1911)

BATEMAN, A. M., *Ore Deposits of Rio Tinto* (*Econ. Geology* vol. 22, 1927)

NASH, W. G., *The Rio Tinto Mine, its history and romance* (London, 1904)

NOSTRAND, I. I., *Two notes on mines in Roman Spain* (*Pacif. Hist. Review* vol. IV, 1935, 281—289)

QUIRING, H., *Kupferzeitlicher Bergbau in Spanien* (*Fortschritte und Forschungen*, vol. XII, 1936, 79—80)

RICKARD, T. A., *The mining of the Romans in Spain* (J. Roman Studies vol. XVIII, 1928, 129—143)

DORY, A., *Las antiguas minas de cobre y cobalto del Aramo* (*Revista minerara, metalurgica y de ingenieria*, Madrid, 1893, 33 ff)

53. FORBES, R. J., *Studies in Ancient Technology* vol. III (Leyden, 1965)

54. FREYDANK, H., *Das Salz und seine Gewinnung in der Kulturgeschichte* (*Kali und verw. Salze*, vol. 23, 1929, 145—181)

HELFRITZ, H., *Die Salzgewinnung in Südarabien* (Kali, vol. 30, 1936)

LANGER, G., *Der prähistorische Bergmann im Hallstatter Salzberge* (*Berg.-, Hüttenmänn. Jahrb.* vol. 84, 1936, 149—170)

KYRLE, G., *Der prähistorische Bergbaubetrieb in den Salzburger Alpen* (*Oesterr. Kunsttopographie* vol. XVII, 1918)

MAHR, A., *Das vorgeschichtliche Hallstatt* (Wien, 1925)

SCHROETER, J., *Das Salz in der Vorgeschichte und in der Antike* (*Ciba Z.* no. 90, 1943, 3154—3160)

NENQUIN, J., *Salt, a study in economic prehistory* (Bruges, 1961)

55. LORET, V., *Le nom égyptien de l'alum* (Rec. Trav. Maspéro, vol. XV, 1893, 199—200)

TESTI, G., *Le antiche miniere di alum e l'arte tintoria in Italia* (Archeion vol. XIII, 1931, 440—448)

56. GALEN, *Opera Omnia* (edit. Kühn) vol. XI, 690—694; XII, 372—375

57. AIGERN, A., *Hallstatt, Kulturbild aus prëhistorischer Zeit* (Munchen, 1911)

MAHR, A., *Das vorgeschichtliche Hallstatt* (Wien, 1925)

FRANZ, L., *Vorgeschichtliches Leben in den Alpen* (Wien, 1929)

PITTIONI, R., *Untersuchungen im Bergbaugebiete Kelchalpe bei Kitzbühel, Tirol* (Band V, 2—3, Mitt. Präh. Komm. Akad. Wiss, Wien, 1947)

KYRLE, G., *Die Gold-Silber-, Blei- und Kupfer-gewinning... in den oesterr. Alpen* (Bl. Gesch. Techn. Heft 1, 1932, 62 ff)

TREPTOW, E., *Der älteste Bergbau und seine Hilfsmittel* (Beitr. Gesch. Techn. Ind. vol. VII, 1918, 155)

PITTIONI, R., *Zur gegenwärtigen Stand der Urgeschichte des Kupferbergwerk-wesens* (Sibrium, vol. IV, 1958/9, 83—96)

EINECKE, G., *Der Bergbau und Hüttenbetrieb im Lahn- und Dill-Gebiet und in Oberhessen* (Wetzlar, 1932)

REINECKE, P., *Bodendenkmäler spätkeltischer Eisengewinnung an der untersten Altmühl* (Dtsch. Arch. Inst. Röm. Germ. Komm, 1937, 128)

PREUSCHEN, E., und PITTIONI, R., *Osttiroler Bergbaufragen* (Festschrift R. Egger, Wien, 1953, vol. II, 64—74)

58. BINDER, I. I., *Die attischen Bergwerke im Altertum* (Laibach, 1895)

CALHOUN, G. M., *Ancient Athenian Mining* (J. Econ. Bus. Hist. vol. III, 1930, 561—584)

ARDAILLON, A., *Les mines du Laurion dans l'Antiquité* (Thorin, Paris, 1897)

CORDELLA, A., *Le Laurium* (Marseille, 1869)

VON ERNST, C., *Über den Bergbau in Laurion* (Berg-, Hüttenm. Jahrb. K. K. Bergakad. Wien, 1902, 447—501)

DAVIES, O., *Bronze Age Mining round the Aegean* (Nature vol. 130, 1932, 985—987)

DAVIES, O., *Two North Greek mining towns* (Cirrha Magoula and Volo Kastor) (J. Hell. Studies. vol. 49, 1929, 89—99)

DAVIES, O., *Ancient Mines in Southern Macedonia* (J. Anthr. Inst. vol. LXII, 1933, 145—162)

GAUL, J. H., *Possibilities of Prehistoric Metallurgy in the East Balkan Peninsula* (Amer. J. Archaeol. vol. XLVI, 1942, 400—409)

SAGUI, CORNELIO L., *The Ancient Mining Works of Cassandra*, Greece (J. Econ. Geol. vol. XXIII, 1928, 671—680)

SAGUI, CORNELIO L., *Economic Geology and Allied Sciences in Ancient Times* (J. Econ. Geol. vol. XXV, 1930, 65—86; Vol. XXVIII, 1933, 20—, 40)

SEIDENSTICKER, A., *Waldgeschichte des Altertums* (2 Bde, Frankfurt, 1886) (Bd. I, 340—344, Bd. II, 363—369)

59. WEHRLI, F., *Straton von Lampsakos* (Basel, 1950)

60. ATHENAEUS, *Deipnos.* VII. 322a

61. CLEMENT ALEX., *Stromata* I. 16. 76

62. STRABO, XV, 1. 30. cap. 700
63. LIVY, XLV. 40
64. DIODORUS, XXX. 9 & 19; XXXI. 14; LIVY, XLV. 40. 1; VELL. PAT. I. 9. 6; PLINY, XXXIII. 56)
65. STRABO, XIII. 4. 17. cap. 631
66. DIODORUS, III. 12—14; PHOTIUS cod. 250
67. STRABO, XII. 3. 40. cap. 562
68. APOLL. RHOD., Argon. II. 1002
69. ARDAILLON, E., Les mines du Laurion dans l'Antiquité (Thorin, Paris, 1897)

BROMEHEAD, C. E. N., Geology in Embryo (Proc. Geol. Assoc. London, vol. 56, 1945, 89—134)

HOPPER, R. J., The attic silvermines in the fourth century B.C. (Ann. Brit. School Athens, 48, 1953, 299—254)

HUDSON, D. R., Some Archaic Mining Apparatus (Metallurgia vol. 35, 1947, 157—164)

SAGUI, C. L., Economic Geology and Allied Sciences in Ancient Times (J. Econ. Geology, vol. 25, 1930, 311—332)

WILSDORF, H., Bergleute und Hüttenmänner im Altertum (Berlin, 1952)

LAUFER, S., Die Bergwerkssklaven von Laureion (2 vols. Wiesbaden, 1955/57)

WILHELM, A., Attische Pachturkunden (Arch. f. Pap. vol. XI, 1935, 206)
70. ALLAN, JOHN C., A Mineraçâo em Portugal na Antiguidade (Boletin de Minas (Lisbon) vol. II, 3, 1965, 1—37)

BATEMAN, A. M., Ore Deposits of Rio Tinto (Econ. Geol. vol. XXII, 1927)

BECKERS, J., Spaniens Erzlager in Zeichen der alten Handelsfahrten (Geogr. Z. 1937, 409—420)

BENOIT, F., Le grenat des Marseillais et les mines des Maures (Riv. Stud. Ligur. XXVI, 1960, 221—232)

BEUTHER, Das Goldland des Plinius (Z. Berg-, Hütten-, Salinenwesen vol. 39, 1891, 55)

BESNIER, M., L'interdiction du travail des mines en Italie sous la République (Rev. Arch. 1919, 31—50)

CUMMINGS, A. D., and MATTINGLY, H. B., A Roman mining document (Mine and Quarry Engineering, August 1956, 339—342)

CUQ, E., Le développement de l'industrie minière à l'époque de Hadrien (J. des Savants 1911, 296 & 346)

DAHM, O., Der römische Bergbau an der unteren Lahn (Bonn. Jahrb. 101, 1897, 117)

CANTACUZÈNE, G., Un papyrus latin relatif à la défense du Bas-Danube (Aegyptus vol. 9, 1928, 75)

DAVIES, O., Roman and Medieval Mining Technique (Trans. Instit. Mining and Metallurgy vol. XLIII, 1934, 3—54)

BROMEHEAD, C. E. N., Practical Geology in Ancient Britain (Proc. Geol. Assoc. London, vol. 57, 1947, 345—367; vol. 58, 1948, 65—76)

DAVIES, O., Roman mines in Europe (Clarendon Press, Oxford, 1935)

GOUGH, J. W., The Mines of Mendip (Clarendon Press, Oxford, 1930)

DUBOIS, CH., *Etude sur l'administration et l'exploitation des carrières, etc. dans le monde romain* (Paris, 1908)

FITZLER, K., *Steinbrüche und Bergwerke im ptolemaïschen und römischen Aegypten* (Leipzig, 1910)

DUBUC, E., *Les mines anciennes de l'Afrique du Nord* (*Géographie* vol. LII, 1928, 303—348)

HARRISON, F. A., *Ancient Mining activities in Portugal* (*Mining Mag.* vol. 45, 1931, 137—145)

JUENGST, E., & TIELSCHER, P., *Vitruv über Baugrube, Baugrund und Grundbau* (Mitt. Dtsch. Arch. Instit. Rom, 1936, 145—180)

HAVERFIELD, F. J., *Romano-British Somerset* (In: W. Page, *Victoria History of Somerset*, Constable, London, 1906)

GSELL, S., *Vielles exploitations minières dans l'Afrique du Nord* (*Hespéris*, 1928)

SCHAMP, H., *Die Bergwirtschaft Aegyptens* (Glückauf, vol. LXXXVII, 1961, 799—803)

LAFFRANQUE, M., *Poseidonius d'Apamée et les mines d'Ibérie* (Pallas V, 1957, 17)

KOLLING, A., *Ueber den Gebrauch der Steinkohle in römischer Zeit* (Germania, vol. XXXVII, 1959, 246—250)

MEHLIS, C., *Norikon* (Arch. f. Anthrop. vol. 50, 1930, 78 & 113)

LAVIOSA, P., ZAMBOTTI, *Miniere e metalli nella preistorica atesina* (Atesia Augusta vol. II, 1940, 2, 17—20)

NEUMANN, B., *Die Metalle, Geschichte, Vorkommen und Gewinnung* (Halle, 1904)

NEUBURG, CL., *Der Zusammenhang zwischen römischen und deutschen Bergbau* (*Z. ges. Staatswissenschaft*, vol. 63, 1907, 161—181)

VON PETRIKOVITZ, H., *Bergbau und Hüttenwesen in der römischen Rheinzone* (*Z. Erzbergbau Metallhüttenw.* (Deutschland) vol. 11, 1958, 594—600)

RICKARD, T. A., *The mining of the Romans in Spain* (J. Rom. Stud. vol. XVIII, 1928, 129)

SCHULTEN, A., *Forschungen in Spanien* (Archäol. Anzeiger 1933, 519)

STROMBOLI, A., *The Metallurgy of the Etruscans* (*Rassegna mineraria, metallurgica e chimica Italiana* vol. 68, 1928, 53)

STRAKER, E., *Wealden Iron* (Bell, London, 1931)

TÄCKHOLM, U., *Studien über den Bergbau der Römischen Kaiserzeit* (Uppsala, 1937)

SCHMID, W., *Norisches Eisen* (Springer, Wien, 1932)

VRYONIS, S., *The question of the Byzantine mines* (Speculum XXXVII, 1962, 1—17)

WEIERSHAUSEN, P., *Vorchristlichen Eisenhütten Deutschlands* (Leipzig, 1939)

CLEMENT, G., WHITTICK, *Roman Mining in Britain* (Trans. Newcomen Soc. vol. XII, 1931/32, 57—84)

71. VARRO, *De Re Rustica* I. 2. 22; TACITUS, *Germania* 43; PLINY, XXXIII. 1. 2

72. DIODORUS, V. 13. 1

73. PLINY, III. 20. 138; XXXIII. 21. 78

74. C. I. L. X. 8073. 3
75. B.G.U. 197; S.P.P. XXII. 48
76. Josephus, *Bell. Iud.* VI. 9. 418
77. Tacitus, *Ann.* 6. 19. 1; Plutarch, *Galba* 5; Suetonius, *Tiberius* 49; Strabo, III. 2. 10
78. C.I.L. II. 5181; translation in T. Frank, *An Economic Survey of Ancient Rome*, Vol. III, Spain, 167 ff (Baltimore, 1937)
79. Pliny, XXXIII. 70—77
80. Bromehead, C. E. N., *Mines and Gems* (Antiquity vol. VIII, 1934, 462—463)
81. Barrow, R. H., *Slavery in the Roman Empire* (London, 1928, 112)

Besnier, M., *L'interdiction du travail des mines en Italie sous la République* (*Rev. Arch.* vol. II, 1919, 31—50)

Calhoun, G. M., *Ancient Athenian Mining* (J. Econ. Bus. Hist. vol. III, 1931, 333)

Clark, J. G. D., *Prehistoric Europe, the economic basis* (London, 1952)

Christescu, V., *Vita econimica a Daciei Romane* (Bucarest 1929, 11 & 137)

Davies, O., *The Roman mines in Europe* (Oxford, 1935)

Diesel, E., *Wald und Mensch im technischen Zeitalter* (Abh. Ber. Dtsch. Museums, vol. VII, 1935, 2, 21—40)

Frank, T., *The financial activities of the equestrian corporations* (Class. Philol. vol. XXVIII, 1933, 4, 7)

Herzog, R., *Zu Xenophons Poroi* (*Festgabe* H. Blümner, Berlin, 1914, 469)

Hirschfeld, O., *Die kaiserlichen Verwaltungsbeamten bis auf Diokletian* (Leipzig, 1905, 145)

Kahrstedt, U., *Staatsgebiet und Staatsangehörige in Athen* (Gött. Forsch. 1934, 19)

Lauffer, S., *Die Bergwerkssklaven von Laureion* (Wiesbaden, 1955/57, 2 vols.)

Lauffer, S., *Prosographischen Bemerkungen zu den attischen Grubenpacht- listen* (Historia vol. VI, 1957, 287—305)

Liek, K. von der, *Die xenophontische Schrift über die Einkünften* (*Diss.* Köln, 1933)

Michell, H., *The economics of ancient Greece* (Cambridge Univ. Press, 1940)

Range, P., *Bergbau und Krieg* (Stuttgart, 1941)

Roeder, J., *Das Werden der Besitzverhältnisse im Mayener Basaltgebiet* (Germania vol. XXXIV, 1956, 248—260)

Rostovtzeff, M., *Social and economic history of the Hellenistic world* (3 vols. Oxf. Univ. Press, 1942)

Rostovtzeff, M., *Gesellschaft und Wirtschaft im Römischen Kaiserreich* (2 vols., Leipzig, 1929)

Frank, T., *An economic survey of ancient Rome* (6 vols. Baltimore, 1933— 1940)

Schönbauer, E., *Vom Bodenrecht zum Bergrecht* (Savigny Z. Röm. Abt. vol. 55, 1935, 183)

Schönbauer, E., *Beiträge zur Geschichte des Bergbaurechts* (München Beitr. Pap. Forschung, vol. XII, 1929, 13)

SCHWAHN, W., *Die xenophontischen Poroi* (Rhein. Mus. vol. 80, 1931, 253)

TARN, W. W., *The Greeks in Bactria and India* (London, 1938, 103)

THIEL, J. H., *Xenophontos Poroi* (Amsterdam, 1922)

82. *Codex Theod.* X. 19. 3.

83. *Codex Theod.* X. 19. 5

84. ENGELBACH, R., *The Problem of the Obelisks* (Fisher Unwin, London, 1923)

EDWARDS, I. E. S., *The Pyramids of Egypt* (Penguin Books, 1950)

LUCAS, A., *Ancient Egyptian Materials and Industries* (Arnold, London, 1962)

CLARKE, S., and ENGELBACH, R., *Ancient Egyptian Masonry, the building crafts* (Oxf. Univ. Press, 1930)

ENGELBACH, R., *The quarries of the western Nubian desert* (Ann. Serv. Antiq. Egypte, vol. XXXVIII, 1938, 65)

ANTHES, R., *Arbeitsweisen ägyptischer Bildhauer* (*Forschungen und Fortschritte* vol. 24, 1948, 169—173)

BRUNNER, H., *Die Anlagen der ägyptischen Felsgräber* (Glückstadt, 1936)

DAVIES, O., *Ancient Roman and Medieval mining technique* (*Trans. Inst. Mining Metallurgy* vol. XLIII, 1934, 3—54)

HARRIS, J. R., *The principles of Egyptian sculpture* (Apollo, Magazine of Arts LXXVII, 5, 1962, 349—355)

LEBEL, P., *Carrières exploitées en Gaule* (*Revue Archéol. de l'Est*, vol. IV, 1953, 360—365)

MACKAY, P., *Cutting and preparation of tomb-chapels in the Theban Necropolis* (J. Egypt. Arch. vol. VII, 1921, 154)

POULAIN, P., *L'extraction et la taille des sarcophages* (*Rev. Archéol. de l'Est* vol. V, 1954, 29—45)

PILLET, M., *L'extraction du granite en Egypte à l'époque pharaonique* (Bull. Inst. Franc. Arch. Orient. vol. XXXVI, 1936/7, 71—84)

ROSENFELD, A., *The Inorganic Raw Materials of Antiquity* (London, 1965, pags. 202—204)

SOMERS CLARKE, *Cutting granite* (Ancient Egypt 1916, 110—113)

ZUBER, A., *Techniques du travail des pierres dures dans l'ancienne Egypte* (*Techniques et Civilisations* vol. V, 1956, 161 & 195)

FISCHER, H. G., *A foreman of stoneworkers and his family* (Bull. Metr. Museum vol. 17, 6, 1959, 145—153)

85. PLINY, XXXVI. 15. 64—74

86. MURRAY, G. W., *Gold mines of the Turin Papyrus* (Appendix I to J. Ball, *Egypt in the Classical Geographers*, Cairo 1942)

87. LUCAS, A., *Building stones and other rocks*

ENGELBACH, R., *Ancient names for Materials* (both in: *Introduction to Egyptian Archaeology*, Egyptian Museum, Cairo, 1946)

HARRIS, J. R., *Lexicographical Studies in Ancient Egyptian Minerals* (Berlin, 1961)

HERMAN, A., *Steine und Steinbrüche der Alten Aegypter* (*Die Umschau* vol. 49, 1949, 271—274)

88. ANDREW, G., *On the Nubian sandstone of the eastern desert of Egypt* (Bull. Instit. Egypte vol. XIX, 1937)

DARESSY, G., *Les carrières de Gebelein et le roi Smendès* (Rec. Trav. Maspéro. vol. X, 1888, 133—138)

89. BROMEHEAD, C. E. N., *The forgotten uses of Selenite* (*Mineralogical Mag.* vol. XXXVI, 1943, no. 182, 325—333)

FORBES, R. J., *Studies in Ancient Technology* (Leiden, 1965, vol. V, 184—185)

90. CRAWFORD, O. G. S., *The quern-quarries of Mayen in the Eiffel* (Antiquity, vol. XXIX, 1955, 68—76)

HÖRTER, P., *Die Basaltlava Industrie bei Mayen in vorrömischer und römischer Zeit* (Mannus vol. VI, 283—294)

LUCAS, A., and ROWE, A., *The ancient Egyptian bekhen-stone* (Ann. Serv. Ant. Egypte vol. 38, 1938, 127—156)

ROEDER, J., *Die antiken Tuffsteinbrüchen der Pellenz* (Bonner Jahrb. vol. CLVII, 1957, 213—271)

SIEGLIN, W., *Die Entstehung des Namens Basalt* (*Forschungen und Fortschritte* vol. XI, 1935, 199)

ROEDER, J., *Zur Lavaindustrie von Mayen und Volvic* (Auvergne) (Germania, vol. XXXI, 1953, 24—27)

HÖRTER, P., *Der Kreis Mayen in ur- und frühgeschichtlicher Zeit* (Mayen, 1928)

91. ENGELBACH, R., *Chephren's Lost Diorite Quarries located* (Ill. London News March 26, 1938, 525)

LITTLE, O. H., *Preliminary Report on some geological specimens from the „Chephren Diorite" quarries, Western Desert* (Ann. Serv. Antiq. Egypte. vol. XXXIII, 1933, 75—80)

MURRAY, G. W., *The road to Chephren's quarries* (Geogr. J. vol. 94, 1939, 97—114)

MURRAY, G. W., *An archaic hut in Wadi Umm Sidrah* (J. Egypt. Arch. vol. XXV, 1939, 38—40)

ROWE, A., *Provisional notes on the Old Kingdom inscriptions from the Diorite Quarries* (Ann. Serv. Antiq. Egypte vol. 38, 1938, 391—396; 678—688)

ZIPPERT, E., *Diorit Steinbrüche in Nubien* (Arch. f. Orientf. vol. XII, 1938, 187)

92. BEHN, FR., *Führer durch die Granitindustrie auf dem Felsberg im Odenwald* (Schneider, Mainz, 1925)

SOMERS CLARKE, *Cutting granite* (Ancient Egypt, 1916, 110—113)

LUCAS, A., and ROWE, A., *The ancient Egyptian Behken-Stone* (Ann. Serv. Antiq. Egypte, vol. 38, 1938, 127—156, 677)

PILLET, M., *L'extraction du granite en Egyype à l'époque pharaonique* (Bull. Inst. Franc. Arch. Orient. vol. XXXVI, 1936, 71—84)

93. SETHE, K., *Die Bau- und Denkmalsteine der alten Aegypter und ihre Namen* (Abh. Berl. Akad. Wiss. Phil. hist. Kl. 1933, 864—912)

94. ANDREW, G., *On the Imperial Porphyry* (Bull. Inst. Egypte vol. XX, 1937, 663—681)

COUYAT, J., *La route de Myos-Hormos et les carrières de Porphyre rouge* (Inst. Franc. Arch. Orient., Caire, 1909)

DELBRÜCK, R., *Antike Porphyrwerke* (Leipzig, 1932)

MEREDITH, D., and TREGENZA, L. A., *Mons Porphyrites, the northwest village and quarries* (Bull. Fac. Arts Cairo Fouad I Univ. vol. XII, 1950, 131—147)

95. LEPSIUS, R., *Griechische Marmorstudien* (Abh. Preuss. Akad. Wiss., Berlin, 1890)

LIBERTI, S., *Sui marmi dei Partenone* (Boll. Inst. Centr. Restauro Roma, vol. II, 1951, 5—8)

DWORAKOWSKA, A., *The quarrying of stone in ancient Greece* (In Polish) (Archaeologia (Warsaw) 13, 1962, 6—55, French summary)

HIGGINS, C. G. and PRITCHETT, W. K., *Engraving techniques in Attic epigraphy* (A. J. A. 69, 1965, 367—371)

POMTOW, H., *Gesteinsproben aus den delphischen Bauten und Weihgeschenken* (Philologus vol. 66, 1907, 260—268)

YOUNG, W. J., *Note on the identification of marbles* (Latomus vol. XI, 1952, 465)

STUDNICKA, F., *Neue archaische Marmorskulpturen, Falsches und Echtes* (Jhb. Dtsch. Arch. Instit. vol. XLIII, 1928, 140—170)

96. SIR JAMES FRAZER, G., *Pausanias' Description of Greece* (Vol. II, London, 1898, 424)

97. PAUSANIAS, III. xxi. 4

98. PLINY, XXXVI. xi. 55—xii. 61

99. PAUSANIAS, VI. 19. 1

100. ARISTOTLE, *De Mirab. Ausc.* 48

101. STRABO, XII. 2. 8. cap. 538

102. STRABO, XII. 8. 14. cap. 577

103. SPRATER, F., *Der Brunhildisstuhl, ein Steinbruch der Mainzer Legionen an germanischer Kultstätte* (Mainzer Z. vol. XXX, 1935, 32)

FITZLER, K., *Steinbrüche und Bergwerke im Ptolemaïschen und Römischen Aegypten* (Leipzig, 1910)

LEHNER, H., *Ein Tuffsteinbruch des ober- und niedergermanischen Heeres bei Kruft* (Germania vol. V. 130—133)

BEHN, FR., *Die Steinindustrie des Altertums* (Berlin, 1926)

PORTER, MARY W., *What Rome was built with* (Frowde, London, 1907)

BLAKE, M. E., *Ancient Roman Construction in Italy from the Prehistoric Period to Augustus* (Carnegie Inst. Washington, Publ. 570, 1947)

BLAKE, M. E., *Roman Construction in Italy from Tiberius through the Flavians* (Carnegie Inst. Washington, Publ. no. 616, 1959)

BROMEHEAD, C. E. N., *Practical Geology in Ancient Britain* (Proc. Geol. Assoc. London, vol. 59, 1948, 65—76)

104. SENECA, *Epist. morales* LXXXVI

105. LIVY, XLI, xxvii. 5; PROCOPIUS, V. xiv. 7—11

106. STRABO, V. 2. 5. cap. 222; TIBULLUS, II. iii. 43—45

107. PAUSANIAS, III. xxi. 4

108. STATIUS, *Silvae* I, 2; I, 5; II. 2; MARTIAL, VI. 42

109. AUSONIUS, *Mosella* 362—364

110. PLINY, XXXVI. 159

111. VITRIVIUS, II. vii. 5—7

112. PLINY, XXXVI. xi. 55

113. M.A.M.A. IV. 7; C.I.L. II, 7024

CHAPTER III

ANCIENT MINING TECHNIQUES

1. *The tools of the Miners*

Generally speaking, the development of new tools for mining proceeded at a very slow pace (1). The functional shapes, invented long ago during the Stone Age, remained; the materials, from which the tools were made, changed with the centuries. The older horn-picks or suitable antlers, products of the chase, were slowly displaced by stone picks. Horn also served to make rakes, but it was too soft a material for attacking rocks and for a time stone picks held their sway. These single-bladed picks were hardly larger than the modern geological hammer. In softer strata such as the Cornish placers flint and wooden tools survived until the Middle Ages. The earliest metal picks were not generally made of copper or bronze, these materials being either softer than stone or more brittle. They were made of iron, such picks were already in use in Siphnos by 500 B.C., but stone picks had a long life in certain centres such as Sinai. According to Sir W. Flinders Petrie the stone tools found there were used for surface outcrops, but they were of little use when sinking shafts into the mountains for which copper chisels were used which left their marks on the rock-surface. Stone pounders, flint grubbers and stone wedges too survived for many centuries, the latter being used as late as the Middle Ages.

Harder rocks were attacked with gad and hammer, the gad usually having a square cross-section. The earliest hammers may have been pounding stones or stones drilled to receive a shaft, but it was the hafted pounding hammer, which displaced the stone pick. These hammers of the rilled type were made of water-worn pebbles, sometimes even disk-shaped, with a striking face on one edge. The groove round the middle served to attach the stone to the handle. In Pliny's days they were gradually being displaced by iron tools in the larger mines, but they were quite efficient tools and finds together with iron tools and coins prove that they were still in use here and there by the fourth century. In the Spanish mines they were certainly still in common use by the first century B.C. and in the Danube region they were not displaced earlier than some two centuries later to survive only in such outposts of the Empire as Wales, though not much beyond the earlier post-Roman period.

The Greeks and the Romans generally used iron tools of a type hardly differing from pre-Roman to medieval times. The single-bladed pick was slightly larger than the modern geological hammer, the 8—9" long blade being slightly curved. Harder rocks were worked with gads and hammers as in Neolithic times. Until recently a miner would take some dozen gads with him every day to be resharpened by a smith after the shift was over. They were sometimes unsocketed, but usually there was a socket-hole near the head through which passed a wooden handle to steady it. The cross-section of all gads was square, the long section on Roman and medieval specimens normally V-shaped. Iron 5—10 lbs hammers were used to strike the gads. Metal crowbars were used to lever off jutting pieces of rock. Battering rams, weighing up to 150 lbs, were used to break up quartz veins according to Pliny.

These were the normal metal tools found at Laurium, the "typis" (iron hammer), the "xois" (gad), the iron pick and the rake or hack made of iron and used to collect the ore. The hack or hoe had a shank bent over at 120°, however, horn and wooden rakes were still very common as were other wooden tools, which have often disappeared. In certain cases they have survived because of fortuitous circumstances such as those encountered by Palmer when he found many old miner's tools preserved at the bottom of an old shaft at Rio Tinto in a liquor rich in cupric and ferric sulphates, which kept metal objects, rope, esparto baskets and other tools in good shape. We know that the spades of pre-Roman and early Roman times were of a flat wooden type with very short handles and objects like a dustpan were used to shovel ore into buckets or bags. The later Roman shovel had the shape of a spoon with handle and blade in one piece, a specimen of which was found at Charterhouse in the Mendips. In medieval times the wooden spade used had a handle which fitted into the flat surface of the blade diagonally at about 60°. By the sixteenth century these shovels had rims cased in iron.

Mining tools have been found at Huelva and Rio Tinto in Spain, at Aveyron (France), Sardinia, Laurium, Cassandra (Macedonia), Cartagena and many other places. Among those finds we have several metal saws of the type discussed in our chapter on ancient quarrying. In the Felsberg quarries a saw, 4.50 M. long and 4 mm thick, was found. A bronze miner's helmet of quite modern style was found in three feet of stiff black leaf-mould at the bottom of a 100' shaft in a Roman lead mine near Cordoba (Sierra Morena), together with a bronze bell of Iberian type.

The notched-trunk ladders and the various forms of baskets and bags used in these ancient mines will be discussed later on. O. Davies has pointed out the continuity of tradition from Roman to medieval times. Certain tools may have evolved independently as products of similar needs, but most mining tools were traditional and handed on from generation to generation from pre-Roman times to post-Roman times. The single-bladed curved pick, the notched ladder and the eyelet gad, held in place by a wooden handle while the end is hammered, are a few obvious examples of this rule. The latter tool, for example, is not only described by Agricola, but it was found in Roman mines at Karacs, Laurium and Iglesias! Again we have a Japanese scroll depicting the work in the Sado gold mine (Japan), which started about 1650 and there too the tools such as hammers and wedges or gads (the latter held by tongs or pincers) differ hardly from those found at Rio Tinto or Laurium.

2. *Pitting and Driving*

In pre-Roman and post-Roman days ore-bodies were often exploited by pitting, e.g. shafts were sunk at regular intervals to explore the ore body. The law often required one or more shafts being sunk in each concession. The section of ancient shafts has been the subject of speculation. Some like Quiring maintain that there was a historical sequence of the different forms which he correlated with the current forms of housing during each period. He claimed that low and broad galleries were Neolithic, high and narrow ones belonging to the Iron Age, whereas the classical form had a square cross-section. However, his reasoning is not very strong, for surely the shaft and level have forms depending strongly on the type of rocks they are to meet, the timbering materials available and such technical reasons. Generally speaking one can only say that as a rule Egyptian and Greek shafts tend to be rectangular and Roman and Etruscan ones to be square. The shafts at Laurium for example measured 1.25—.40 by 1.50—1.90, the average depth being 50 M. At Cassandra (Macedonia) they were less regular, whereas in Spain and Sardinia they were sometimes no more than 1 M in diameter. Though walling a circular shaft will make it more secure these square and rectangular shafts are far more common in Roman times. Round shafts were used in pre-Roman and post-Roman Central

Europe, but they were not popular in the classical world. The Romans, like the Greeks at Laurium, used a peculiar type of shaft, the "twisted" shaft, on certain occasions, the square shaft was sunk in sections each at a slight angle to each other, so that in descending the shaft turns as much as 90° on its axis like a screw.

An unfinished, almost square shaft near San Roque (Linares) shows us how such shafts were sunk. The miner first picked vertically and soon cut deeper than the side of the vein, where the rock would split at the contact, so that the striations on the side-walls became more and more diagonal. The wall opposite the vein was not immediately cut back to its final limits, but from time to time about 2″ of the rock was scraped away to prevent it from contraction. This wall therefore has vertical tool marks. Beam-holes were cut as the shaft descended at about 2′ intervals in the opposite walls, wooden baulks being hammered into them to form a ladder. This was often set on one side of the shaft so as to leave room clear for the buckets. In Etruria these baulks were spaced at wider intervals. Porters must have sat on them and handed the buckets of ore up to the next man. Roman mines usually had relays of men stationed in the narrower galleries to transport the ore to winding or hoisting machinery in the main shafts. The depths of such shafts is of course variable but they frequently go down more than 200 meters. The casing was interrelated with the section of the shaft. Wood requires rectangular shafts, circular shafts being ideal for stone casing.

We do not possess much information of the methods used in driving galleries. Often one side of the rock-face was cut out by a channel some 1″ wide and 5″ deep, and then the rest of the face was chipped away (2). When a vein was followed the rock was chipped up to the hanging or foot-wall, which would easily split, as at Linares. The absence of tool marks in some places suggest the use of wedges, probably wooden ones expanding when wetted. In compact rock the above-mentioned method of cutting a groove down the left side of the gallery-face with iron tools and breaking the rest away seems to have been quite common, it was practised at Laurium and a great many other places.

The ancient galleries were low, this saved time in driving and using a number of slave-porters was much cheaper. The galleries at Laurium are mostly 2—3′ high and 2—2.5′ wide; the section is usually regular with the corners neatly cut away. Roman and Medieval galleries are generally trapezoidal, somewhat narrower at the top, and sections of 4′ by 8′ are not uncommon. The Romans, as far as we know, avoided pitting and preferred orderly systematic underground workings with frequent communication between the galleries and with the surface. The galleries with a section like a Gothic arch cut off horizontally just below the point seem to be of post-Roman date, the Romans sometimes made rectangular or even oval galleries, but generally stuck to the trapezoidal type.

The levels of Greek mines usually branch off from the shaft at depths varying from 10 to 25 M. The Romans also exploited some mines by levels, four at Andros. At Rio Tinto we find no less than eight levels, about 25′ apart. At Cartagena there was a central shaft with exploratory galleries at various depths, but on the other hand many Roman mines are just unplanned disorderly mazes for reasons which we discussed earlier. Mining with the help of numerous shafts is typical for early prehistoric times as well as for post-Roman Saxon mining areas, but we must also remember that even at Laurium one finds over 2000 shafts connected with over 140,000 meters of tunnels!

When attacking a vein the Romans drove down a sloping adit; if the vein was shallow the adit was often connected with the surface by means of shafts at regular intervals. When the ore was close to the surface like in Bosnia a gallery would have been more costly, for it required more timbering and more sterile rock would have to be removed. Such was also the case for the ochre-mines of Rio Tinto (3) and the copper-mines of Göllheim (Pfalz). To some extent a new shaft was made to be connected at a certain depth with the old one by a horizontal drift. In other cases there was a central shaft with galleries radiating off at various depths. In later Roman times the "cave-and-gallery" method was sometimes used, a cave in the hillside with either a broad or a narrow entrance served to house the miners and narrow galleries ran off it following small veins of ore.

The Romans also made use of drainage adits, which had to be level, but as there was no wheeled trolley in a mine before the Renaissance galleries need not be horizontal all through the mine. The breaking up of a vertical traverse by horizontal drifts to speed up the work was first discussed by Agricola. At Linares and Sotiel Coronada we find level from the surface two prospecting adits occasionally stepped upwards, where a vertical shaft would have cost much less. Entrances were usually steep or even vertical, as in most cases the water was being collected below the shaft and then bailed out to the surface. On the other hand at Huelva an adit of over 1800 meter was made and at Rio Tinto one of 2,000 meter.

We have already mentioned that timbering was sometimes used when

Table XIII – *Mining Terms*

English	Egyptian	Coptic	Greek	Latin
prospecting	'ḏ'w (I. 238. 19)	—	diakrino, gatomeo	scrutor
prospector	bj3 (I. 438. 12)	—	metalleutes	
mine (gold, copper) (also quarry)	ḥ3. t (III. 360. 11)	ϧн, ϧιτ	metallon	
„ ("terrace on coast", Sinai, Lebanon)	ḥtjw (III. 349. 6)	—		
surface deposits	bsj (I. 474. 8,9)	—		
vein		—	phlebes, rhabdos	vena
start mining	š3' k3. t (V. 99. 19)	—	kainotomeo	seco
sink a shaft		—	anasatto	—
hole, gallery	{ št3 (IV. 354. 14) / št3 (IV. 554. 12)	—	{ hyponomos, diadysis / dioryx, orygma	
shaft		—	phrear, katatome	
air-shaft		—	psychagogia	
tap subsoil minerals	ḥ3j (II. 473. 10)	—	pnigomai	
strike subsoil water	bsj (I. 474. 14)	—	ekbolades	
barren rock		—	aster	
selvage		—	aetos	
rock ceiling		—	mesoktrineus, ogmos	
supporting pillar, prop		—	xylon	
pit-timber		—	typho	
fire-setting		—	anapsycho	
ventilate		—	diorytto	
pierce (through)	ḥbḥb (V. 67. 8)	ⲕⲁϧⲕⲟ	diorytto, elayno	
hew out, extract		—	ekmetreo	
survey		—	ogmos	
area, concession limit		—	stomion	
mouth of pit (or shaft)		—	orytto	
wind (raise, hoist)		—	metallon, ergasimon	
mine in full exploitation				

	Egyptian	Coptic	Greek	Latin
mining industry	ws' (I. 370. 17)	—	metalleia, siderourgeia	metallicus
miner	ḳwr (V. 21. 9)	—	metalleus, diorytton	
„ (ores)	—	—	metallikos	argentifodina
worker in stamping-mill	—	—	kopeus	arenifodina
foreman in mines	—	—	metallarches	—
silvermine	—	—	argyreios	
sandquarry	—	—	—	
ochre mines	—	—	miltoruchia	
quarry (general term)	ikw (I. 139. 12)		—	
„ (stones)	št3 (IV. 554. 12)			
„ (open)	{ ḥ3. t (III. 360. 13)	ϧⲏ		
	{ ḥ. t (III. 359. 6)			
„ (underground chambers)	{ ḥt. t (III. 203. 18)	ϧⲓⲉⲓⲧ, ϧⲓⲧ		
	{ ḥ. t. t (III. 6. 6)			
stone-quarry	p3 š3d inr. w (IV. 415. 5)	—		
quarry in Elephantine	bj3. t (I. 438. 14)			
quarrymen	khkhw (V. 67. 9)			
„	ḫrtj nṯr (III. 394. 14)			
rocktomb quarrier	t3j bs3 (V. 348. 1)			
stone cutter (mason)	wšbw (I. 372. 12)			
„	ms. '3. t (II. 138. 19)			
stone-dresser	mdh. w (II. 190. 12)			
stonemason (incising inscriptions)	ḥm' (III. 282. 8)			
men towing stones	3ḥ' (I. 19. 12)			
to dig (well, minerals)	mnj (II. 77. 1), šr (IV. 550. 13)	ⲱⲓⲕⲉ		
to quarry	š3d(IV. 414.11;IV.415.3)	ϣⲱϫⲓ ⲕⲁϧⲕⲟ	kopto, typto	frangere
	wḥ3 (I. 346. 15)			
to separate slabs (blocks) of stone	ḳḥḳḥ (V. 67. 8)	ϥⲱϫⲓ ϣϫⲟⲧ		
dressing stone blocks	pg3 (I. 562. 1)	ϣⲟⲩϣⲧ		
	š'd (IV. 422. 13)	—		
crushing stone	ḥšb (III. 339. 6)			
broken stone	ḥšḥš (III. 339. 7)			

Mining Terms III

English	Egyptian	Coptic	Greek	Latin
grinding stone (ore)	tš3 (V. 329. 17)	ⲧⲟⲩ		
„ „	wšf (demot.)	ⲟⲩⲟ̄ⲟⲩⲧ		
mining technique	—	—	metallike techne	
mining machinery	—	—	metallika, mechanemata	
mining tools	—	—	lithourgika, sideria	
wedge	—	—	sphen, sphenarion	
pick-axe (pointed)	tr3t (pap.)	ⲧⲟⲣⲉ	skalis	
„ (broad)	—	ⲝⲁϫⲟⲙ	makella, dikella	
crowbar	—	—	mochlos	
gad	md3. t (II. 188. 5)	ⲙⲁϫⲓ	kopeus, xois, glaris	
chisel	—	—	glaris, toros	
cleaving hammer	—	—	krotaphis	
(pointed) hammer	—	—	kestra	
iron hammer (maul)	—	—	typis	
scraper	wšj (I. 358. 10)	ⲟⲩⲉⲓⲥⲉ, ϩⲓⲥⲉ	xystron	
saw	—	—		
tongs	—	—	karkinos	
leather bags (baskets)	h'r (III. 244. 9)	ϣⲁⲁⲣ	thylakos, sakkos	
water buckets	—	—	gaulos	
Archimedian screw	s'k (IV. 314. 14)	—	cochlias	cochlea
(mill-stone) grind	bnwt śwgm (IV. 76. 11) / s3s (III. 422. 6)	ⲥⲓⲕⲉ	chupto	mulitare
mill-stone	nd (II. 369. 11) / śśm (IV. 292. 9)	ⲛⲟⲩⲧ		
whetstone	inr r dm (V. 448. 15)	ⲧⲱⲙ		
washing ores	—	—	plyno, syro, hygraino	lavare
oredressing (washing) plant	—	—	katharisterion, kegchreon	
sorting (ores)	—	—	exaireo	
hand-sorting (sifting)	—	—	ekkathairo, diakrino	cernere
sieve	—	—	salax	
sieving crushed ore, screening	—	—	diasetho, diatheo	

sinking shafts or driving galleries. *Propping* was resorted to in dangerous grounds only. Even in prehistoric flint mines we find exhausted galleries and shafts filled with the debris of mining and flint knapping. This was even extended to galleries connecting chambers on sites rich in nodules. But even then accidents did happen and several skeletons of miners and their tools have been found on spots where the roof caved in. In classical Greece supports of a simple nature were often used, baulks between the hanging wall and the foot ground were fairly common and mortized olive-wood props are occasionally found at Laurium. On account of the danger of the roof caving in "arched supports are left at frequent intervals to bear the weight of the mountain", says Pliny (4). Such natural pillars, called "hormoi" of "mesokrineis", were mined last starting with those furthest away from the entrance of the mine. In such cases the country rock was left to subside, but in many cases filling was resorted to, for sometimes caves of 70—80 by 2,000 M had been completely emptied. The necessary material was carried down in the same baskets or bags used to transport the ore to the surface.

Underground surveying seems to have been a very difficult problem. There is hardly a trace of it in pre-classical days, and in Greek or Roman mines the surveying must have been extremely inaccurate in certain cases if any! When tunneling close to the earth's surface, for instance when piercing a mountain to prepare a duct for water (Samos!), the classical engineers could achieve very good results, but surveying at some depth seems to fail and tunnels make unnecessary detours. Adits usually follow valleys and where possible the direction of a gallery was preserved by sinking shafts to meet the gallery at regular intervals of 50—400 feet (Sotiel, Linares, S. Spain). The galleries usually deviate but slightly to the right of such shafts and this is then corrected. At Sotiel Coronada fairly accurate results were obtained by squaring. We are certain that geodetical instruments were used. At Mount Pangaeum fragments of an ingenious surveying table and metallic rods were picked up, which Sagui pieced together. Also Agricola reports that such instruments were used to survey adits and shafts and we know of course that the Greeks and Romans were competent surveyors from their tunnels, aqueducts and many other pieces of engineering. Therefore the practical results of mine surveying seem rather disappointing.

At this point it is worth while drawing attention to the wide range of mining terms (Table XIII) in ancient languages, which again proves that the Egyptians as well as the Greeks and Romans had much experience in the mining and quarrying of a great variety of mineral products.

3. *Extracting and Transportation*

Extracting the desired product from placers or open-cut mines did not commonly present great difficulties. We saw that the tools in use to loosen these products, hammers, gads and chisels or wedges, were known, and that then the coarser rocky components, the gangue and the desired product could be separated by pounding, grinding, washing and sieving. However, the extraction of the mineral or ore from the vein in galleries deep down presented more difficulties. Here "the miners meet with flinty rocks which they break up by heating them and pouring vinegar on them or more often, for steam and smoke make the air in the galleries unbearable, they hew them out with battering-rams fitted with iron heads weighing one hundred and fifty pounds, and they bear out the debris on their shoulders" according to Pliny (5).

This passage refers to the older method of "*fire-setting*", when the

Fig. 22.
Fire-setting in a mine (After G. Agricola, De Re Metallica)

rock-face as too hard to be tackled by pounding and chiseling. It was certainly in use for many centuries, for in Stone- and Bronze-Age mines sooty rock-surfaces, typically fractured pieces of rock and remains of charcoal and charred wood have often been found. The latter do not always point to fire-setting in flint mines, where such drastic measures seem hardly necessary in view of the soft strata to be worked.

Such a fire burned badly at the end of a gallery. Hence at Mitterberg one finds galleries with V-shaped longitudinal sections rather than with parallel floor and ceiling. The use of such fires was only possible if there was a good draught, it made the mine uninhabitable for some time and it was therefore little used if speed in working was essential. Moreover it was not of much use in much-fissured rock, so it was rarely use at Laurium. Also fuel had to be plentiful, this was so in the Alps, but

Fig. 23.
Cross-cut of a mine showing fire-setting (After Löhneysser's Bergwerck)

not in the Mediterranean in classical times and therefore fire-setting was not too common in Roman Spain. After the heating the rock was rapidly cooled with water. In certain cases there were arrangements of wooden pipes to bring water to the galleries for the rapid cooling of the heated rock-face (Mitterberg) and the galleries were planned to give a good draught to draw the smoke away. The addition of vinegar to this water has puzzled many.

The effect of the cold water on the heated rock was described by Pliny in the passage given above as "rumpere", and Livy (6), who tells us that Hannibal used the same method of fire-setting in making his way over the Alps, uses the verb "putrefacere" in this passage: "Since they had to cut through the rocks, they felled some huge trees that grew near at hand, and lopping off their branches, made an enormous pile of logs. This they set on fire, as soon as the wind blew fresh enough to make it burn, and pouring vinegar over the glowing rocks, caused them to crumble. After thus heating the crag with fire, they opened a way in it with iron tools...". The essential point of throwing water on the heated rock is to make use of the forces of contraction evoked through sudden fall of temperature. The vinegar is evidently believed to enhance the effect, for one could hardly hold that Hannibal's soldiers wanted to dissolve the limestone rocks (if any) in acetic acid. Still this vinegar in water is recommended by Apollodorus of Damascus for breaking ramparts after heating them with braziers (7). Similar methods of fire-setting continued in use during the eighteenth century in the Cumberland mines (8) and they were still used in Norway about 1885 and even more recently in Korea and the Gold Coast, in Bangalore and the Central Provinces of India. The Gold Coast miners held that the fetish of the gold mines would be offended if the reef were broken up with gunpowder instead of by fire-setting. In most cases vinegar was added to the water when cooling the rock rapidly (9). The method is still in use in Northern Italy in road-building. There the author was assured that the vinegar was "a very cold substance", which would strengthen the water's effect, for did not a drop of strong vinegar on the top of the hand cause an icy feeling?

The force of a strong current of water to break down softer beds of ore, especially when dealing with high-level alluvia, was used by the Romans on a fairly large scale. This method, called "*hushing*", was applied in Asturias in northern Spain (10) and Granada, in Gogofau and Dolaucothy in Wales (11), in Crvena Zemlja (Bosnia) (12), in Korabia and on the Zsil in Hungary (13). In these cases canals or aqueducts, sometimes many miles long, were built, discharging their water from cisterns onto the soft auriferous clays. The muddy water flowed into settling tanks, here the gold was deposited and separated from the sand. This method could be used along certain rivers of north-western Spain, near Granada, and on the Vrbas, but when treating auriferous quartz veins or quartzite which could not be disintegrated (Asturias, Dolaucothy, Korabia) the aqueducts were constructed to wash the ore at the pithead in order to avoid costs of transport of ore to the river-head. It is said that "the Romans brought the river to the ore, the Saxons the ore to the river" and it is certain that this latter method is characteristic of the post-Roman and medieval miner, whose individualistic system was opposed to the centralized "capitalist" system of the Romans and their equestrian companies exploiting mines with large sums of money at hand. The "arrugiae" in the gold-bearing districts of Spain are ably described by Pliny in the following passage (14):

"Gold dug up from shafts is called "channelled" or "trenched" gold; it is found sticking to the grit of marble, not in the way it gleams in the lapis lazuli of the East or the stone (granite) of Thebes and in other precious stones, but sparkling in the folds of the marble. These channels or veins wander to and fro along the sides of the shafts, which gives the gold its name; and the earth is held up by wooden props. The substance dug out is crushed, washed, fired and ground to a soft powder. The powder from the mortar is called the "scudes" and the silver that comes out from the furnaces the "sudor" (sweat), the dirt thrown out of the smelting-furnace in the case of every metal is called "scoria" (slag). In the case of gold the scoria is pounded and fired a second time, the crucibles for this are made of tasconium, which is a white earth resembling clay. No other earth can stand the blast of air, the fire, or the intensely hot material.

The third method will have outdone the achievements of the Giants. By means of galleries driven for long distances the mountains are mined by the light of lamps — the spells of work are also measured by lamps, and the miners do not see the day-light for many months.

The name for this class of mines is arrugiae (from the Greek "orysso, to dig?"), also cracks give way suddenly and crush the men who have been at work, so that it actually seems more venturesome to try and get pearls and purple-fishes out of the depths of the sea: so much more dangerous have we made the earth! Consequently arches are left at frequent intervals to support the weight of the mountain above. In both kinds of mining masses of flint are encountered, which are burst asunder ("rumpere") by means of fire and vinegar, though often, as this method makes the tunnels suffocating through heat and smoke, they are broken to pieces with crushing machines carrying 150 lbs of iron, and the men carry the stuff out on their shoulders, working night and day, each men passing them on to the next man in the dark, while only those at the end of the line see the daylight. If the bed of flint seems too long, the miner follows along the side of it and goes round it. And

yet flint is considered to involve comparatively easy work, as there is
a kind of earth, which is almost impossible to overcome. They attack
it with iron wedges and the hammer-machines mentioned above; but
this kind of potter's clay mixed with gravel, called "gangadia" is thought
to be the hardest thing that exists except for the greed for gold, which
is the most stubborn of all things. When the work is completely finished,
beginning with the last, they cut through, at the tops, the supports of
the arched roofs. A crack gives a warning of a crash, and the only person
who notices it is the sentinel on a pinnacle of the mountain. He by
shout and gesture gives order for the workmen to be called down and
himself at the same moment flies down from his pinnacle. The fractured
mountain falls asunder in a wide gap, with a crash which it is impossible
for human imagination to conceive, and likewise with an incredibly
violent blast of air. The miners gaze as conquerors upon the collapse
of Nature. And nevertheless even now there is no gold so far, nor did
they positively know there was any gold before they began to dig; the
mere hope of obtaining their coveted object was sufficient inducement
for encountering such great dangers and expenses.

Another equally laborious task involving even greater expense is
the incidental operation of previously bringing streams along moun-
tain-heights frequently a distance of 100 miles for the purpose of washing away the debris of this collapse; the channels made for this purpose
are called "corrugi", a term derived I believe from "conrivatio", a unit-
ing of streams of water. This also involves a thousand tasks; the dip of
the fall must be steep, to cause a rush rather than a flow of water, and consequently it is brought from very high altitudes. Gorges and crevasses
are bridged by aqueducts carried on masonry; at other places impassable
rocks are hewn away and compelled to provide a position for hollowed
troughs of timber. The workmen hewing the rock hang suspended
with ropes, so that spectators viewing the operations from a distance
seem to see not so much a swarm of strange animals as a flight of birds.
In the majority of cases they hang suspended in this way while taking
the levels and marking out the line for the route, and rivers are led by
man's agency to run where there is no place for a man to place his foot-
steps. It spoils the operation of washing if the current of the stream
carries mud along with it: an earthy sediment of this kind is called
"urium". At the head of the waterfall on the brow of the mountain reservoirs are excavated measuring 200 feet each way and 10 feet deep. In
these are left five sluices, in order that when the reservoir is full, the
stopping-barriers may be struck away and the torrent of water may

burst out with such violence as to sweep forward the broken rock (gold-bearing debris). In order to avoid the "urium" they have guided the water over flint stones and pebbles before letting it into the reservoirs. There is yet another task to perform on the level ground. Trenches are excavated for the water to flow through — the Greek name for them means "leads", and these, which descend by steps, are floored with gorse, this is a plant resembling rosemary, which is rough and holds

Fig. 24.
Section of a Roman shaft in the Esperanza mine (Rio Tinto, Spain) showing footholds for climbing.

back the gold. The sides are closed with planks; and the channels are carried on arches over steep pitches. Thus the earth carried along in the stream slides down into the sea and the shattered mountain is washed away; and by this time the land of Spain owing to these causes has encroached a long way into the sea. The material drawn out at such enormous labour in the former kind of mining is in this latter process washed

out, so as not to fill up the shafts. The gold obtained by means of arrugiae does not have to be melted but it is pure gold straight away. In
this process nuggets are found and also in the shafts even weighing
more than ten pounds. The gorse is dried and burnt and its ash is washed on a bed of grassy turf so that the gold is deposited on it. According
to some accounts Asturias and Gallaecia and Lusitania produce in this
way 20,000 lbs of gold a year, Asturias producing the largest amount."

The *transport of the ore* extracted underground was one of the most
important problems to be solved. When seams were close to the sur-

Fig. 25.
Roman winding machinery (Nemi Museum)

face, it was customary to arrange for ladders or series of steps to be cut
out of the shaft-face intervening between the galleries and the surface,
or a series of shallow ladders were installed for the same purpose,
which was the carrying of bags or baskets on the backs of men or
women. Some of these ladders were notched tree-trunks. Ladders were
used where timber was more plentiful. More elaborate ladders sometimes had two prongs at the base to fix them firmly in the ground
(Mitterberg, Ajustrel). At Dean a plank was found with holes through
which the feet could be stuck when climbing this solid ladder (15). In
other cases piece of wood were let into the walls of the shaft at 2'—3'

distance to form a ladder. Trough-like wooden vessels, sometimes
with a leather handle or grip, and sometimes shod with two iron bands,
were dragged along the gallery floor to transport the ore to the shaft
(Aramo, Mitterberg, Jura). At Cartagena the ore was carried to the
adits in esparto buckets, some 20 cm in diameter and 17 cm high, and
in a few mines with narrow galleries bronze bowls were used for this
transport. In Laurium and in Central Europe leather sacks, carried
like "Rück-sacks", about 77 cm high and provided with straps and
strengthened with ribs of ash, were used. They were easy to tip when
arrived at the top of the mine without detaching the straps. Baskets
woven from strong grasses like esparto and ordinary leather bags were
used in sizes mostly adapted to the nature and specific gravity of the
ore collected.

The transport in the galleries with the help of wheeled trolleys became possible in the days of Agricola. However, this involved more engineering works to ensure level tracks in drainage adits, which were high and wide enough. Sometimes standard axle-lengths were used, even in

Though most of the earlier mines, and even some later ones had
relays of porters bringing the ore to the surface (Spain, Cyprus), the
mouths of the shafts in many mines clearly show the traces of ropes on
the lip (Cassandra (Macedonia), Campiglia, Paros, Batignano (Tuscany),
Aramo). With increased depths the baskets or corves were made larger,
which after being filled with ore, were attached to a hemp rope and
wound to the surface by means of capstans, winches or animal power.
Every 100 feet increase in depth halved the output per shift and more
than doubled the price of the product. In the Nurra mines (Sardinia)
the remnants of a capstan have been found and cranes and other mechanical devices for hoisting have been described in many details by
Vitruvius and other classical authors, they were in common use in
architecture. As long as such hoisting machinery depended entirely on
human, animal or water-power (the latter having been introduced in
the days of Agricola) the load of ore per wind was limited and it remained almost stationary until the introduction of steam as a source of
power by the end of the eighteenth century.

The transport in the galleries with the help of wheeled trolleys became
possible in the days of Agricola. However, this involved more engineering works to ensure level tracks in drainage adits, which were high
and wide enough. Sometimes standard axle-lengths were used, even in
conjunction with parallel lengths of stones or rutways with a 4′6″—5′4″
gauge. Often we find a single line of way with shunting places as a
measure of economy when such traffic in the mine was not too heavy.

In 1788 John Curr of Sheffield introduced wooden tubs, cages and
shaft-guides for winding in coal-mines thus obtaining increased winding speeds and greater safety. He also introduced the division of shafts

by vertical partitions, which assisted ventilation and prevented the collision of the cages in the shafts. The modern systems of cages constructed from an iron frame guided by rails was introduced in 1834.

In the ancient quarries the blocks were usually fastened on a kind of sledge, sliding on a double set of rollers. At Paros the marble blocks cut underground were raised along inclined planes. Rows of strong pins were fixed solidly on both sides of the inclined plane at convenient distances. Three differential capstans were employed for rolling up the weight, and were shifted upward from one pin to another. A similar system was generally used in lowering blocks from quarries on to the road. Only in this case no capstan was used, but three strong ropes were turned three or four times around the pins and slowly released as the weight descended. The friction of the ropes against the pins acted as a break on the speed of the block lowered. This classical method is still in use in the Carrara marble quarries.

4. *Illumination, Ventilation and Drainage*

Illumination was the easiest of these three problems which the ancient miners had to solve, they simply applied the types of lighting which were used in their houses and buildings (16). Some of the remains of charcoal and charred wood in ancient flint mines may derive from fires used for lighting (Champignolles, Grime's Graves, Petit-Garonne), but in Cissbury and certain pits in Grime's Graves round stone bowls were found placed in niches, identical with the limestone bowls, filled with whale-oil and a wick of moss, still used by the Eskimos. A lamp of this type was recently recovered at Lascaux. At Aramo resinous torches or pieces of skin, soaked in fat, were used. In Hallstatt two types of splinters were found. The flat, broad type, still made in the region and used for lighting fires, is frequent. All specimens found were charred at one end and we are not sure whether they may have been used in bundles. The second type of splinter is round, it has a diameter of about 1 cm. Such splinters, 50—100 cm long, were bundled to form "Buchel" or "Buchelfackel" and used as torches. Several of such torches were found made of fir or pine and held together with rings of linden-bast. Their manufacture was a special trade until very recently. Such torches were also used in the mines of Hallein, Mitterberg and Japan.

In the scroll illustrating the gold mines of Sado (c. 1650) the miners carry torches, and in one case a lamp, when travelling about, but like in classical mines, at all working places small lamps are placed on ledges.

For as Pliny said "lamps serve to measure the spells of work and for many months together the workers are without the light of day". These lamps were simply shallow dishes of terracotta or stone with a small wick floating in it. The cup with a pinched rim for wick support and a widened footring is a later type also used in Egypt and Carthage. In the Greek homeland a lamp of this type was found in the workings of a Thracian gold mine dating back to about 350 B.C. Similar lamps were found in mines at the Isle of Seriphos, Thasos, Laurium (with pentagram decoration!), Transsylvania, Spain, Sardinia and Tunis. The Greeks and Romans placed these lamps in niches about 5 cm deep and they stuck these lamps with clay. Some of these lamps in the form of a fish or inscribed with the word "Ichtus" are taken as proofs that Christians worked in the mines (Rio Tinto). We have no proof that lamps were ever fastened to the forehead of the miner notwithstanding Diodorus' testimony (III. 12. 6). Ancient lamps would not have been very satisfactory if worn by the miners themselves like our electric lamps. Though we have one or two picture of a lamp hanging from the roof of a gallery no such evidence was found in the mines themselves. The so-called "frog-lamp", perforated to fit on to a vertical stick, appears in Saxon times only.

Ventilation was a very serious problem in ancient mining as we saw in the preceding pages. The shafts and galleries were narrow and many of the minerals collected gave off noxious gases or were poisonous like the ore from the realgar-mines of Pontus Strabo described. This is certainly one of the reasons why the Romans preferred open-cast workings. Bundles of twigs found at Hallstatt may have served as fans and "if the air at great depth begins to act injouriously, they try to improve it by the constant waving of cloth flaps" according to Pliny (17). Still in the mines of Aramo, Laurium, Hallstatt, Konia and Spiennes the remains of miners were found, some of whom were certainly suffocated. The bad air down below was worsened by fire-setting. Some shafts at Laurium descend from the bottom of a short slope, and could only be meant for ventilation, for they would be useless for haulage. There are other examples of real ventilation shafts built to improve the air (Sinai), mostly rising from galleries. Vitruvius devotes a special paragraph of his book to the testing of air in wells, etc. (18). We do not know whether the ancients used the later device of building a partition in the shafts, one half of which then functioned as a ventilation shaft, but seeing their dimensions, this seems doubtful. The "Wetterscheider" would seem to be of sixteenth-century date or even later.

When long adits were constructed to dewater the mine, a series of shafts were often opened along them, as at Sotiel Coronada, south-west of Rio Tinto, in order to maintain the air supply near the working-front. Later such shafts along the line of adits and galleries would provide good ventilation, notably when combined with intercommuni-cating parallel galleries (Cissbury). There was also a system of sinking parallel pairs of shafts, one of which had a ledge before entering the gallery-system. On this ledge a fire could be built to maintain a draft in the underground maze (Laurium, Mitterberg, Rio Tinto). Sometimes the same effect seems to have been obtained by building a chimney on one of the two shafts. Traces of such chimneys are reported from the Mount Pangaeum mines. Adits at different levels intercommunicating and even doors used to direct the air currents towards different parts of the mine are mentioned in reports on ancient mines. But there was no solution with the help of some mechanical device like blowers.

Drainage was certainly by far the most difficult of the three problems we are discussing. The ancient miner must have been powerless against sudden floodings of his mine and he was definitely limited in exploiting the veins much below sea-level in most cases. It was beyond his power to lower the subsoil water-level substantially, but he gradually developed means to overcome the danger of flooding to some extent. The cost and inefficiency of ancient drainage machinery made it difficult to work a mine well below the subsoil water-level, hence the work at Laurium stopped at about sea-level and at Astoescoria in the Pyrenees the miners went but five fathoms below the river-level (19). The most primitive way of getting rid of the water was simple diverting it into side-galleries (20) or to dig a hole in one part of a gallery into which it would then flow (Neolithic flint mines). Some of the adits in older mines have a water-channel along their side. A good way of getting rid of this water was driving a cross-adit where the configurations of the hill-side permitted such a method though it might prove expensive. Galen (21) reports on such an adit to tap the mineralized waters oozing from old workings at Soli. The water collected in a pool at the further end of the gallery, from which it was bailed out and carried to the surface by relays of slaves. Hand-bailing in relays was common like trans-porting ore to the surface with relays of slaves (22). This bailing involved the use of bronze buckets, such as found at Sotiel Coronada and Posadas, esparto buckets lined with pitch and set in a frame of wood (Cartagena), simple wooden buckets (Mitterberg), or baskets woven of birch twigs and yarn, which became tight by swelling during use. In Spain the pottery jugs used in some mines are ovoid and tip to fill easily when lowered in the water. The esparto buckets look like haulage baskets with a pointed base, which are easily tipped and re-filled, and strengthened by 4 or 6 wooden ribs with a V-shaped cross-bar as a handle (23).

The porous rock at Laurium or the dry climate of Egypt did not make drainage adits necessary there, and at the deepest levels fissures could sometimes be used to get rid of the water. The paucity of adits for drainage purposes at Cartagena and other early Roman workings suggests that their use was the result of a gradual development. Good efficient drainage adits date from a later period (Centenillo, Transsyl-vania, Savoy, Rio Tinto), in the latter area in two cases two parallel and intercommunicating galleries were cut, the lower one used for drainage purposes. If the formation of the hillside permitted it, the working was drained by a cross-cut at a deep level (Minas de Mouros, Madenokhorio, Dolaucothy), of which type no less then 13 were found at Rio Tinto. At Centenillo adits meet the vein at depths of 150, 210 and 250 M. In the second Table of Ajustrel we find the Roman govern-ment constructing and repairing a large drainage adit for the use of the concessionaires who were not allowed to touch it!

During the classical period the ancient mining engineers began to apply machinery to difficult drainage problems. There was of course a wealth of irrigation and water-lifting machinery available, which had hitherto been used in agriculture only (24). In his tenth book Vi-truvius discusses the "tympanum", which is nothing but the ancient compartment-wheel or tâbût of the Egyptians, the "rota" or the bucket-wheel (the Persian wheel or sâqija), mill-wheels or water-wheels, the cochlea or Archimedean screw and the "water-machine of Ctesibius" which is nothing but a force-pump (25).

The earliest device to be introduced into the Spanish mines was the cochlea or Archimedean screw, and this is what Diodorus (26) has to tell about them: "All the ground in that region of Spain is a tangled network of veins which wind in many ways. And now and then, as they go down deep, they come upon flowing subterranean waters, but they overcome the might of these rivers by diverting the streams which flow in on them by means of channels leading off at an angle. For being urged on as they are by expectations of gain, which indeed do not deceive them, they push each separate undertaking to its con-clusion, and what is the most surprising thing of all, they draw out the waters of the streams they encounter by means of what is called by men the Egyptian screw, which was invented by Archimedes of Syracuse at the time of his visit to Egypt; and by the use of such screws they carry water in succesive lifts as far as the entrance, drying up in this way the spot where they are digging and making it well suited to the furtherance of their operations. Since this machine is an exceptionally ingenious device, an enormous amount of water is thrown out, to one's astonishement, by means of a trifling amount of labour, and all the water from such rivers is brought up easily from the depths and poured out on the surface".

Fig. 26.
Pompeiian wall-painting showing a slave moving an
Archimedean screw with his feet.

It is said that Archimedes, when visiting Egypt about 220 B.C., saw such screws in action for pumping water onto the fields, and they are still in use throughout the Nile Valley for irrigation purposes. The British Museum has a terracotta of a slave working a cochlea with his feet, supporting himself on a pole and turning the inclined barrel like a tread-mill. He thus "screws" the water up some six feet. At Pompeii a wall-painting was discovered by Halbherr in 1927 showing a similar scene. The lift of such a cochlea depends of course on its length and inclination, and strangely enough some of the screws found in Spanish mines are set at an angle of 15° only, thus giving a lift of some two feet only, whereas in Japanese mines (Sado) they are fixed at 35—40°, and they have a length of some 3.60 M, some being 48 cm in diameter.

The introduction of the cochlea in the Spanish mines seems to have taken place in the first century B.C. Some of these screws have a wooden core on which are set screw-vanes of wood (Alcaracejos) or copper (Posadas, Centenillo), the whole being encased in a barrel of planks. The screws are pivotted by wooden pins on iron beams, some have an iron shoe. Some are worked by rotating the barrel, some by rotating the screw with a crank. If set at a reasonable slope like 40° a 12' long screw would give a lift of about 8', but usually the slope is but 15—20° and the lift but two feet. On the other hand such screws could be set in series, one man could work them and they gave a steady flow of water, whereas the larger wheels would have to be worked by treadmills,

Fig. 27.
Oak Archimedean screw found in Sotiel mine
(Now in Liverpool Institute of Archeology)

moved by two to three or even more men. It is clear that both ways of drainage were costly and paid only when the ore was rich.

Randall described an oak screw found at the Cerro Muriano mine near Cordoba which was 5' long and 6—7" in diameter, with a barrel of sheet lead, but it is doubtful whether this screw was really of Roman date. At the Coronada workings three Archimedean screws were found some 3.60 M long and 48 cm in diameter, placed in a series, one above the other. The most perfectly preserved example of a cochlea was re-covered at the Centenillo mines near Linares (27). It consists of a wooden core, 8" in diameter, into which a copper helix, 1/8" thick, is fixed. This is in turn attached to the longitudinal laths of a barrel, a cylinder 20" in diameter and 14' long. Each end of the barrel was centered in an iron point pivoting in a socket set in the timber. In the

Castulo group of workings no less than five such screw pumps have been recovered. The report says that "it is likely that as many as twenty were in use at one time in the deepest parts of the Roman workings".

Auden discovered an oak screw at the Sotiel mine, now in possession of the Liverpool Institute of Archaeology. The central axis is 24″ in diameter, the helix projects about 2.4″ and is over 1″ thick. It is built up from slabs 1/8″ thick, ½″ wide and over 1″ long, glued together vertically; the pitch at the top of the blades is some 7″. A Roman screw, some 8 M long and 30 cm in diameter, made of chestnut timber, was found at Beaune (Haute Vienne) (28).

Fig. 28.
Compartment-wheel used by the Romans to drain the mine
at Rio Tinto, S. Spain. (After Palmer)

It is interesting to mention that in 1637 Soho, a hydraulic engineer introduced the "tatsudoi" in Japan, wooden Archimedean screws about 8′ long and 1′ in diameter. Jerome Cardan (Cardanus) claims in his De Rerum Subtilitate that in his days (about 1550) a smith from his home town, Pavia, rediscovered the cochlea! This can hardly be true seeing the fact that Vitruvius, one of the most popular authors in those days, describes it in detail!

Bucket-wheels have been found in Spanish and Transsylvanian mines but they required much labour and seem to have been found less efficient than compartment-wheels. In the northern workings of Rio Tinto such a wheel with fragments of rope still adhering was found in one of the galleries and described by Palmer in 1926. This was a reversed undershot wheel, 14.5′ in diameter with 24 compartments 15″ × 7″ × 5″, fastened by wooden dowels, rotating on an axle of leaded bronze.

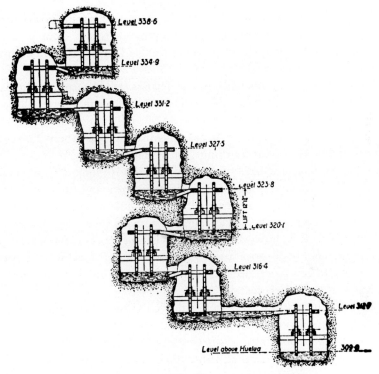

Fig. 29.
Nest of eight wheels recovered at Rio Tinto in 1920/21
giving a lift of 97 feet (After Palmer)

Probably such wheels were turned out by a sort of rudimentary mass-production since they were made of identical pinewood, not indigenous in Andalusia. The hubs were of oak. Usually they were placed parallel in pairs, each worked by a slave in a treadmill. A reconstructed wheel was found to raise $13\frac{1}{2}$ lbs of water per minute through 12′ with an overall efficiency of 61%.

In 1919—1921 a whole nest of such water-wheels was found in the

Rio Tinto mine. The remains of eight pairs were identified. To give a constant direction of flow the wheels in each pair revolved in opposite directions and the discharge from each couple was carried to the sump of the next pair above. The average diameter of the wheels was $4\frac{1}{2}$ M, the total lift of the set was 30 M. The lift varies considerably, thus wheels found at Planes lift only 6—8' and at Rudo $9\frac{1}{2}'$. In a shaft at Logrono (Old Castile) a 15' water-wheel was found, turned by men walking on the outer-rim. In Leon the wheels measured over 20', two rows of ten slaves could have walked inside. The shafts at this mine go down to 700' but the limit of drainage by pumping does not seem to have reached yet. One of these water-wheels is said to be in a museum in Madrid.

Similar wheels have been found at Tharsis (Huelva) and in the San Domingos mines in Portugal fourteen such wheels in a series along a gallery dipping at 40° raised the water 44 M to a height at which natural drainage was possible. In the Minas dos Mouros in northern Portugal Harrison found ancient workings, in which narrow water-roads 16" deep had been channelled at the side of galleries 16' square. At intervals these widen into pumping stations. In the centre and floor of such a room there was placed a square block of granite around which there is a worn circular track such as might have been caused by an animal-driven whim. It is, however, doubtful whether this late-medieval type of arrangement really goes back to Roman times. Typical Roman compartment-wheels like those in Spain were also found in Transsylvania at Ruda (29) and Verespatak.

The conquistadores, who were still well aware of the drainage machinery of the Romans in Spain carried the water-wheel to the New World. In 1896 the Espiritu Santo mine in Darien was reopened, which had been previously worked from 1665—1727. Woaks describes the finds in these words: "Five treadwheels were found here, some in a very perfect state of preservation. They were about 12' in diameter and evidently raised the water by stages of about 30' (?) each. There were all built on the same principle. The small drum about 4' in diameter is mounted on the spokes of the big wheel, and round it the endless chain of buckets is hoisted, the buckets dumped into a dugout launder, inserted under the rim of the small wheel, through which the water was conveyed to the sump of a similar wheel and again raised another stage. We know that by this means the Spaniards raised about 80 gallons of water per minute to a height of well over 100'. The buckets were made of leather."

A similar contrivance with a chain of basket-work carrying earthen pots is used in Cyprus and the Near East for irrigation purposes, a horizontal drum rotating on a vertical axis by the power of a mule or donkey moving in a circular track provides the motive power to the waterwheel. Only in late-medieval times were underground halls cut in which a rotating animal could work a chain-pump with buckets (salt-mines of Reichenhall). As far as we know horses were not used underground before the fourteenth century.

As to the suction-pump or force-pump of Ktesibios described by Vitruvius, examples of such pumps have been found in the ruins of Castrum Novum (Marinello, Etruria) (30) and Bolsena. Both in China and Japan wooden bamboo suction pumps of this type were used, but it is doubtful whether they play any part in the drainage of classical mines.

5. *Dressing the Ore*

Though the crushing, sifting and washing of ores are in reality preparatory phases of metallurgy, a few pages will be devoted to their discussion, as sites, where such operations were conducted, very often accompany ancient mines and shafts. The ancients generally picked or enriched the ores before transport and hence such operations were mostly conducted at the pit-head and not in metallurgical centres. Demosthenes makes a distinction between the mines and the plants where ores were dresses (31), which in some cases only were far apart. The words of the Ajustrel Table "expedire, frangere, cernere, lavare" show that the ore was pounded, hand-sorted and washed before being smelted by the "scaurarii" and refined by the "testarii". Other texts have "quod est tunditur, mulitur in farinam, lavatur, uritur" and the Greek authors have the same sequence (32).

Pounding tools were of course easily made from boulders (gabbro, diorite, quartz, etc.) found in brooks and rivers. In prehistoric times ores were usually pounded with rilled hammers or spherical and pear-shaped mullers on cup-marked querns, and then rubbed and ground with stone rollers. Pounding by hand was still practised in Roman Dacia and in medieval Britain. Later, however, the hand-sorted ore was crushed and ground, stone rollers becoming obsolete in later prehistoric times. After the gangue (ekbolades) had been removed the ore was put in mortars of trachite or quartzite and crushed with iron pestles. Usually the ore was first ground to the size of grains of millet (kegchros) in the plant called "kegchrion" by the Greeks, to be milled to flour later on.

The Assyrian smelters also used their ᵃḤAR. AD. BAR or erû ad-bari (mill of lava) and other forms of hand-mills or the larger animal-driven mills such as the ᵃḤAR. DUK. KA. BUR, the erû paḫari or potter's mill (roller mill) and other forms of crushing machinery besides mortar and pestle such as agricultural techniques had developed (33). Such hand-mills of hard stone were used in Egypt, Spain, Laurium and all over the classical world and they continued in use for many centuriers after the Roman Empire had fallen. Schürmann reported that some hundreds of granito-diorite mill-stones were found next to over a hundred miner's shelters at Wadi Ballat in the eastern desert. Here as in Roman Cerro Muriano and other mines in Spain these mechanical

Fig. 30.
Querns for grinding gold ore in an ancient Nubian mine.

processes were carried out near the placer or pit-head, even the smelting furnaces are often found nearby and only raw material or refined metal would have to be transported.

Diodorus in quoting Agatarchides' description of the Nubian gold mines (34) says that the quarried stone was first reduced to the size of a vetch in mortars with iron pestles, then milled to the consistency of the finest flour, then "in the last steps the skilled workmen receive the stone which has been ground to powder and take it off for its complete and final working for they rub the stone which has been worked down upon a broad board which is slightly inclined, pouring water over it all the while; whereupon the earthy matter in it, melted away by the action of the water, runs down the inclined board, while that which contains the gold remains on the wood because of its weight. And repeating this a number of times, they first of all rub it gently with their hands, and then gently pressing it with sponges of loose texture they remove in this way what is porous and earthy, until there remains only the pure gold dust" which was then smelted and refined.

However, before washing the ore must be jigged (sifted) for the grains to be washed should be of the same size approximately. Sieves made of hazel-twigs have been found at Kelchalp and in the pre-classical world basket-work and linen sieves were of course well-known. The washing is a gravity-concentration and therefore particularly effective for galena, tin ore and gold (all with high specific gravity), but it was also used for iron ores disseminated in clays.

The ordinary washing tables were rectangular sloping constructions,

Fig. 31.
Remains of tables for washing galena at Laurium.

often with a cemented surface. At Laurium they had storage cisterns at their head whence the water flowed out. In northern Sudan the water was raised in buckets and poured out on the tables. If the stream is regulated, most of the heavy ore would be left on the table, that which is carried away could be caught in various settling tanks. At Laurium the ore was washed at least three times on tables of different slopes and planes to deal with grains of different density and size, though jigging must have already concentrated the grains of equal size. Strabo claims that five-fold washings took place at the gold-mines of Spain (35):

"The gold of Turdetania is not only mined, but is also washed down; that is, the gold-bearing sand is carried down by the rivers and the torrents, although it is often found in the waterless districts too, but in these districts it can not be seen, whereas, in the flooded districts the gold-dust glitters. Besides they flood the waterless districts by conducting water thither, and thus they make the gold-dust glitter; and they also get the gold out by digging pits; and by inventing other means for washing the sand; and the so-called "gold-washeries" are now more numerous than gold-mines. The Gauls hold that their own mines, both those in the Cevennes and those situated at the foot of the Pyrenees themselves, are equal to those of Turdetania; the metals of

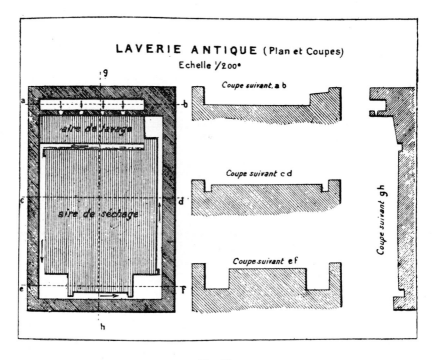

Fig. 32.
Plan of the washing tables at Laurium (After Ardaillon)

the latter, however, are held in greater esteem. And in the gold-dust, they say, nuggets weighing as much as half a pound are sometimes found, which are called "palae", and they need but little refining. They further say that when the stones are split they find small nuggets resembling nipples and when the gold is smelted and refined by means of a sort of styptic earth (containing alum and vitriol) the residuum thereof which contains a mixture of gold and silver, is smelted, the silver is burned away, while the gold remains. For the alloy-type is easily fused and stonelike. For this reason too, gold is preferably melted with chaff-fire, because the flame on account of its softness, is suitable to a substance, that yields and fuses easily; but the charcoal fire consumes much of it because, owing to its intensity overmelts the gold and carries it off as vapour. The soil is carried along in the streams, and is washed nearby in troughs, or else a pit is dug, and the soil that has accumulated there is washed...

The Turdetanians cut their shafts aslant and deep, and, as regards the streams that meet them in the shafts, oftentimes draw them off with the Egyptian screw... Among the Artabrians, who live farthest on the north-west of Lusitania, the soil "effloresces" with silver, tin and "white gold", for it is mixed with silver. This soil, however, is brought by the streams, and the women scrape it up with shovels and wash it in sieves woven basket-like. Such, then, is what Poseidonius has said about the mines... (according to Polybius) the silver-bearing ore (of New Carthage), carried along in the streams, is crushed and by means of sieves disengaged in water; then the sediment is again crushed and again strained through (the water meantime being poured off), and crushed; then the fifth sediment is smelted, and after the lead has been poured off, yields the pure silver...".

Bromehead, in his discussion of ancient mining processes, rightly claims, that Strabo has compressed this description into nonsense. No amount of sieving would affect the proportion of metal in the powdered rock. He telescoped into one the two different processes of classifying and of sizing, both effected with water. On the washing tables the gravity-concentration took place, the sieves sorted out grains of a like size!

The same kind of gravity-concentration was used to wash gold from placers and debris in rivers and brooks. Asiatic tribes use round wooden basins for this purpose, the Dajaks of Borneo have trays about 54—68 cm in diameter and 12—18 cm deep. Planks with a raw surface or sheepskins have been used for such purposes. The Sarts of Central Asia sometimes cut the hairs of such skins away over 15 mm at distances of about 5 cm and put them in the water with the shorn strips across the stream. The rounded quartz and sand participles wash away over the sheepskin, but the greasy wool catches the gold particles. This process may be at the base of the story of the Golden Fleece for such methods were also used in Colchis to obtain stream-gold. In Macedonia wooden channels with ribbed bottoms were in use. In the case of tin ore, the loamy stream-tin holding masses were broken up with rods, then mixed with water in pools and decanted, the residue being washed in the stream to remove the loam.

6. *The social and legal status of the miner*

We will say only a few words about this subject, which actually belongs to the social and economic history of the ancient world rather than to that of technology in Antiquity. Moreover a number of good books and essays on this subject are now available (36). However, as these various aspects of ancient history interlink on many points and our subject cropped up several times in the previous chapters, some of the main problems will be indicated here.

There is no doubt that the miner's craft was not regarded as a healthy and pleasant one, moreover, as so many criminals and slaves were set to work in the mines, it stood low on the social scale (37): "For although it is true that the working of mines cannot be highly regarded since most of it is carried out by employing malefactors or barbarians, some of whom are kept in chains and done to death in damp and unwholesome places, still, when compared with the public confiscations of Sulla and the making of contracts where fire is raging, it will appear in a more favourable light".

Strabo mentions the sulphurous fumes which poison the air at the pit-head: "They build their silver-smelting furnaces with high chimneys, so that the gas from the ore may be carried high into the air, for it is heavy and deadly", and Pliny says that "the exhalations from silver mines in Spain are dangerous to all animals but especially to dogs", by which he probably means carbon dioxide. Many authors comment on the paleness and sickly appearance of miners in general, which Lucretius and Aristotle ascribe to the fumes of sulphur and pitch. The Scaptensula mentioned on this passage of Lucretius was a mining town in Thrace already known to Thucydides and Herodotus: "When men following up the veins of gold and silver, probing with the pick deep into the hidden parts of earth, what stenches Scaptensula breathes out underground? And what poison gold mines may exhale! How strange they make men's faces, how they change their colour! Have you not seen or heard how they are wont to die in a short time and how the powers of life fail those whom the strong force of necessity imprisones in such work? All these effluences, then, earth sends steaming forth, and breathes them out into the open and the clear spaces of heaven".

Most of the labour employed mines was unskilled, sometimes, as we have seen criminals or slaves, but a number of experts must have been present to direct the work, certainly in historical times. Agatarchides tells us that there was a technical director of the gold mines of Nubia, who may have been a descendant of the "prospectors" and "organizers", who accompanied the Pharaonic expeditions to the Sinai mines and the eastern desert. There were certainly expert mining engineers in Greek times, we have already mentioned Gorgus of Eretria, the "metalleutes", whom Alexander the Great took to India according to Strabo (38): "And gold and silver mines are reported in other Indian mountains, not far away, as has been shown by Gorgus the mining expert (metalleutes). But since the Indians are inexperienced in mining and smelting, they also do not know what their resources are, and handle the business in a rather simple manner", and Atotas, a mining engineer, held a responsible post at Laurium (39).

We have little information on such technical men working in Roman mines. It is clear from the following passage from Pliny (40), that prospecting must have been a skilled profession:

"Gold in our part of the world, not to speak of the Indian gold obtained from ants or the gold dug up by griffins in Scythia, is obtained in three ways: in the detritus of rivers, for instance in the Tagus in Spain, the Po in Italy, the Maritza in Thrace, the Sarabat in Asia Minor and the Ganges in India, and there is no gold that is in more perfect state, as it is thoroughly polished by the mere friction of the current. Another method is by sinking shafts; or it is sought for in the fallen debris of mountains. Each of these methods must be described.

People seeking for gold begin by getting up "segullum" (Spanish segullo), that is the name of the earth that indicates the presence of gold. This is a pocket of sand, which is washed, and from the sediment left an estimate of the vein is made. Sometimes by a rare piece of luck a pocket is found immediately on the surface of the earth, as occured recently in Dalmatia, when Nero was emperor (e.g. c. AD 60), one yielding fifty pounds weight of gold a day. Gold found in this way in the surface crust is called "talutium" if there is also auriferous earth underneath. The otherwise barren, dry mountains of the Spanish provinces which produce nothing else whatever are forced into fertility in regard to this commodity".

In certain cases (41) the sub-procurator of a mining area was a skilled engineer, in one case a freedman who had acquired much experience in Transsylvania. A military engineer, not of high rank, was sent for when tunnels for the Claudian aqueduct failed to meet in the middle

(42) and the mining district of Rio Tinto seems to have functioned almost as a school of mines whence skilled men were called elsewhere to perform engineering jobs.

Eusebius informs us that in late-Roman times a mining official was in charge of Cyprus, Lebanon and Palestine and we have the impression that at this date the choice was rather a mining expert than the financial director usually appointed to such posts in the early Empire. In 377 skilled prospectors were sent to Thrace to look for gold mines, so Ammianus tells us, but they went over to the enemy (43): "Besides these there were not a few who were expert in following out veins of gold, and who could no longer endure the heavy burden of taxes; these were welcomed (by the Goths) with the glad consent of all, and rendered great service to the same, as they wandered through strange places, by pointing out hidden stores of grain, and the secret refuges and hiding places of the inhabitants".

By that time experts were already sometimes lent to barbarian states and the "sub-procurator aurarium" in Dacia probably had technical duties during this period. Through the lack of skilled engineers the Romans probably often abandoned mines, because exploitation at deeper levels would only pay if one was not dependent on unskilled labour only. The skilled staff required made it impossible to work in provinces where ores were rare, hence the term "non-mining provinces". In certain cases, e.g. the gold placers on the Rhine and in the Austrian Alps, working were abandoned before exhaustion, but in these cases mostly for political reasons. Anyhow, we get the impression that mining was not yet a career appealing to promising young engineers such as were certainly numerous in the Roman Empire. Exploitation of mines with insufficient technical staff did not pay on the long run.

We still know little about the evolution of the economic and legal aspects of mining, such as claims, ownership of mining rights, etc. Certainly labour costs did not figure as the main factor of the budget of ancient mining and in most mines there was little overhead. Hence the ancients could work small placers and deposits which we could not work with any profit nowadays. On the other hand the mining and smelting techniques were still too primitive to work ores which we now consider rich and the slags or rejects of many an ancient mine has been re-worked with profit recently both in Spain and in Greece.

We have little information about the economics and organisation of the mines of the Hittites and the Armenian mountains from which the inhabitants of Mesopotamia for centuries received most of their minerals and ores. More information can be derived from Egyptian records.

The distinction between the ownership of the soil and that of the minerals beneath its surface could only arise with a well-developed mining-industry. In the early days of open-casts and pitting it was probably necessary to buy the land from the owner before starting exploitation of such minerals. It seems that during the later dynasties of Pharonic Egypt the idea took root, that the King of Egypt was master of all soil and mines (Fitzler), but as he gave away part of the land to temples and private individuals they could start the exploitation of mines on their lands directly without craving for permission from the King. During the Ptolemaic period a change of opinion is clearly noticeable. Probably it was already held that the king remained in the possession of all mineral products underground even if he gave the surface away, but quarries were merely a monopoly of the king as they formed part of the soil, which anybody could buy, own and exploit. So private quarries were already exploited and also some were leased by the king. The mines were owned by the state. In Hellenistic monarchies there seems to have been no ultimate distinction between ownership of the soil and underground stones or minerals, except in Egypt. Roman law recognized private possession of "metalla" and so quarries and mines in Roman Egypt were partly state and partly private affairs.

In Pharaonic Egypt only free people worked in the quarries and mines for the number of banished and criminals employed there was small. Gardiner (44), the eminent Egyptologist, has pointed out that "slavery is a term that requires careful definition and I am not aware, that its existence in the Old and Middle Kingdom has yet been satisfactorily demonstrated. None of the over thirty expressions for "statute labour" in some form or other can be explained to mean "forced labour in the mines". Miners were often specialists, some of them have high titles". This opinion is supported by the lists of the members of the expeditions sent to the Sinai mines and other workings. In Ptolemaic Egypt mines worked by the state employed criminals and forced labour, which demanded military supervision, different from the troups sent along with the expeditions to Sinai to guard them from wandering nomads and desert robbers. In Roman times the "damnati ad metallum" were slaves in the worse sense of the word.

In the Greek homeland the ownership and revenue of the mines seem to have belonged to the state, in extra-territorial areas private ownership was permitted to a certain extent. We are well-informed about the situation of the miners of Laurium through the excellent publications by Ardaillon and Lauffer. They furnish us with many details about the organisation of labour, the rights of the state and its lessees and the various conflicts which arose during the last six centuries B.C. Twice the mining population, varying from 10,000 to 20,000, revolted, but they were by no means all slaves. Citizens and metics worked their own concessions, more particularly during the last two centuries. The slaves at Laurium were much better treated than in Roman times and they had their barracks above-ground. In the early days the technical officers such as the "epistratai" and "archepistrates" may have been slaves, but they were certainly accorded privileges

Fig. 33.
Greek miners at work, from a pinax from Penteskouphia near Corinth (c. 550 B.C.)
(After Rickard, Man and Metals)

because of their technical abilities, the Romans even calling them "philosophi"! We hear that prospects were sold for ten years, working mines for three. Generally speaking, conditions at Laurium were such that most work was properly and efficiently done in the mines and the smelting sites nearby. Conditions such as led to the revolts mentioned above were exceptional and temporary only.

In Italy quirite ownership was considered valid, but the senate claimed the right to interfere in mining ventures. In the provinces there was no general rule, ownership of the soil seems to have included that of the subsoil. The jurists of the later Empire developed some rudimentary theory of mining royalty, the state reserving the ownership of the subsoil leaving the owner the precarious ownership of the surface or tenure. Under medieval law (and partly under Roman too) the metallic mines were state-owned, quarries and iron-mines belonging to the owner of the soil. The latter exception was probably due to the extensive bog-iron industry in the provinces which dated back to pre-Roman days.

The Roman Republic farmed its mines to publicani; this saved trouble and obviated a large staff with which ancient governments were incompetent to deal. In some cases Augustus leased the placers of the Salassi to contractors who also bought the river-water from the gov-

Fig. 34.
Roman miners and inspector.

ernment. Spain was overrun by private adventurers but the larger undertakings were let to companies of equites, as only rings of Roman bankers could provide the capitals needed to run such large workings as Almaden, Sierra Morena and Cartagena. In the latter district over 40,000 slaves worked according to Polybius and in republican times many contractors worked here too, nearly all ingots being stamped with the names of private individuals (45) or as Strabo says:

"The silver mines of New Carthage are still worked at the present times, they are not state-property, however, either at New Carthage or anywhere else, but have passed over to private ownership. But the majority of the gold-mines are state property". Diodorus (46) describes this "gold-rush" in the following passage: "After the Romans had made themselves masters of Iberia, a multitude of Italians have swarmed to the mines and taken great wealth away with them, such was their greed. For they purchase a multitude of slaves whom they turn over to the overseers of the workings of the mines; and these men, opening shafts in a number of places and digging deep into the ground, seek out the seams of the earth which are rich in silver and gold; and not only do they go into the ground a great distance, but they also push their diggings many stades in depth and run galleries off at every angle, turning this way and that, in this manner bringing up from the depths the ore which gives them the profit they are seeking".

Fig. 35.
Miner on early Christian monument.

The Romans frequently used slaves and criminals in their mines, also forced labour in certain provinces. Free contracting labourers are known at Verespatak and probably provincials from Spanish towns agreed to work underground at Rio Tinto for periods of six months. It is not clear whether the soldiers employed by Claudius at Ems (47) acted as miners or merely in charge of technical operations, for "Curtius Rufus had opened a mine in search of silver-lodes in the district of Mattium (Wiesbaden-Homburg). The profits were slender and short-lived, but the legions lost heavily in the work of digging out watercourses and constructing underground workings which would have been difficult enough in the open".

Military control is evident in mines in the Mendips, Shropshire and Yorkshire and this is also the case in the provinces along the Limes. Roman miners were sometimes well-treated. At Ajustrel and Dolaucothy pit-head baths and other facilities were at their disposal. But normally authorities had little consideration with them and thirty was the average age of the miners whose bodies were found in Roman mines. They lived mostly underground and the entrance to the mines was usually steep and narrow, except in England where they were easily accesible.

The procurators were mostly equites or freedmen, assisted by "tabularii" and "commentarienses", they dealt mainly with the financial side, and only during the later Empire were technical officers appointed procurators or were procurators appointed to supervize the entire mining operations. This was only the case when the mines were worked by gangs under military supervision. The unity of design and the vast scale of the operations at Rio Tinto or Minas de Mouros suggests centralized control.

Elsewhere conductores, and sometimes larger lessees, rented important mines, the smaller ones usually being worked on a percentage basis and controlled by imperial officers. The larger conductores, often equites or curiales, are found in documents as far back as the first century B.C., mostly in charge of iron mines. The smaller conductores have left fewer memorials except the Ajustrel Tables, which give and illuminating glimpse of their organization.

At Ajustrel (Portugal) two bronze tablets were found (48) giving the regulations by the emperor Hadrian for these "Vipasca mines". Here the procurator let small concessions to groups of two or three poorer miners, who lived in mining villages, usually extra-territorial communities controlled by the procurator, who granted the licenses for trading monopolies and managed all details of the life of the mine. Sometimes he had even mine-coinage struck, with a special checkmark, for local use. This system was the ancestor of the cost-book companies at the Cornish stanneries (49) in the Middle Ages and after.

Lessees of gold and silver mines were not allowed to form "collegiae" or guilds; only seldom does one find a contractor in this type of mining, such as the contractor of Narbonne (50). In Roman times, however, certain communities of free miners such as the Pirustae of Albania and the "leguli aurariarum" (gold-washers) of Transsylvania (51) may have continued to exist for a time. However, the tendency in larger under-takings was certainly for centralisation under the control of an imperial officer or procurator. In Cyprus Augustus had found Ptolemaic direct management, but in other provinces procurators became general only under Tiberius or Vespasian. There was, however, no central office or administration at the capital Rome and controllers of large areas were appointed much later only, as we have seen. In the later Empire, when Cyprian mentions the decay of several gold and silver mines, we find Valens offering better terms to private persons (52) and under Gothic rule free miners in Italy were offered free State contracts probably for a share in the proceeds (53).

Often it is difficult to decide when Roman mines were abandoned and when such mines were opened again, also the date of many medie-val mines is still uncertain. In Central Europe more continuity may have existed than we imagine. Davies, comparing Roman and medieval mining techniques, mentions that the Saxons were the principal miners of Central Europe in medieval times, being summoned as far south as Italy and the Balkans to work as experts. They may have started mining in subjection to their territorial laws, but they soon became largely autonomous communities under State supervision and paying duties to the State, like their predecessors, the Roman conductores, had done.

Another great story still remains to be written, the part which the ancient mines and deposits or ores played in political history. It is clear that this part was as important then as it is nowadays and the ancients knew this, for is it not written (54): "Now Judas had heard what the Romans had done in the country of Spain for the winning of the silver and the gold which is there"? Still most ancient historians neglect this factor in history. The absence of all technological subjects in general education in Antiquity may be spotted by a few prominent engineers, who ask for a better training of professional man, but, generally speaking, the ancient philosophers might note a few technical achieve-ments without bothering much about their social possibilities. They treat the mining engineers with pity and may be contempt like Aristo-phanes in his "Clouds" (ll. 187—194) deals with the geologist. When Strepsiades, the main character in this comedy, visits the "thinking house of sapient souls", one of the philosopher's schools, and a student shows him around, he notices a group of men and asks "What makes them fix their eyes so on the ground?". His host mentions that "they seek things undergrond" and immediately Strepsiades believes that he knows what they are after and starts a long story on how to look for truffles. Then he notices a second group stooping down very deeply, of whom his guide says that "they are diving down deep into the deepest secrets", into the darkness below Tartarus. Strepsiades has no idea what the guide is hinting at for he asks: "Then why's their rump turned up towards the sky?" at which stupid question the student has nothing to say but "It's taking private lessons on the stars". Unfortunately both geology and mining remained very much neglected in Antiquity and the practical experience gained in the field was not supported by guidance from scientific theories and observation.

7. *Note on precious and semi-precious stones*

The preceding notes on ancient geology and mining also cover what is known on ancient gem mining, as precious and semi-precious stones were collected from placers and open-casts or obtained by mining in the same way as other minerals were. We have also seen that proper identification and characterization of such gems by their physical, chemical and mineralogical characteristics did not begin until some 200 years ago and hence the ancient classifications often led to false conclusions.

Indeed, even now we have no precise information on the variety and number of ancient gems in our museums and it is high time that they were properly identified by experts, for this would give us statistical-chronological data on the use of various gems all throughout Antiquity, which may enable us to write an proper history of gems and which might also help us to identify the many unknown or dubious terms, such as Caley and Richards rightly pointed out in their edition of Theoprastus' On Stones. This identification is sorely needed to understand many ancient texts the point of which escape us now. Though we have many books on ancient gems (55) the archaeological and philogical data published are not always reliable. As we pointed out in our chapter in ancient mineralogy Ball's survey, for example, is excellent as far as the modern data go, but it is definitely weak in the archaeological and philological part, basing itself on the completely antiquated version of Pliny's thirty-seventh book written by Philemon Holland in 1601! Fortunately the modern edition of this book in the Loeb Classical Library, edited by D. E. Eichholz is now available and whatever the charm of Holland's edition may be it can no longer form the basis of a discussion of our subject.

Meticulous research on the history of gems is much needed. We have

Table XIV

The most important precious stones of preclassical Antiquity

	Egyptian	Sumerian	Accadian	
Amethyst ḥsmn	(III. 163. 25)	^{na_4}al-ga-mes (?)	algamišu (?)	Gr. amethyson
Emerald w3ḏ w3ḏ n b3ḥ	(I. 267. 8) ? (I. 267. 8) ?	—	barraktu	Hebr. bârĕkĕth Syr. bâr'ḳa
Beryl w3ḏ w3ḏ n b3ḥ	(I. 267. 8) ? (I. 267. 8) brgt ?	—	burallu	beryllus
Carnelian ḥrś. t ḥ. t	(III. 150. 9) (III. 359. 5) ?	^{na_4}gug	sâmtu	Gr. sardion
Coral	—	^{na_4}ḫar-ḫum-ba-SIR	baḫru	Gr. korallion
Jasper mḫn (m)t	(II. 132. 4) ?		^{a}iaśpû	Hebr. iâs'pheh Gt. xanthe, aimatites
Lapis lazuli ḫsbd tfrr	(III. 334. 1) (V. 300. 2) (Turfan?)	^{na_4}ZA. GÌN	uknû	Gr. chytos, kyanos

Egyptian		Sumerian	Akkadian	Greek
nmḥ. f	(II. 268. 17)			Gr. iaspis?
		na₄dug-ši-a KA. GIN. NA	dušû / šadanu	Gr. krystallos
Rockcrystal				
irḳbš	(I. 116. 4) ?			
mnw ḥd	(II. 72. 4; V. 123. 5)			
Sapphire		na₄za. gin. duru₅ ?	zagindurû ?	—
	—			
Turquoise		záZA. GIN	abnî biruti ? / uknû	
mfk3. t	(II. 56. 1)			
ḥb	(III. 62. 1)			
w3d̲ n b3ḫ	?			

Unidentified Egyptian stones

ḫnm. t	(III. 294. 4) (red)
ḥkm	(III. 174. 21) (red) (ḥm 3ḳ?)
mjnw	(II. 44. 5) (= mnw?)
mḫn	(II. 132. 2) (blue)
ḳˤ	(V. 18. 2) (= haematite?)
d̲r. t. t	(V. 598. 10) (carnelian?)

already mentioned Pliny's "adamas" which seems to have different meanings in the various passages where the term is used. Though Laufer holds that the "adamas" in the prodemium of the twentieth book of Pliny's Natural History is no doubt the diamond and identical with the Chinese "kun-wu" (later "kin-kang") it is doubtful whether the "adamas" in the thirty-seventh book is a diamond at all. Bromehead thinks that it was probably corundum, in its less pure form called emery and hailing from Naxos. Such questions are not purely academic, in this case it is an important point to know what the hardest material was, which the ancient engravers of gems and other stones knew, in order to judge the merits of their work. Up to now we have no definite data proving that diamonds were known or used in the Mediterranean area to any appreciable scale in classical times, one or two may have crept in an consignement of gems from Ceylon, but we simply do not know.

We know, however, that the inhabitants of ancient Mesopotamia were familiar with certain precious stones (Table XIV) like the Egyptians and that their jewellers and lapidaries (ZADIM, zadimmu, sasînu) must have had considerable knowledge of such stones. Their skill can be judged from a curious document in which two jewellers guarantee Ellil-šum-iddim, that an emerald set in a golden ring will not come off within ten years on pain of paying him ten minae of silver in case it does (56). The map we append to this note gives the possible sources of these ancient gems rather than proven placers or workings, though many of them are indeed mentioned in the ancient texts. However, before the problems of terminology have been cleared properly, nothing much can be done about the study of the craft and trade of the lapidary and the jeweller.

This study would be fascinating from another point of view too. It is doubtful, whether aesthetical valuation predominated in the choice of gems in those days. There is a possibility that fashions changed and a closer study of such fashions might be the outcome of the investigation of museum objects we proposed above. On the other hand the precious and semi-precious stones were probably seldom chosen for decorative purposes only. Their imaginary qualities, enhanced by religious, magical, astrological and medical beliefs, must have been preponderant, and this lore of precious stones is still very much alive. The handbooks have shown less energy in trying to identify the stones mentioned than in repeating these ancient fables over and over again. Their stories are still too much an account of the follies and fancies of mankind rather than the tracing of the slow accumulation of scientific data and theories about such stones, which is definitely more interesting to us moderns.

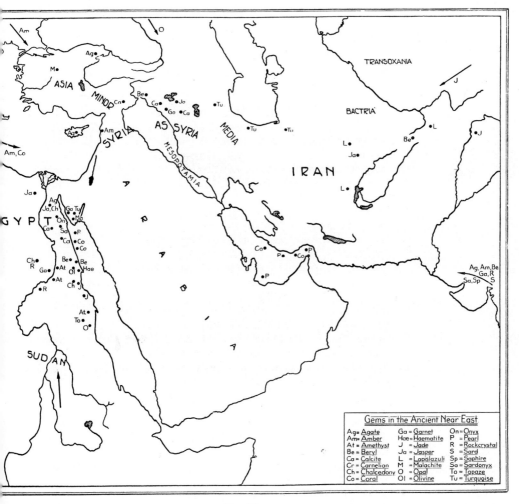

Fig. 36.
Map of the deposits of gems in the Ancient Near East.

BIBLIOGRAPHY

1. HAUSSCHILD, A., *Die Entwicklung der Tiefbohrtechnik* (Urania vol. 19, 1956, 470—475)

ALLEN, T., *Coal mine illumination* (Min. Congress J. vol. 26, 1940, 44—47, 59—61, 76)

BLACK, A., *The story of tunnels* (MacGraw Hill, London, 1937)

BÖRGER, K., *Die Entwicklung der Tiefbohrtechnik bis um die Mitte des* 19. Jahrhunderts (Kali XXX, 1936, 101—104; 115—117; 125—127; 134—137)

BRIGGS, H., *The development of mine surveying from early times to* 1850 (Trans. Mine Surv. Inst. vol. VI, 1925, 19—32; 77—83; 118—124) (Colliery Guardian, 1925, 391—393; 465—466; 510—511)

BROMEHEAD, C. E. N., *Ancient Mining Processes* (Antiquity vol. XVI, 1942, 193—207)

BROWN, T., *The development of mine surveying* (Leeds Univ. Mining Soc. J. no. 2, 1923, 38—50)

CHAMPAUD, CL., *Notice sur trois types d'outils gallo-romans retrouvées dans l'exploitation minière d'Abbaretz* (Loire Inf.) (*Not. Archéol. armor.* (Rennes), 1955, 293—299)

GORDON CHILDE, V., *The antiquity and function of antler axes and adzes* (Antiquity vol. XVI, 1942, 258—264)

CUMMINGS, A. D., and MATTINGLY, H. B., *A Roman mining document* (*Mine and Quarry Eng.*, August 1956, 339—342)

DAVIES, O., *Roman and medieval mining technique* (Trans. Inst. Mining Metallurgy, vol. XLIII, 1934, 3—54)

DEBONO, F., *Pics en pierre de Sérabit el-Khadim* (Ann. Serv. Antiq. Egypte vol. 46, 1947, 265—285)

DESMED, R., *Le vinaigre employé par Hannibal dans les Alpes* (*Promethée* (Bruxelles) April 1957, 1060—1063)

EVANS, E. M. F., *Ancient Mining* (Antiquity vol. XVII, 1943, 52)

FRASER, A. D., *Splitting rocks with cold water* (Class. Weekly vol. XV, 1921/22, 168)

FREISE, R., *Geschichte der Bergbau- und Hüttentechnik* (Springer, Berlin, 1908)

GEER, R. M., *Livy xxi.* 37. 2—3 *once more* (*Class. Weekly* vol. XXII, 1929, 160)

GONZALO Y TARIN, *Descripcion minera de la provincia de Huelva* (Madrid 1888, 17)

HÖRTER, P., *Vorgeschichtliche Werkzeuge der Basaltlava-Industrie bei Mayen* (Mannus, vol. VII, 1917, 83)

HÖRTER, P., *Der Kreis Mayen in ur- und frühgeschichtlicher Zeit* (Mayen, 1928)

Howat, D. D., *Fire-setting* (*Mine Quarry Engineering* vol. 4, 1939, 239—245)

Hudson, D. R., *Some archaic mining apparatus* (Metallurgia 1947, 157—164)

Inge, C. H., *Toolmarks, Tell El-Duweir, Palestine* (Antiquity vol. XIII, 1939, 88)

Joube, G. R., *Catalogue de l'outillage lithique provenant des tombes d'Abou Roach* (Kemi vol. VII, 1938, 71—113)

Johannsen, O., *Die erste Anwendung der Wasserkraft im Hüttenwesen* (Stahl Eisen, 1916, 1226)

Knowles, Sir Francis H. S., *Stoneworker's Progress, a study in stone implements* (Oxf. Univ. Press, 1953)

Lauffer, S., *Bergmännische Kunst der antiken Welt* (In: H. Winckelmann, *Der Bergbau in der Kunst*, Essen, 1958)

Lee, C. H., *Early mining transport* (*Colliery Engineering* vol. XV, 1938, 224—226)

Morton, Fr., *Grubenbeleuchtung in der Urzeit* (*Berg-Hüttenm. Jhrb.* vol. 75, 1927, 114—116)

Pittard, J. J., *La recherche et l'exploitation des mines au Moyen Age* (Rev. Polyt. vol. XXXV, 1933, 2451—2453; 2459—2461)

Posepny, F., *Zwei römische Schöpfräder aud den Gruben Verespatak in, Siebenburgen und S. Domingos in Portugal* (Wien, 1877)

Sanders, Horace W., *On the Use of the Deer-horn Pick in Mining Operations of the Ancients* (Archaeologia vol. LXII, 1910, 2)

Sanders, Horace W., *The Linares bas-relief and Roman Mining Operations in Baetica* (Westminster, 1905)

Taube, E., *Mining terms of obscure origin* (Scient. Monthly vol. 58, 1944. 454)

Treptow, E., *Der altjapanische Bergbau und Hüttenbetrieb, dargestellt auf Rollbildern* (Jhb. Berg- Hüttenw. Kön. Sachsen, 1904)

Treptow, E., *Der älteste Bergbau und seine Hilfsmittel* (Beitr. Gesch. Techn. Ind. vol. VIII, 1918, 155—191)

Treptow, E., *Deutsche Meisterwerke bergmännischer Kunst* (Abh. Ber. Dtsches Museums vol. I, 1929, 1—46)

Wilsdorf, H., *Bergleute und Hüttenmänner im Altertum* (Berlin, 1952)

Whitcombe, W. H., *All about mining* (New York, 1938)

ANON. History of Mine winding (*Colliery Engineering* vol. 20, 1943, 25)

Vercoutter, J., *The gold of Kush, two gold-washing stations at Faras East* (Kush vol. 7, 1959, 120—153)

2. Sagui, C. L., *Economic Geology* vol. 23, 1928, 671

3. Palmer, *Trans. Inst. Mining Metallurgy* vol. XXXVI, 1926/7, 299

4. Pliny, XXXIII. 21. 70

5. Pliny, XXXIII. 21. 71

6. Livy, XXI. xxxvii. 2—3

7. Schelenz, *Z. ges. Schiess- und Sprengstoffwesen* vol. IV, 1909, 288

8. Raistrick, *Trans. Newcomen Soc.* vol. 7, 1926/7, 81

9. Evan Sage, T., *Splitting rocks with cold water* (*Class. Weekly* vol. 16, 1922/23, 73—76)

10. Breidenbach, *Z. f. prakt. Geologie* 1893, 16
11. Williams, *Cambrian Register*, vol. 3, 1815, 31
12. Rücker, *Goldvorkommen in Bosnien*
13. Teglas, *Foldtani Közlöny* vol. 22, 1892, 82
    Teglas, *Ungarische Revue* vol. 9, 1899, 323
14. Pliny, XXXIII. 21. 68—78
15. *Proc. Antiq. Soc.* London 2, 2, 323
16. Forbes, R. J., *Studies in Ancient Technology* Vol. VI (Leiden, 1966)
17. Pliny, XXXI. 28
18. Vitruvius, VIII. vi. 13
19. Daubrée, *Rev. Archéol.* 1868, 1, 298
20. Diodorus, V. 37. 3
21. Galen, *Simpl. Med.* IX. 3. 34
22. Pliny, XXXIII. xxi. 71
23. Engel, *Revue Etd. Anc.* 1899, 249; Sandars, *Archaeologia* 59, 311
24. Forbes, R. J., *Studies in Ancient Technology* vol. II (Leiden, 1965)
25. Vitrivius, X, iv—vii
26. Diodorus, V. 37. 3
27. *Early Mining in Spain* (Metallurgia vol. 33, 1946, 293—300)
28. Sevensma, P. H., *Les Gisements d'or de la région de St. Yrieix* (Geneva, 1941)
29. Posépny, *Sitz. ber. Anthrop. Ges.* Wien, 1892, 44
30. Beck, H., *Geschichte des Eisens*, Vol. I, 578
31. Demosthenes, *Contra Pantaenetum* 26—29
32. Diodorus, III. 13; Strabo, II. 2. 10
33. Forbes, R. J., *Studies in Ancient Technology* vol. III (Leiden, 1965)
34. Diodorus, III. 14. 1—3
35. Strabo, III. 2. 8—10. cap. 146—147
36. Andreades, M., *Geschichte der griechischen Staatswirtschaft* (2 vols. Berlin, 1931)
    Arndt, A., *Zur Geschichte des Bergregals und der Bergbaufreiheit* (Freiberg, 1916)
    Arnold, G., *Historia Christianorum ad metalla damnatorum* (Frankfurt, 1696)
    Besnier, M., *L'interdiction du travail des mines en Italie sous la République* (*Rev. Archéol.* vol. LIL, 1919, 31—50)
    Binder, I. I., *Die Bergwerke im römischen Staatsrecht* (*Z. f. Bergrecht* vol. 32, 1891, 32 & 216)
    du Bois, H., *Die soziale Stellung des deutschen Berg- und Hüttenmannes…* (*Technik und Kultur* 1926, 205)
    Burthe, J., *Note on the bronze tables found in the mine of Ajustrel* (Ann. des Mines, vol. 13, 1928, 24—25)
    Cagnat, R., *Lex Vipascensis* II (J. des Savants, n. s. vol. 4, 1906, fasc. 8)
    Cuq, E., Vipasca II (C.R. Acad. Inscr. Belles Lettres 1907, 95)
    Ritter von Friese, F., *Das römische Berggesetz von Vipasca* (Oesterr. *Z. f. Berg- und Hüttenwesen*, vol. 35, 1887, 317)
    Heyner, C., *Disputatio de damnatione ad metalla* (Lipsiae, 1794)

HIRSCHFELDT, O., *Die kaiserlichen Verwaltungsbeambten bis auf Diokletian* (Berlin, 1905)

HOPPER, R. J., *The attic silvermines in the fourth century B.C.* (Ann. Brit. School Athens, 48, 1953, 200—254)

HORN, M., *De metalli fodinarum iure* (Vittenbergae, 1703)

HÜBNER, E., *Adnotationes ad legem Vipascam I, cum commentario Theodori Momseni* (*Emphemeris epigraphica* 1877)

HURE, O., *Die Bergarbeiter* (2 vols. Düsseldorf, 1910)

JUNGIUS, H., *De iure salinarium, tum veteri tum hodierno, liber singularis* (Göttingae, 1748)

KAHRSTEDT, U., *Staatgebiet und Staatsangehörige in Athen* (Göttinger Forschungen, Stuttgart, 1934)

KNÖTZSCHKER, L., *Von Verdammung der Missetäther zur Bergarbeit* (Leipzig, 1795)

LAUFFER, S., *Die Bergwerkssklaven von Laureion* (2 vols. Wiesbaden, 1955/57)

LOMMER, CH., *Bergmännischer Beitrag... "Wie waren die Bergwerke bey den Alten beschaffen"* (Freiberg, 1785)

MENZEL, A., *Soziale Gedanken im Bergrecht* (*Oesterr. Z. f. Berg-Hüttenwesen* vol. 40, 1892)

MOTZ, F., *Ueber die Metallarbeiter der heroischen Zeit* (Meiningen, 1868)

NEUBURG, CL., *Der Zusammenhang zwischen römischen und deutschen Bergbau* (*Z. f. ges. Staatswissenschaft* vol. 63, 1907, 161—181)

NEUBURG, CL., *Zur Lex metalli Vipascensis II* (*Lexis Festschrift*, Tübingen, 1907)

OIKONOMOS, P., *Eine neue Bergwerksurkunde aus Athen* (*Athen. Mitt.* 35, 1910, 274—294)

ROSTOVTZEFF, M., *Geschichte der Staatpacht in der römischen Kaiserzeit bis Diokletian* (Berlin, 1902)

SCHÖNBAUER, E., *Beiträge zur Geschichte des Bergbaurechtes* (München, 1929)

TÄCKHOLM, U., *Studien über den Bergbau der römischen Kaiserzeit* (Uppsala, 1937)

TITIUS, G., *De iure metallorum* (Lipsiae, 1695)

TUSCANI, J., *Beiträge zur Geschichte der ältesten bergrechtlichen Urkunden* (*Z. f. Bergrecht* vol. 18, 1877, 336)

VOELKEL, C., *Die beiden Erztafeln von Vipasca* (*Z. f. Bergrecht* vol. 55, 1914, 182—243)

WILHELM, A., *Attische Pachturkunden* (*Arch. f. Pap.* vol. 11, 1935, 206)

WILMANNS, G., *Inschrift von Vipasca* (*Z. f. Bergrecht*, vol. 19, 1878, 217—232)

WILSDORF, H., *Bergleute und Hüttenmänner im Altertum* (Berlin, 1952)

ZYCHA, A., *Das Recht des ältesten deutschen Bergbaus* (Berlin, 1899)

37. PLUTARCH, *Comparison of Nicias and Crassus I*; STRABO, III. ii. 8. cap. 146; PLINY, XXXIII. xxxi. 98; LUCRETIUS, VI. 808—815; ARISTOTLE, *De Sensu et Sensili* V. 444b, 30; XENOPHON, *Memor.* III. 6. 12; SILIUS, ITALICUS, I, 233; STATIUS, *Silvae* IV. 7. 15; LUCANUS, *Pharsalia* IV. 298

38. STRABO, XV. i. 30. cap. 700

39. C.I.G. 2. 3260b
40. PLINY, XXXIII. xxi. 66—68
41. C.I.L. 3. 1088
42. C.I.L. 8. 2728
43. AMMIANUS, XXXI. 6. 6
44. GARDINER, A., *Z. f. aeg. Sprache* vol. 43, 1906, 43
45. STRABO, III. 2. 10, cap. 148; C.I.L. 2. 6247
46. DIODORUS V. 36. 4
47. TACITUS, *Annals* XI. 20
48. *Z. f. Bergrecht* vol. 19, 1976, 207; *Oesterr. Z. Berg-Hüttenw.* 1907, 39
49. MISPOULET, *Nouv. Revue Hist. Droit Franc. et Etr.* 1907, 345
    LOUIS, *Univ. Durham Phil. Soc.* vol. 6, 1921, 2, 33
50. C.I.L. 12. 3336
51. C.I.L. 3. 1307
52. *Codex Theod.* 10. 19. 3
53. CASSIODORUS, 9. 3
54. MACCABEES I., 8. 3
55. ANDRÉE, K., *Der Bernstein und seine Bedeutung in Natur- und Geistes-wissenschaft...* (Königsberg, 1937)
    ARKELL, A. J., *Cambay and the Bead Trade* (Antiquity vol. X, 1936, 292—306)
    BALL, S. H., *A Roman Book on Precious Stones* (Los Angeles, 1950)
    BALL, S. H., *Historical Notes on Gem-mining* (*Econ. Geol.* vol. 26, 1931, 681—738)
    BLAKE, R. P., and DE VIS, H., *Epiphanius de Gemmis* (London, 1934)
    BLECHSTEINER, R., *Altpersische Edelsteinnamen* (*Wiener Z. f. Kunde Morgenl.* vol. XXXVII, 1930, 93—104)
    BOLMAN, J., *De edelsteenen uit de Bijbel* (Paris, Amsterdam, 1938)
    BOLMAN, J., *De Edel- en Siersteenen* (Paris, Amsterdam, 1938)
    BOLMAN, J., *Welcher Edel- oder Schmuckstein ist das* (Brill, Leiden, 1942)
    BOLMAN, J., *The mystery of the pearl* (Brill, Leiden, 1941)
    BROMEHEAD, C. E. N., *Mines and Gems* (Antiquity vol. VIII, 1934, 462)
    CALEY, E. R., and RICHARDS, J. F. C., *Theophrastus On Stones* (Columbus, 1956)
    COHN, D., *Die Technik der griechisch-römischen Gemmenschneider und ihr Ursprung* (*Dtsche Goldschmiedeztg.* vol. XXIV, 1927, 127)
    DENMAN, C., *Jade, a comprehenisve bibliography* (J. Amer. Orient. Soc. vol. 65, 1945, 117—126)
    EICHHOLZ, D. E., *Theophrastus peri lithon 25 (tanon, smaragdus)* (*Class. Review* vol. VIII, 1958, 221—222)
    EVANS, J., and SERJEANTSON, M. S., *English Medieval Lapidaries* (London, 1933)
    FARRINGTON, O. C., *Amber* (*Field Museum Nat. Hist.* Chicago, 1923)
    FARRINGTON, O. C., & LAUFER, B., *Agate* (*Field Museum Nat. History*, Chicago, 1927)
    FRANKFORT, H., *Cylinder Seals* (Macmillan, London, 1939)
    FÜRTWÄNGLER, A., *Die antiken Gemmen* (Leipzig, 1900, 3 vols.)

GETTENS, R. J., *Minerals in art and archaeology* (Smithsonian Report for 1961 (1962), 551—568)

HERRMANN, A., *Edelsteine* (Reallex. Antike Christentum vol. IV, 1958, 505—552)

HOLWERDA, F., *Short introduction to the Roman ambertrade* (BVAB XXXVIII, 1962, 66—67)

HARRIS, J. R., *Lexicographical Studies in Ancient Egyptian Minerals* (Berlin, 1961)

KING, C. W., *Precious Stones and Metals* (London, 1867)

KING, C. W., *Gems and Decorative Stones* (London, 1867)

KUNZ, C. F., *Curious Lore of Precious Stones* (London, 1913)

KUNZ, G. F., *Precious and Semi-Precious Stones* (London, 1917)

KRAUS, H. E., & HOLDEN, E. F., *Gems and Gem Material* (New York, 1936)

LAUFER, B., *Notes on Turquoise in the East* (*Field Mus. Nat. Hist.* Chicago, 1913)

LAUFER, B., *The Diamond, a study in Chinese and Hellenistic Folklore* (*Field Museum Nat. Hist.*, Chicago 1913)

LAUFER, B., *Sino-Iranica* (Chicago, 1919)

LEEMANS, W. F., *Ishtar of Lagaba and her dress* (Brill, Leiden, 1952)

MAENCHEN-HELFEN, O., *Two notes on the diamond in ancient China* (J. Amer. Orient. Soc. vol. 70, 1950, 187—188)

LÖW, I., *Der Diamant* (*Festschrift Heller*, Budapest, 1941, 230—238)

LORET, V., *Le turquoise chez les ancient Egyptiens* (*Kemi*, vol. I, 1928/30, 99)

MADHIHASSAN, S., *Cultural words of Chinese origin* (*Bhâratîya Vidya* vol. XL, 1950, 1 & 2, 31—39)

MEADOWS, J. W., *Pliny on the smaragdus* (*Class. Review* 1945, 50—51)

DE MÉLY, F., *Les lapidaires de l'Antiquité et du Moyen Age* (3 vols., Paris, 1896—1902)

MENGHIN, O., *Weltgeschichte der Steinzeit* (Wien, 1931, 645—647)

NEEDHAM, J., *Science and civilisation in ancient China* (Cambridge, 1959, vol. III)

PAZZINI, A., *Le pietre preziose nella storia della medicina e nella legenda* (Mediterranea, Roma, 1939)

QUIRING, H., *Die Edelsteine im Amtsschild des jüdischen Hohenpriesters* (*Südhoffs Archiv* vol. 38, 1954, 193—213)

QUIRING, H., *Zur ältesten Geschichte des Bernsteins* (*Bl. Technikgesch.* vol. 16, 1954, 44—50)

REICHELT, H., *Geschichte der Obersteiner-Idar Edelsteinindustrie* (*Beitr. Gesch. Technik* vol. XXI, 1920/21, 74—78)

OVERWEEL, C. J., *A Petrography of 23 Commemorative Scarabs of Amenophis III* (Oudh. Med. XLV, 1964, 1—14)

SCHEIL, V., *Vocabulaire des pierres et objects en pierre* (*Revue Assyr.* vol. XV, 1918, 115—125)

SCHMIDT, L., *Geschichte und Technik des Bernsteins* (Dtsch. Museum Abh. Ber. vol. XIII, 1941, Heft 3)

ARNOLDS SPEKKE, *The Ancient Amber Routes* (Stockholm, 1957)

THOMPSON, R. C., *A Dictionary of Assyrian Chemistry and Geology* (Oxford, 1936)

TOMKEIEFF, S. I., *Ueber den Ursprung des Names Quarz* (*Mineral Mag.* vol. 26, 1942, 172—178)

THORNDIKE, L., *The Pseudo-Galen de Plantis* (Ambix XI, 1963, 87—94)

ULLMAN, B., *Cleopatra's Pearls* (*Class. J.* Vol. LII, 1957, 193—201)

VARILLE, A., *Quelques données nouvelles sur la pierre Bekhen des anciens Egyptiens* (Bull. Inst. Franc. Arch. Orient, vol. 34, 1934, 92—102)

WATSON, C., *The drill style on ancient gems* (Ann. Arch. Anthr. vol. XXIII, 1936, 51—55)

WELLMANN, M., *Die Stein- und Gemmenbücher der Antike* (*Quellen, Stud. Gesch. Naturw. Med.* vol. IV, 1935, 86—149)

WENDEL, C. H., *Ueber die in ägyptischen Texte erwähnten Bau- und Edelsteine* (Leipzig, 1888)

56. CARDASCIA, G., *Les Archives des Murasû* (Paris, 1951, 185)

CHRONOLOGICAL BIBLIOGRAPHY OF ANCIENT AUTHORS ON
GEOLOGY AND MINING

For the benefit of those readers who wish to consult the original works
of ancient authors, whose passages on geology and mining we quoted in
the course of these pages we append a list of the editions of their works which
are readily available. The pre-Socratic philosophers are only vaguely known,
the books by Burnet and Freeman which we have quoted belong to the most
authoritative collections of the fragments of their teachings which we posses.
For most of the other ancient authors proper editions of their work and
English translations have been published in the Loeb Classical Library, here
indicated by LCL. These, then, are the authors who have important data
on our subjects:

Thales (624—548 B.C.) — On "water" as the archè, knowledge of loadstone
Anaximander (c. 545 B.C.) — On changes of the earth's surface by "thicken-
ing" (pyknosis) and "thinning" (manosis)
Xenophanes (sixth cy. B.C.) — On fossils and rock formation (quoted by
Origen)
Anaximenes (c. 546 B.C.) — On stones and rocks formed from "pneuma"
Heracleitus (c. 500 B.C.) — Earth and rocks formed by condensation of "fire"
Melissus of Samos (c. 440 B.C.) — Stones formed from "water"
Hippon of Samos (c. 450 B.C.) — On the hydrological cycle
Anaxagoras (c. 460 B.C.) — On cosmology and the hydrological cycle
Pindar (522—442 B.C.) — Important data in his Odes (LCL)
Oenopides of Chios (c. 425 B.C.) — Theory of the flooding of the Nile
Democritus of Abdera (c. 420 B.C.) — On earthquakes and the salt in the sea
Herodotus (484—425 B.C.) — Data in his History (4 vols. LCL)
Thucydides (460—400 B.C.) — Data in his Peleponesian War (4 vols. LCL)
Ctesias (c. 400 B.C.) — "Indika" (edit. J. W. McCrindle, Calcutta, 1882)
Plato (428—347 B.C.) — Theories mostly in his Timaios and his Critias (both
in the LCL)
Aristotle (356—323 B.C.) — Theory in his Meteorologica (LCL) and in the
"De Mirabilibus Auscultationibus" and "Liber de Elementis, both as-
cribed to him (LCL)
Theophrastus (372—288 B.C.) — On Stones (edit. Caley and Richards, Colum-
bus, 1956) and On Plants (LCL)
Strato (c. 290 B.C.) — A lost work on "Mining Tools and Machines"
Metrodorus of Chios (fourth cy. B.C.) — Wrote an "On Nature"
Ephoros (c. 350 B.C.) — Fragments given by Schwartz (Pauly-Wissowa, vol.
XI, 1907, 1—16)
Agatarchides (c. 250 B.C.) — Data collected by Schwartz (Pauly-Wissowa
vol. I, 1893, 739—741)
Poseidonius (c. 135—51 B.C.) — On volcanic eruptions (see W. Capelle in
Hermes vol. 48, 1913, 321)

Philon — A lost work "on Mines and Metals"
Lucretius (95—55 B.C.) — De Natura Rerum (LCL)
Cicero (106—43 B.C.) — De Natura Deorum and De Divinatione (both in LCL)
Vitruvius (died 26 B.C.) — "On Architecture" (LCL)
Diodorus Siculus (c. 40 B.C.) — Many data in his History (12 vols. LCL)
Strabo (64 B.C. — AD 19) — Many data in his Geography (8 vols. LCL)
Seneca (4 B.C. — AD 65) — Naturales Quaestiones (LCL)
Anon. (first century) — "Aetna" (Text in Minor Latin Poets, LCL)
Anon. (first century) — "Periplus of the Erythaean Sea" (edit. W. H. Schoff, New York, 1912)
Pliny (23—79) — Natural History (10 vols. LCL)
Dioscorides (c. 50) — Materia Medica (edit. R. Gunther, Oxford, 1934) on stones
Ovid (43 B.C. — AD 18) — "Metamophoses" and "Fasti" (both in LCL)
Silius Italicus (25—101) — "Punica" LCL)
Plutarch (46—120) — "Lives" and "Morals" (both in LCL)
Statius 40—96) — "Silvae" (LCL)
Tacitus (55—117) — "Histories" and "Annals" (both in LCL)
Suetonius (70—160) — "Lives" (LCL, 2 vols)
Aulus Gellius (c. 150) — "Attic Nights" 3 vols. LCL)
Apuleius (c. 153) — "Apologia" (Trans. H. E. Butler, Oxford, 1909)
Dio Cassius (150—235) — "Roman History" 9 vols. LCL)
Lucian (115—200) — "Imagines" (8 vols. LCL)
Pausanias (c. 175) — "Description of Greece" (LCL)
Philostratus (c. 200) — "Imagines" (LCL)
Polybius (62—120) — "Histories" (6 vols. LCL)
Clement (160—215) — "Recognitions" (Trans. T. Smith, Edinburgh, 1867)
Hippolytus (third cy.) — "Philosophumena" on Xenophanes (edit. F. Legge, London, 1921)
Ausonius (310—395) — "Mosella" (LCL)
Procopius (c. 530) — "History of the Wars" (7 vols. LCL)
Epiphanios (315—403) — "Liber XII de gemmis" (transl. Blake & Vis, London, 1934)
Ammianus Marcellinus (325—391) — "Rerum Gestarum" (LCL)
Orosius (c. 420) — "History of the World" (edit. J. Bosworth, London, 1859)
Augustine (c. 400) — "City of God" (7 vols. LCL)
Varâmihira (c. 500) — "Summary of astronomy and astrology" (Pâncasiddhântikâ) (edit. Finot, les lapidaires indiens, Paris, 1896)
Cosmas Indicipleutes (c. 535) — "Christian Topography" (edit. Hakluyt Soc., no. 98, London, 1897)
Isidore of Seville (560—636) — "Etymologarium" (Oxford, 1911, vol. 2)
Beda (672—735) — "De Natura Rerum" (edit. Giles, London, 1843, vol. VI)
Anon. (c. 850) — Das Steinbuch des Aristoteles (J. Ruska, Heidelberg, 1912)
Al-Jâhiz (c. 850) — "Book of Animals" containing germ of evolution theory (Carra de Vaux, Penseurs de l'Islam, vol. I, 293 & 352)
Al-Mas'ûdî (c. 950) — "Meadows of gold mines and precious stones (edit. De Meynard & De Courteille, Paris, 1864)

Ikhwân al-ṣafâ (950) — "Encyclopedia of the Brethern of Purity" (edit. Fr. Dieterici, Leipzig, 1886)

Ibn Sînâ (Avicenna) (980—1037) — Kitâb al-Shifâ (E. J. Holmyard, Nature vol. 117, 1926, 305)

Psellos (1018—1078) — "Monodie" (P. Würthle, Rethorische Studien 6, Paderborn, 1917)

Adelard of Bath (c. 1100) — "Quaestiones Naturales" (H. Gollancz, Dodi Ve-Nechdi, London, 1920)

Neckham (1157—1217) — "De Natura Rerum" (T. Wright, Rolls Series, London, 1863)

Michael Scotus (c. 1235) — "Mensa Philosophicus" (See C. H. Haskins in Isis, vol. IV, 1921, 250—275 and Amer. Hist. Rev. vol. 27, 1922, 669) (L. Thorndike, Michael Scot, Nelson, London, 1965)

Albertus Magnus (1193—1280) — "De Mineralibus et Rebus Metallicis Librae Quinque (Opera Omnia, edit. Borgout, Paris, 1190, vol. V)

R. Higden — "Polychronicon" (edit. Babington, Rolls Series vol. I, London, 1865)

Georg Agricola (1494—1555) — "De Re Metallica (edit. (English) H. C. & L. Hoover, London, 1912 and (German) Schiffner, Berlin, 1929) (See also his "De Ortu et Causis Subterraneorum", "De Natura Eorum...", "De Natura Fossilium", "De Veteribus et Novis Metallis", "Bermannus", most of them now available in the Freiberger Forschungshefte, Akademie Verlag, Berlin in German translation)

Conrad Gesner (1516—1565) — "De rerum fossilium, lapidum et gemmarum" (Zürich, 1565)

Bernard Palissy (1510—1589) — "Resources, a Treatise on Water and Springs" (transl. E. E. Willett, Brighton, 1876)

INDEX